D1338105

PETRARCH'S
SECRETUM

Medieval Academy Books, No. 94

PETRARCH'S
SECRETUM

Its Making and Its Meaning

HANS BARON

The Medieval Academy of America

Cambridge, Massachusetts

1985

The publication of this book was made possible by grants of funds to The Medieval Academy of America from the Carnegie Corporation of New York.

CONTENTS

AN INTRODUCTORY NOTE

For nearly a generation, in everything connected with the *Secretum*'s
"making" — that is, its genesis, growth, and chronology — a true
revolution has been taking place, a revolution which, though irre-
versible in some of its major results, could also lead us astray if un-
checked. This means that a fresh analysis of the work cannot avoid a
reexamination of what has happened in *Secretum* research during the
last thirty years. This is the basic reason for the conspicuous role
played in this book by critical discussions of the right or wrong of
past scholarship.

What I want to stress in these prefatory remarks, however, is that
despite the ample attention paid in my study to the "making" of the
Secretum, this feature is presented here not as an end in itself but
rather as a means of defining the period in which Petrarch first drafted
and then expanded his work. For about six years in the middle of his
humanistic career, his thinking differed both from the humanism of
his youth and from the mature thought of his last two decades; it is
an interlude for which no other writing of Petrarch's is more informative than the *Secretum.* To make this period better understood in-
tellectually and spiritually and to augment our intimate picture of
Petrarch in those years through his letters and some of his poems are
goals as important to our study as the tracing of the history of the
Secretum's composition. The Petrarch that stands before us in his
middle years is in some vital respects not the person known from his
conduct and ideas before and afterwards; and since a change in our
perspective of the *Secretum* inevitably leads to a redrawing of our
image of Petrarch's life and work, the reader should be aware from
the start that the distinctive character of Petrarch's middle years will
gradually become the second major topic of this book as the investigation unfolds.

H.B.
Cambridge, Massachusetts
February 1984

vii

ACKNOWLEDGMENTS

I would certainly not have been able so late in life to write a work of historical and literary criticism like the one offered here without the help of my daughter, Renate Baron Franciscono. During a collaboration of more than five years, she not only succeeded in putting an untidy, partly German manuscript into a stylistically acceptable form, but as my first reader and critic proved her worth in countless particulars. She also relieved me of the burden of compiling the indices.

This book came into being in Cambridge, Mass., among the treasures of the Widener Library, another aid without which my studies would hardly have been possible. I wish to thank Harvard University for its hospitality, and especially Giles Constable, formerly in the History Department of Harvard, Dante Della Terza of the Department of Romance Languages and Literatures, and Morton Bloomfield of the English Department, who by the interest they showed during difficult phases of the work gave me more encouragement than they could know.

The same is true of Ronald Witt of the History Department of Duke University, who read my manuscript through at two different stages and offered gratefully accepted advice.

H.B.

CHAPTER ONE

A Glance at the Past Study
of the *Secretum*

(1) Crossroads in Early *Secretum* Scholarship

Until recently, the study of the chronology and growth of the *Secretum* lagged far behind that of most of Petrarch's other major works. This was due not to any lack of interest in the *Secretum* but to the seemingly unequivocal information found in the sources; no extraordinary philological effort seemed necessary. Given that autobiographical details in the *Secretum* clearly attribute Augustine's imaginary visit with Petrarch in the Vaucluse (the setting for the *Secretum* conversation) to the winter of 1342–43 and that the visit is said to have taken place "not so long ago" (*nuper*), the work was assumed to have been composed during, or shortly after, that winter. And since some phrases in the text seemed to point to the beginning of Petrarch's stay in Milan (he moved there from Provence in mid-1353), it was thought for generations that, in accordance with his usual habit of making corrections and additions over the course of many years, he still made occasional changes in the *Secretum* during the early part of his residence there.

The first step toward the recognition that the *Secretum* was completed gradually was taken by Remigio Sabbadini as late as 1917, when he tried to identify a number of allusions in the *Secretum* to writings and events apparently belonging to later years.[1] Although most of Sabbadini's conclusions failed to stand the test of time,[2] he was the first to propose that changes such as are found in most of Petrarch's writings also appear in the *Secretum*.[3]

---

[1] Remigio Sabbadini, "Note filologiche sul 'Secretum' del Petrarca," *Rivista di Filologia e di Istruzione Classica* XLV (1917), pp. 24–37.

[2] See my appraisal of Sabbadini's contribution in Hans Baron, *From Petrarch to Leonardo Bruni: Studies in Humanistic and Political Literature* (Chicago, 1968; hereafter cited as Baron, *From Petrarch to Leonardo Bruni*), pp. 53–56.

[3] Changes were modest, Sabbadini concluded, since "il Petrarca non sottopose il

At the same time it became clear to Sabbadini that the mysterious years listed at the end of Petrarch's autograph — 1353, 1349, 1347, in that order — could not be the respective dates of the three books of the *Secretum*, as earlier scholars, from Lorenzo Mehus in the eighteenth century to Georg Voigt in the nineteenth, had speculated. Sabbadini assumed that the three unexplained dates indicate three years in which an original text of 1342–43 was enriched by additions, and that the final autograph was prepared in 1358, five years after Petrarch moved from Provence to Milan.[4]

For almost fifty years, Sabbadini's essay, however imperfect, served as a basis for critical studies of the growth of the *Secretum*. A more systematic textual analysis, undertaken by me in 1963,[5] resulted in the conclusion that Petrarch substantially changed at least three extensive sections of his text. To my surprise, the dates which seemed most probable for those changes and additions were precisely 1349 and 1353, two of the years listed by Petrarch at the end of his manuscript. One major aim of my investigation was to determine whether Petrarch's interpolations mirror his changing environment. They most assuredly do, provided that due note is taken of Petrarch's sojourns in Italy, away from the Vaucluse. Another finding of my study was that most of the detectable changes appear in a few extensive portions of text, where demonstrable interpolations are dense — "disturbed areas," as I called them.

To point to an example, in the third book, the advice given to Petrarch by the imaginary Augustine, that he should leave Provence for good and travel in Italy in order to free himself from his love for Laura, flatly contradicts the usual contention in the *Secretum* that Petrarch can achieve spiritual seriousness only by avoiding the distractions to be found away from the solitude of the Vaucluse. Equally important are the changes that appear in two paragraphs of the second book, where Augustine tries to show that Petrarch's dangerous entanglement in some of the Seven Deadly Sins is a major cause of his incapacity for pious concentration. In connection with *avaritia*

---

dialogo a un vero rimaneggiamento, ma vi introdusse soltanto qua e là poche giunte parziali" (Sabbadini, "Note filologiche," p. 37).

[4] Baron, *From Petrarch to Leonardo Bruni*, p. 91.

[5] "Petrarch's *Secretum:* Was It Revised — and Why? The Draft of 1342–43 and the Later Changes," *Bibliothèque d'Humanisme et Renaissance* XXV (1963), pp. 489–530. Reprinted with minor changes in Baron, *From Petrarch to Leonardo Bruni,* pp. 51–101.

and *accidia,* he accuses Petrarch of having forgotten the blessings that
the solitude of the Vaucluse brought to him earlier, before he became
a captive of city life. This is the diametrical opposite of the critique in
the Laura section of Book III, in which Augustine is said to have
looked down mockingly from on high at Petrarch's attempts to find
inner peace in Provence, where everything reminds him of Laura
and kindles his love.

The earliest date when Petrarch could sadly have recalled his
years in the Vaucluse and felt himself to be a captive of city life is
1353, that is to say, the second half of that year, when his long stay in
Milan began. No other explanation is possible (as my analysis of
1963 tried to bring out) but that the two long passages on *avaritia* and
accidia were added or altered in Milan in 1353. Conversely, Augustine's counsel that Petrarch should flee from the Vaucluse to Italy
must have been added in 1349, another occasion when Petrarch lived
in Italy.

My discovery of three "disturbed areas" in Books II and III was
not directly contradicted by the results arrived at in the comprehensive work on the *Secretum* published by Francisco Rico in 1974. His
work cannot be called a simple continuation of earlier analyses or
ideas regarding the genesis of the *Secretum*. To some extent it calls
into question any biographical approach that deals with the *Secretum*
as an expression of Petrarch's changing life and thought; it views the
Secretum rather as a piece of literary art and, perhaps, medieval symbolism. Not without reason does Rico present his work — the *Lectura
del "Secretum"* — as the first volume of a trilogy with the striking title
Vida u obra de Petrarca, life *or* (not "and") work of Petrarch.[6] Even more
important are the specific methods which — for better or worse —
he follows.

(2) The Thesis That the *Secretum* Was Drafted in 1347,
Not 1342–43: Its Necessity and Consequences

In some respects, to be sure, Rico's work starts from problems already
tackled or anticipated in preceding scholarship. This applies to three

[6] Francisco Rico, *Vida u obra de Petrarca,* vol. I, *Lectura del "Secretum,"* Ente Nazionale
Francesco Petrarca: Studi sul Petrarca 4 (Padua, 1974; hereafter cited as Rico, *Lectura*). For the perspective on medieval symbolism see p. 175, n.56, below.

of the major grounds on which his chronological revision is based.

In the first place, a weakness of the 1342–43 dating of the *Secretum* had always been the almost total lack of sources other than the *Secretum* to support the assumption that Petrarch underwent a religious crisis at that time[7] — the one exception being his *Psalmi Penitentiales,* which shows clear parallels to the *Secretum* and was long believed to have also been written in 1342–43. In the course of the last twenty years, however, it has become evident that these psalms were composed about 1348,[8] and Rico had this knowledge at his disposal when he worked out his own chronology. The only apparent major basis outside the *Secretum* for assuming that Petrarch passed through a religious crisis of any kind about 1342–43 had thus already been lost when Rico took up his studies.

Second, there is the fact that Petrarch's first large work after 1342–43 was the *Rerum Memorandarum Libri* of 1344–45, a vast, soon abandoned project of classical (not religious) interest. If the *Secretum* was written in 1342–43, the *Rerum Memorandarum* would have almost directly followed it and would thus clash with the *Secretum*'s ending, where Petrarch vows henceforward to use his time and energy to complete the *Africa* and *De Viris* quickly and afterwards turn to a more spiritually oriented life. This, too, was bound to arouse uncertainty regarding the date of 1342–43 for the *Secretum.*

Third, it must have been an often felt embarrassment among scholars that a number of classical authors with whom Petrarch was unfamiliar before the mid-1340s are cited in the *Secretum* without any recognizable sign that the citations are interpolated. Here was still another source of uneasiness concerning such an early date.

During the 1950s and 1960s, before the strong impact made by Giuseppe Billanovich's revision of the chronology of the early *epistolae familiares* (in his *Petrarca letterato* of 1947), such doubts remained basically without issue. A breakthrough for the exploration of the *Secretum* occurred when Rico proposed using Petrarch's treatment of

---

[7] This was Carlo Calcaterra's thesis, first proposed in 1939. See Baron, *From Petrarch to Leonardo Bruni,* p. 25.

[8] The three more recently proposed dates of the *Psalmi* are 1347, 1348, and 1349. See Baron, *From Petrarch to Leonardo Bruni,* p. 57; Rico, *Lectura,* pp. 340f., 498; and Francisco Rico, "Precisazioni di cronologia petrarchesca: Le 'Familiares' VIII 2-5, e i rifacimenti del 'Secretum,'" *Giornale Storico della Letteratura Italiana* CLV (1978), p. 516.

his early correspondence as a model for dealing with the *Secretum*. According to Billanovich, the letters contained in the first three or four books of the *Familiares* were actually written or rewritten during the early 1350s, thus serving Petrarch as an invented correspondence for the 1330s and 1340s. For instance, the famous *Fam.* IV 1 describing his ascent of Mont Ventoux in 1336, a topic related in many respects to those in the *Secretum*, was written in or about 1353. Rico posed the question whether the same pattern of preparing the text and giving it an imaginary dating might not apply to the *Secretum;* whether there was not a parallel between Augustine's visit, intimated in the dialogue to have occurred in 1342–43, and the composition of the letter on the ascent of Mont Ventoux, freely ascribed to 1336. Everything considered, do not the *Secretum* and the first few books of the *Familiares* equally reflect Petrarch's mind during the biennium he spent in Provence from mid-1351 to mid-1353?

Guided by this theory, Rico made a number of discoveries which have thrown entirely new light on the *Secretum*. In the first place, he put the utmost emphasis on those above-mentioned contradictions in our information which make the origin of the *Secretum* in 1342–43 implausible. And he supplemented this negative evidence, which excludes 1342 but does not point to a specific later year or years, by proposing a new interpretation of Petrarch's notation of the three years 1353, 1349, and 1347: since 1342–43 is not mentioned by Petrarch, it must be excluded from consideration. Finally, he provided a new and necessary philological framework. In general and in minute detail he showed that there was much in Petrarch's state of mind in 1347 which encourages the attribution of the initial draft of the *Secretum* to that year. In 1347 Petrarch had just written the *De Otio Religioso* for his brother Gherardo, a Carthusian monk. It is a guidebook which, among other things, makes it clear that however deeply Petrarch himself was longing for some kind of monastic life, his inborn nature and literary occupations demanded that he find a different way for himself. If there was any time in Petrarch's life when one would expect him to have worked out a program for his future, it is the months following his depiction of monastic life for Gherardo in the *De Otio Religioso*.

Rico not only drew this conclusion in theory but provided it with a solid foundation: the demonstration that the *Secretum* shares one of its most important inspirations with the *De Otio Religioso,* namely, a deep admiration for and detailed knowledge of Augustine's *De Vera Religione*. Now, it is true that this Augustinian work had been available to Petrarch since about 1335, but its fullest impact was not felt until 1347. The *De Vera Religione* is the most dualistic of Augustine's religious writings, culminating in the opinion that life on earth is filled with "phantasmata" and "figmenta" that make it difficult for those who come in contact with them not to forget man's heavenly origin. As Rico proved through careful study of Petrarch's manuscript copy of the *De Vera Religione*, which is filled with his marginal notes, the doctrine of earthly "phantasmata" and "figmenta" seized Petrarch's imagination while he was working on the *De Otio*. This dualistic mood is reflected in both the first and third books of the *Secretum*, particularly in the *amor* section of Book III, where Augustine's disparagement of the idea that Petrarch's love for a creature of God (Laura) might lead him upward to the love of the Creator is rejected in the same emphatic terms used in Petrarch's marginal notations in his copy of the *De Vera Religione*.

The consequences of the strong dependence of the *Secretum* on the *De Vera Religione* are obvious. It is next to impossible to believe that the ideas in the *Secretum* just mentioned could have been formulated before the time when Petrarch was preparing the *De Otio* — that is, the early part of 1347. Together with Rico's reinterpretation of Petrarch's dating note and his various observations discounting the origin of the *Secretum* in 1342–43, this makes for an uncommonly round and consistent demonstration of the necessity to transfer the original date of the *Secretum* to the late 1340s.[9]

[9] The basis for all these conclusions is a special paper by Rico on Petrarch's marginal notes in his copy of Augustine's *De Vera Religione*, "Petrarca y el *De vera religione*," *Italia Medioevale e Umanistica* XVII (1974), pp. 313–364.

One point may still cause uneasiness. Is there a reason why Petrarch decided in his narrative of 1347 to choose the surprisingly early date of 1342–43 for his imaginary disputation with Augustine? The answer, first given by Rico, will be discussed in the chapter dealing with Petrarch's truthfulness, pp. 208–210 below.

After my manuscript was sent to the publisher, I became acquainted with Bortolo Martinelli's book *Il "Secretum" conteso* (Naples, "Finito di stampare nel dicembre 1982"), which includes an attempt to refute the theory that the first draft of the *Secretum* was written in 1347, not 1342–43. I can only state here that, in my judgment, none of Martinelli's relevant arguments carry conviction. The reader who wants to form his own opinion should consult Rico's reply to Martinelli, "Sobre la cronología del *Secretum:* Las viejas leyendas y el fantasma nuevo de un lapsus bíblico," in *Studi Petrarcheschi,* nuova serie, I (1984), pp. 51–102.

(3) Misconceptions That Emerged When the *Secretum* Was Redated

I

Although we lack external evidence that the first draft of the *Secretum* was written precisely in 1347 — except for the inclusion of that year in Petrarch's somewhat enigmatic chronological note — the various theories in favor of 1342–43 proposed by scholars in the past are now obsolete in view of the strong ties linking the *Secretum* to the *De Otio Religioso* of 1347.

The certainty of this conclusion must be stressed all the more because Rico has ventured upon a further, questionable claim: that the attribution of the earliest *Secretum* draft to 1347 is ultimately confirmed by allusions to the *Secretum* in other writings of Petrarch's between 1347 and the early 1350s, whereas no such hints are found in the years following 1342–43. As Rico puts it, it is the appearance of allusions to the *Secretum* from 1347 onward that makes it "impossible to maintain the mirage of the composition of the *Secretum* in 1342 or 1343. For it cannot be by chance that the transcription [of Petrarch's dating note] places the first stage of the work in 1347 and that the first allusion to it corresponds to the same year." [10] During the early 1350s, references to the *Secretum* "multiply," says Rico; "sí lo anunció en repetidas ocasiones," and "one finds clear references to it [*anuncios claros*] in *Familiares,* I 1," that is, in the introduction (written in 1350) to the book edition of the letters, as well as a half dozen minor — to Rico equally unquestionable — allusions elsewhere. [11]

The assumption that Petrarch alluded to the *Secretum* in a number of his writings from 1347 onward, which is an integral part of Rico's approach, has serious consequences: beyond testifying to the existence of the *Secretum* in 1347 or soon afterwards, it also presents us with the stark contradiction that Petrarch averred in the *Secretum* proem that the work was for his eyes alone and yet invited readers of *Fam.* I 1 to learn about his personality by reading the *Secretum*. Should we, therefore, with Rico, question the trustworthiness of the *Secretum*? Or must we not rather ask whether *Familiaris* I 1, and perhaps other writings of his, really alludes to it?

[10] Rico, *Lectura,* p. 482.
[11] Ibid., pp. 33, 483.

II

Epistola Familiaris I 1 is largely concerned with the reasons why Petrarch anticipates bitter attacks against his letters by unsympathetic readers, attacks which Ludwig van Kempen (Petrarch's "Socrates"), to whom the collection of the *Familiares* is dedicated, will find it difficult to oppose. "At least defend these unsophisticated and improvidently released pieces [of letter writing] against such impudence by not giving them too much visibility," Petrarch concludes. He then adds abruptly: "However, that other [work], which is not, as Cicero puts it, a Phidian Minerva [that is, not his greatest work, as the Minerva was Phidias'] but offers something of an image of my soul [*animi mei effigiem*] as well as a true representation of my talent carried out with great dedication [*ingenii simulacrum multo michi studio dedolatum*] — if that [work], I say, ever receives its finishing touches from me and reaches you, you may place it without concern [*secure . . . constituito*] on whatever acropolis you choose [as Phidias' Minerva was placed on the Acropolis of Athens]."[12] Put differently, this other work may be given the wide visibility the collected letters should not have, at least not as long as they must stand alone without the guidance provided by the former.

What is this other work of Petrarch's? During the last fifty years, many scholars have identified it with a first draft of the later *Epistola Posteritati*.[13] As Rico rightly says, this need not be the last word on the matter. But if one ventures, as he does, to reject the *opinio communis* of many eminent Petrarch students and assumes rather that the allusion in *Fam.* I 1 is to the *Secretum*, one must offer a convincing

[12]"Adversus hanc proterviam latebris saltem tuis horridula hec atque improvide nobis elapsa defendito. Illam vero non Phidie Minervam ut ait Cicero, sed qualemcunque animi mei effigiem atque ingenii simulacrum multo michi studio dedolatum, si unquam supremam illi manum imposuero, cum ad te venerit, secure qualibet in arce constituito" (*Fam.* I 1 [37]). See Francesco Petrarca, *Le Familiari,* ed. Vittorio Rossi, vol. I [Edizione Nazionale delle Opere di Francesco Petrarca 10–13, Florence, 1933–42]; hereafter, in references to Petrarch's *familiares,* the numbers in brackets or parentheses refer to the paragraphs of Rossi's edition).

[13]Both Rossi and Arnaldo Foresti suggested the letter *Posteritati* as early as 1928. Giuseppe Billanovich accepted the thesis for his reconstructions in *Petrarca letterato,* vol. I, *Lo scrittoio del Petrarca,* Edizioni di "Storia e Letteratura" 16 (Rome, 1947). Among later Petrarch students, the identification with *Posteritati* was accepted by Ugo Dotti.

argument. I confess not to understand why Rico believes that the mere fact that the first version of the *Secretum* dates to 1347 proves such an assumption. *Fam.* I 1, he states, "alludes to the *Secretum* with sufficient clarity," and "I think . . . that only the long routine acceptance of an erroneous date for the *Secretum* has impeded the recognition of the allusion. Yet to . . . identify it turns out to be highly revealing. For Petrarch calls the work in question 'multo studio dedolatum,' but not finished . . . in January 1350." "This agrees with all we have concluded: the 'multum studium' took place chiefly in the versions of 1347 and 1349 . . . and the desire to complete the enterprise carefully was to culminate in the intense reworking of 1353."[14]

It may be granted that the identification of the unnamed work as the *Secretum* could not have been proposed before the latter was redated. But this does not prove that *Fam.* I 1 alludes to the *Secretum*. Petrarch himself reminds us in his letter that he had partially completed not only one major work but several "which, already interrupted for some time and awaited by many, I have in hand" (*de manibus meis pendent*); and more than one of these was resumed soon after *Fam.* I 1 was composed, mainly during Petrarch's last sojourn in Provence in 1351–53. In other words, the pattern of extensive writing during the 1340s and resumption around 1353, which characterizes Petrarch's labors on the *Secretum*, is applicable to several of Petrarch's early writings. If there is any criterion for choosing among these unfinished projects, it will have to be discovered by tracing the ideas found in *Fam.* I 1.

The burden of the letter to Socrates, as indicated, is Petrarch's fear of laying himself open to impatient criticism for having thus far given to the public only vernacular poems and a nascent collection of Latin letters. He thus appeals to Socrates, as the recipient of the corpus of the *Familiares*, not to defend him on the basis of his letters alone, but to wait instead for a more representative creation. Why do his letters not appear to him to be an adequate ground for defense? *Fam.* I 1 offers several reasons. Letters must vary in spirit according to the personality, age, fortune, and education of the recipient and his capacity to understand the writer. To be correctly and sympathetically understood by an addressee should be the prin-

---

[14] Rico, *Lectura*, pp. 479–480.

cipal concern of a letter writer, the consequence being, Petrarch admits, that as a correspondent "I myself have the impression that I have said contradictory things now and then." Sometimes, indeed, he simply could not remain loyal to himself: "multum a me ipso differre compulsus sum." To this must be added that in their original form missives often give the same news to different people, thus making it necessary when collecting them to omit, repeat, or make changes, thereby creating the impression for those who know the original versions that the opinions of the writer have changed and that the texts are unfaithful. This impression is enhanced by Petrarch's adherence to the program of letter writing advocated by Cicero, who insisted that a letter should not be a small philosophic treatise but a piece of literary art recreating in words domestic and public events and giving a picture of the writer's fluctuating moods. Last but not least, Socrates is asked for the time being to restrain his defense of Petrarch because the latter has not yet released any major work that Socrates might show to critics as an epitome of his true persuasions concerning life and its values. To repeat: when the unnamed work which reveals his "animi effigiem atque ingenii simulacrum multo . . . studio dedolatum" has finally been given its finishing touches, it may be raised high and visible on an "acropolis." The work to which *Fam.* I 1 alludes must, therefore, be one which is capable of demonstrating not only Petrarch's "ingenium" as a scholar and writer but also the true and lasting bent of his mind, in contrast to his largely receiver-oriented letters — a work substantial enough to give a clear idea of Petrarch the man and the scholar.

With these criteria as a guide, we recognize that Petrarch's reference can hardly have been to the *Epistola Posteritati*. It was certainly not a major work worth placing on an acropolis. Moreover, this fragment (the extant self-portrait is about 600 words in length) cannot have been written earlier than 1368. If it were the work which Petrarch had in mind, we would have to assume that he had drafted, but not finished, another self-portrait in 1350, one whose elements may or may not be preserved in the letter *Posteritati;* this, indeed, is the conclusion accepted by Ernest H. Wilkins.[15]

[15] Ernest H. Wilkins, "On the Evolution of Petrarch's Letter to Posterity," *Speculum* XXXIX (1964), pp. 304, 308. See p. 212, n.62, below.

But Petrarch could not have been referring to the *Secretum* either. For the *Secretum,* whose introduction states that, unlike normal literary products, it is destined to remain with its author and not be read by others, is the very opposite of a work meant to be placed on an acropolis as a widely visible guide to his mind. Rico was not entirely unaware of this formidable obstacle to any attempt to make the *Secretum* fit this role. In a footnote he remarks that such assurances of Petrarch's as those found in *Fam.* I 1 and the *Secretum* preface must be understood as nothing more than "mohínes retórices, decorativos."[16] This, of course, leaves him with the burden of proving the unreliability of Petrarch's affirmations, and we shall see later (in Chapter 7) the unfortunate consequences of his attribution of cynicism to the *Secretum* preface. Under the circumstances, if there should be another work by Petrarch which gives us an adequate "effigies" of his mind without forcing us to make unreasonable assumptions, that work would have to take precedence.

III

Could the work in question be either the *Africa* or the *De Viris Illustribus*? Even as late as the early 1350s they occupied Petrarch's mind more than any other of his writings. But the *De Viris* is a historical work, not an "animi mei effigies"; it is not the sort of book that could reveal his personal outlook on life. The *Africa* epic, on the other hand, is one of Petrarch's most ambitious undertakings and tells us more about his perennial aspirations. The role of the poet — celebrated in the person of Ennius, Scipio's admirer and eulogist and, in this respect, Petrarch's forerunner — and the poet's relationship to men of action are subjects discussed on many of its pages. Furthermore, at the beginning of the 1350s, Petrarch still hoped to finish the *Africa* quickly. Not until 1352 did he begin to wonder whether he would ever be able to complete his "magnum opus." Before that time he felt the *Africa* to be by far his most important work, as is realized by every student who reads in the *Secretum* that when, during a serious illness in 1343, Petrarch thought he was dying, he almost burned the *Africa,* because the poem was liable to shape the opinion that poster-

[16] Rico, *Lectura,* p. 479, n.85.

ity would have of him, and nobody could perfect it after his death. Finally, no one who reads Petrarch's characterization of the *Africa* in the *Secretum* as "preclarum nempe rarumque opus et egregium" — a conviction with which Augustine himself is made to agree[17] — will doubt that this was a work Petrarch would indeed have been happy to place on an acropolis.

Nevertheless, there are obvious obstacles to the acceptance of the *Africa* as the work Petrarch had in mind. The crucial phrase in *Fam.* I 1 is the assurance that the reader of the letters will find Petrarch's own "animi effigies" in the announced work; and although Petrarch and the poet's vocation have their place in the *Africa,* these are much less than the view and evaluation of life one would expect after reading the reference in *Fam.* I 1. There is a psychological reason, too, why the allusion is probably not to the *Africa.* In cases in which a classical model for a humanist's phrasing is known, the motivation of the model often throws light on the imitator's motives. There can be no doubt that Petrarch's reference to "Minerva Phidiae" was made in free imitation of a passage in the preface to a minor work of Cicero's, his *Paradoxa Stoicorum.* This pamphlet, dedicated to Marcus Junius Brutus — the recipient as well of a magnum opus of Cicero's, the *Brutus: De Claris Oratoribus* — is here admitted not to be the kind of work worthy of being put on an acropolis like Phidias' Minerva; it is praised merely as a product of the same famous "workshop" (*officina*) which produced the *De Claris Oratoribus.*[18] The sense of the words used in the *Paradoxa* is clear: "Minerva Phidiae . . . tale ut in arce poni possit" means a magnum opus, but the *Paradoxa* can only claim minor status. Is it probable that if Petrarch had had the *Africa* in mind when he wrote *Fam.* I 1 he would have chosen as his model the sentence in the *Paradoxa* in which Cicero talks of its being *not* a "Minerva Phidiae" but something less important from the same smithy? Is it not more likely that Petrarch was not thinking of his "Phidie Minerva" — that is, the *Africa* — at all, but like Cicero in the *Paradoxa,*

---

[17] See Enrico Carrara's edition of the *Secretum* (hereafter cited as Carrara), in Francesco Petrarca, *Prose,* ed. Guido Martellotti et al., La Letteratura Italiana: Storia e Testi 7 (Milan, 1955; hereafter cited as *Prose*), p. 194.

[18] For Cicero, the *Paradoxa* pamphlet "non est tale ut in arce poni possit quasi Minerva illa Phidiae, sed tamen ut ex eadem officina exisse appareat."

of a work which contained some of his philosophical ideas without being (as the *Africa* would have been) his supreme accomplishment?[19]

The only other work which the author of *Fam.* I 1 could have had in mind is the *De Vita Solitaria* of 1346; and it is, indeed, difficult to imagine a single point where this work of Petrarch's fails to meet the necessary qualifications. To begin with, the *De Vita* must have been one of the several nascent books to which Petrarch alluded in *Fam.* I 1 as being expected from him but not yet completed. Moreover, Petrarch did not consider the *De Vita* the greatest and most important of his works. For in its preface he states in plain words that when he began the *De Vita* he felt he was taking a brief vacation "from the greater and older tasks which beset me and ring incessantly in my mind"[20] — these "greater tasks" being the *Africa* or, probably, the *Africa* and *De Viris* together. Finally, the *De Vita* also fits the chronological conditions which have made the *Secretum* appear a candidate in Rico's eyes. For, like the latter, the *De Vita* was drafted a few years before 1350 and by that year needed only some finishing touches to be ready for readers.

In one decisive respect, moreover, the *De Vita Solitaria* is superior to all its rivals: it alone can explain how it happened that in his dedication of *Fam.* I 1 to Socrates (Ludwig van Kempen), Petrarch considered it unnecessary to give the title of the work to which he was so secretively alluding. Van Kempen did not need to be told what the work in question was. He had lived near Petrarch in Provence; in 1347, according to the papal registers in Avignon, Petrarch petitioned the pope for some kind of arrangement that would enable him to settle permanently with Ludwig in the neighborhood of the

---

[19] Even though Rossi's commentary on *Fam.* I 1 refers to the *De Oratore* rather than the *Paradoxa,* Petrarch is following the latter. Only there does Cicero bring together Phidias' Minerva and its placement on the acropolis (*arx*) of Athens. Rico accepts this (Rico, *Lectura,* p. 479), and it was known before him (see *Briefe des Francesco Petrarca,* trans. Hans Nachod and Paul Stern [Berlin, 1931], p. 352, where reference is made to *Paradoxa,* Prooem. 5). This is not to say that Petrarch was thinking only of the *Paradoxa.* He also had *Orator* II 8–10 in mind, since he took some of the key words for his phrasing from there (see Paul Piur, in Konrad Burdach, *Vom Mittelalter zur Reformation: Forschungen zur Geschichte der deutschen Bildung,* vol. II 2 [Berlin, 1928], p. 143f.). But the basic inspiration came from the *Paradoxa.*

[20] ". . . indutias petens ab aliis maioribus et antiquioribus curis meis, que me obsident atque circumsonant . . ." (*Prose,* p. 294).

Carthusian monastery of Montrieux, to which Petrarch's brother Gherardo belonged. The petition makes mention of Ludwig as Petrarch's "precarissimi socij et confamiliaris sui in domo domini Cardinalis [Colonna] et qui semper sibi extitit loco fratris et secum usque ad mortem inseparabiliter esse cupit."[21] Had it succeeded, they would have lived together from that year onward in a kind of common "vita solitaria," and it is natural to infer that the *De Vita* must have appeared to this friend to be Petrarch's most relevant literary work, the one whose completion and publication he was impatiently awaiting.

What is still missing from this argument is final evidence that Petrarch actually regarded his *De Vita Solitaria* as an "animi mei effigies," as he characterized the unnamed work in *Fam.* I 1. It comes as something of a surprise, after the many attempts to identify this "effigies" with the much later *Epistola Posteritati,* the *Africa,* or the *Secretum,* to read at the end of Petrarch's introduction to the *De Vita* that we will learn "what ideas I am wont to harbor when I reflect on this whole subject of the solitary life" — not by setting forth a great multitude of doctrines but by selecting "such as may let you recognize, as in a reduced mirror image, totum animi mei habitum." In other words, what in the letter of 1350 is called "animi mei effigies" and "ingenii [mei] simulacrum" is described in the book of 1346 as "totus animi mei habitus," viewed "parvo velut in speculo." Everything points to the conclusion, therefore, that the *De Vita Solitaria* is Petrarch's unnamed work. If this should not be accepted, however, the only serious competitor would be the *Africa* — but hardly the *Secretum*.

IV

Three things should be stated at the end of this opening chapter. One is that *Fam.* I 1 is basically different from all the other writings in which, according to Rico, Petrarch "announced" the existence of the *Secretum* to his readers. For in *Fam.* I 1 Petrarch recommends in so many words that some other (unnamed) work should, after its completion, be read together with the *Familiares.* If that other work were the *Secretum,* this recommendation would directly contradict

---

[21] Ernest H. Wilkins, *Studies in the Life and Works of Petrarch* (Cambridge, Mass., 1955), p. 14.

Petrarch's contention that the *Secretum* was to remain with him and not be read by strangers. The question whether Rico's identification of this unnamed work with the *Secretum* is tenable is thus of great significance for everything connected with the problem of Petrarch's truthfulness. Since none of the other suspected allusions to the *Secretum* include such an invitation to read it, they would have no bearing on Petrarch's veracity even if we had no doubts about them whatever; for they would then still be couched in terms so enigmatic that no reader before Rico has ever claimed to recognize them. Under the circumstances, it should be sufficient here to state summarily that there is no proof that Petrarch alluded to the *Secretum* in *Fam.* I 1 or anywhere else. The evidence on which this opinion rests is described and evaluated in the appendix to this chapter.

The second point to be made is that to contend that allusions to the *Secretum* do not appear in Petrarch's writings after 1347 is not to deny that early bibliographical listings of Petrarch's works include references to the *Secretum*. Such references are available from the late 1340s onward, although they use the name "dialogus" rather than "Secretum." The reasons for this are too complicated to be set forth in a few words. They will be discussed in Chapter 7 on Petrarch's truthfulness.

Finally, how does it happen that after redating the *Secretum* from 1342–43 to 1347 so judiciously, Rico could err so persistently with respect to the related subject of allusions to the *Secretum*? The answer, it seems to me, must largely be sought in his methodology. The comparison he draws between the growth of the *Secretum* and the treatment of the letters in the first few books of the *Epistolae Familiares* results in many keen observations on his part but also in a good measure of dogmatism. His method of deducing the history of the *Secretum* from the procedure followed in the preparation of the *Familiares* easily leads to error, since it depends upon parallels between objects very different in kind. As we shall find out, the alleged discovery of references to the *Secretum* in other writings of Petrarch's between 1347 and 1353 is only one of many illusions arising from the use of dubious models; it gives us warning of submerged rocks, as it were, which we should be prepared to sound out and evade. While we must be deeply grateful for the pioneering impulse given by the lately charted course, we will have to pilot it with much greater care.

Appendix
Some Further Misconceptions

Now that we have found the presumed allusion to the *Secretum* in *Fam.* I 1 does not in fact exist,[22] what can be said about the contention that identifiable allusions to the *Secretum* begin to appear in 1347 in other writings of Petrarch's?

The most interesting example of such a supposed reference is found in the *De Otio Religioso*. There, in the part originally written in 1347, we read that Augustine's *Confessiones* has often proved to be a consolation and model in Petrarch's restless life: "In the midst of my fluctuations — if I ever begin to get ahead of them, I too will have to write a huge book of confessions — I came across Augustine's book of *Confessiones*."[23] Does this strangely contorted sentence mean that Petrarch was planning to write a book like Augustine's *Confessions* and that this could be the *Secretum* as we now know it?

For Rico, there is no doubt that this is so. "In those lines," he says, "the *De Otio* presupposes that Petrarch was contemplating the scheme of the *Secretum* at that time," and this is thus "the earliest attestation" to it.[24] But is Petrarch really speaking about the work we know as the *Secretum*? He mentions two characteristics of the book he has in mind. It will be a "liber ingens" — which is surely not the right appellation for the dialogue he was to write a month later and entitle his "Secretum." And it will be written after he has emerged from the "fluctuationes" of his life — a contention that suggests a hope for the distant future which is in glaring contrast to a book dealing with his present "conflictus curarum suarum." In the course of our discussion, we shall see that Petrarch still planned as late as 1358 to compose a work describing his eventual victory over his sins and passions. At that time it was to comprise six books, including three "de secreta pace animi," and most important, was to be written in the distant future, that is, after he had reached port.

There are only two possible explanations of the *De Otio* passage, both devastating to the assumption that in February–March 1347 (the date of the

---

[22] See in particular pp. 11, 14f., above.

[23] ". . . inter fluctuationes meas — quas si percurrere cepero et michi confessionum liber ingens ordiendus erit — Augustini *Confessionum* liber obvius fuit" (*De Otio Religioso,* ed. Giuseppe Rotondi, Studi e Testi 195 [Vatican City, 1958], p. 104). I have used dashes in place of commas to clarify this complicated sentence.

[24] ". . . el *De otio,* en esas líneas, supone que Petrarca rumiaba entonces el esquema del *Secretum*" (Rico, *Lectura,* p. 481). "En el *De otio,* pues, se halla la más temprana atestación del *Secretum* . . ." (ibid., p. 482).

De Otio) Petrarch was alluding to the work he was to draft a few weeks later. One explanation is that Petrarch did not yet have any clear plan for the *Secretum* in mind and was dreaming instead of a completely different sort of book from the one he was soon to compose. The other possibility is that the reference to an autobiographical "liber ingens" in the *De Otio* passage is not a reflection of Petrarch's mind in 1347 at all but an interpolation from the time when he intended to change the *Secretum* into a vast autobiography culminating in his final triumph over worldly passions — the plan about which he reported in 1358 in his autograph of the *Secretum*.[25] To be sure, there is no external evidence of an interpolation, but the singularly awkward structure of the quoted *De Otio* passage invites us to consider the possibility of an insertion. Whichever of the two alternatives is correct, however, the *De Otio* passage cannot be used as proof that Petrarch was already anticipating and "announcing" the *Secretum*.

The *De Otio* passage has a revealing counterpart in *Fam.* IV 1, the report on Petrarch's earlier ascent of Mont Ventoux, written or rewritten about 1353. In the letter, one of the thoughts attributed to Petrarch on the mountaintop concerns the still imperfect spiritual progress he had been making in the decade preceding the ascent. "Nondum enim in portu sum, ut securus preteritarum meminerim procellarum. Tempus forsan veniet, quando eodem quo gesta sunt ordine universa percurram, prefatus illud Augustini tui: 'Recordari volo transactas feditates meas et carnales corruptiones anime mee. . . .'"[26] Here, just as in the *De Otio* reference to a "confessionum liber ingens" once he has arrived "in portu," he plans to write an autobiographical history, modeled on Augustine's *Confessions,* and to report his progress from sin to salvation, so that (as he puts it) "in security I might remember the past assaults on me." By 1353, the *Secretum* had been completed, or the last touches were just being added to it while *Fam.* IV 1 was being written. The quoted sentence from *Fam.* IV 1 tells us, therefore, that when Petrarch mentioned his plan to record the story of his spiritual development after reaching port, as Augustine did in his *Confessions,* he must have been thinking of something more extensive than the three books of the *Secretum* he had written by 1353.

Another letter of Petrarch's has also been described as an "inequívoco anuncio del *Secretum*" and as a source that "anunciaba el debate en torno a Laura de la tercera jornada [of the *Secretum*]."[27] *Fam.* II 9, of which I am speaking, and which like *Fam.* IV 1 belongs to the group of letters written

[25] See pp. 72ff., below.
[26] *Prose,* p. 838.
[27] Rico, *Lectura,* pp. 473, 483.

or rewritten during the early 1350s, is a defense against the accusation that Petrarch's great love for Laura-laurel ("Laurea") and admiration for Augustine were both simulated. As he says in reply, against that Laura which he is alleged to have invented, he might, after all, be greatly helped by that other fabrication of his, Augustine. ("Adversus hanc simulatam, ut tu vocas, Lauream, simulatus ille michi etiam Augustinus forte profuerit.")[28] This is a play on words, of course: his supposedly fake devotion to Augustine will help him in the future to overcome his love for "Laurea," namely, his "desiderium famae" as well as his "amor."

Could this really be an allusion to Augustine's role in Book III of the *Secretum*? Not only is there not the slightest hint of the scene in the *Secretum* in which Augustine descends from heaven to visit Petrarch in his solitude, but the letter actually describes the manner in which Augustine is expected to exert his influence: through Petrarch's study of Augustine's writings ("Simulatus ille michi etiam Augustinus forte profuerit. Multa enim et gravia legendo multumque meditando, antequam senescam, senex ero").[29]

Rico asks us even more confidently to believe that Petrarch "alude al *Secretum*" in a work which is roughly contemporaneous with the 1353 version of the *Secretum* — the third book of the *Invective Contra Medicum*.[30] What he means is that the program of studies recommended by Augustine in the *Secretum* conforms to the same standard followed by Petrarch in his attack on the education of physicians in the *Invective*. Both emphasize meditation on death, knowledge of oneself, renunciation of poetry, and the correction of one's faults in old age. What is surprising, however, is not this parallelism in Petrarch's general attitude and specific motivations but Rico's manner of describing and evaluating it. Petrarch, he says, "proclaimed" in the *Invective* "that he was busy with some work that was substantially similar in form to the *Secretum* as we have it today" (*voceaba estar atareado en un escrito coincidente en forma sustancial con el Secretum hoy conservado*). I cannot see that Petrarch is referring here to the *Secretum* or to any other of his works, and I can only imagine that Rico's opinion is the product of a fervent desire to find such a reference. The simple fact is that the text of the *Invective* "alludes" to the *Secretum* as little as do the phrases in the *De Otio*, *Fam.* I 1, *Fam.* IV 1, and *Fam.* II 9, or any of the even less significant ones in other writings of Petrarch's that Rico has in mind when he contends that the "referencias" to the *Secretum* "se multiplican" in the early 1350s.[31]

---

[28] *Prose*, p. 824.
[29] Ibid.
[30] Rico, *Lectura*, p. 511.
[31] Ibid., p. 483.

CHAPTER TWO

How Much of the *Secretum* — Known from an Autograph of about 1353 — Existed in the Late 1340s? An Attempt at Restoration

(1) Some Guidelines for the Study of the *Secretum*'s Evolution

I

The transfer of the initial draft of the *Secretum* from 1342–43 to 1347 not only changes its chronology but also necessitates a change in the methods required for studying its early history. The long-accepted date of 1342–43 — between October 1342 and March 1343, to be precise[1] — was not a mere inference of modern scholars but sprang from Petrarch's own intimation of the period in which the conversation with Augustine is imagined to have taken place, a period gradually identified by hints given in the conversation. Since, moreover, it is said in the dialogue that Augustine's visit occurred "nuper," scholars seemed to face a relatively uncomplicated task: to discover later alterations and insertions by hunting down passages, quotations, and larger sections (if there were any) that fail to fit a context or a literary conceit possible as early as 1342–43. The hermeneutics of the *Secretum* at that time seemed a simple matter.

The clues we find in the *Secretum* today are no longer as clear and simple as they appeared at the time when Petrarch's fictitious dating of Augustine's "visit" in the year 1342–43 was used as a basis. For once the chronological note at the end of the final autograph listing the three years 1353, 1349, and 1347 is used in place of the references within the dialogue, we can no longer base our conclusions on a single established date: although some passages or paragraphs can now be dated 1347 instead of 1342–43, others may have been written in either 1349 or 1353. A major consequence of the redating of the original

---

[1] See Baron, *From Petrarch to Leonardo Bruni,* p. 52.

Secretum, therefore, is that the successive phases of the work can no longer be traced by the detection of interpolations alone. A one-dimensional procedure has to give way to a more complicated form of critical analysis. As with so many other literary works, the reader must first form a reasonably clear idea of the original appearance of the text before he can attempt to define the successive changes.

II

Little of this methodological concern is found in Rico's investigations. While he is revolutionary in insisting that Petrarch's concluding list of dates, "1353. 1349. 1347," must replace the questionable hints made within the conversation, his procedure is limited mainly to the observation of similarities between the *Secretum* and other, more or less contemporaneous works of Petrarch's, especially the fictitious letters contained in the early books of his *Epistolae Familiares.* But why should the existence of even numerous parallels with letters of the early 1350s favor 1353 as the year when the entire surviving text of the *Secretum* was composed? Might not the real explanation for such parallels be that motifs appearing in both works were expressed in the *Secretum* as early as 1347 and subsequently inspired the letters of the early 1350s? Only through some familiarity with the 1347 and 1349 versions of the *Secretum* could we tell.

This is not to minimize the importance of the similarities that have been discovered between certain *familiares* of the early 1350s and the *Secretum.*[2] It may be true that these two works sometimes express the same phase of Petrarch's intellectual development. In Rico's confident words, they often show "similar inspiration and tendencies"; they "complement each other" and "the *Secretum* finds a harmonious place within the environment defined by the *Familiares* up to 1353." Both are marked by a similar autobiographical and introspective curiosity and a "yearning for dialogue" that expresses itself in Petrarch's imaginary conversations with great men of antiquity — classical Romans in the letters and the church father Augustine in the *Secretum.* Because of these parallels, Rico concludes, we should look upon the late 1340s and early 1350s as a coherent period in Pe-

---

[2] Rico's volume on the *Secretum* is to be followed by another on the *Familiares.*

trarch's development, extending from his discovery of Cicero's *Epistolae ad Atticum* in Verona in 1345 (the "catalyst" for Petrarch's heightened autobiographical interest) to the fictitious letter of 1353 on his ascent of Mont Ventoux and the last version of the *Secretum*.[3]

But although the observation of uniformities in Petrarch's writings of the 1340s and 1350s is welcome, it does not help us with the problem of the evolution of the *Secretum*. Quite to the contrary, the greater the uniformity in Petrarch's thinking during the period from the mid-1340s to 1353, the less we would expect the *Secretum* of 1347 to appear so unacceptable to its author in 1353 that he would discard everything he had written earlier. Yet next to the shifting of the *Secretum*'s date of inception from 1342–43 to 1347 and the detection of some striking analogies between the *Secretum* and certain *familiares* of the early 1350s, nothing characterizes the revolt initiated by Rico against the older views of the *Secretum* more than his claim that as we know it today it is not a work of 1347 but a total "reelaboración de 1353."[4] As he summarizes his conclusions: "In everything that makes [the *Secretum*] organic, in all that concerns its unity and its sense of coherence . . . [it] can be considered a creation of 1353."[5]

It must be one of our major tasks to find a way out of this apparent dilemma.

III

Since we do not know from manuscript evidence what the text of the *Secretum* was like before 1353, it is natural to apply the methods by which classical philology has long learned to distinguish the successive layers of the works of ancient authors that survive only in a final version. Now, it cannot be denied that confidence in the results of those methods has been diminishing during the past few decades, largely because we live in a period in which historical skepticism has made deep inroads into critical scholarship. The questioning attitude of some recent students toward all sorts of problems in the study of the genesis of the *Secretum* must certainly be viewed against this widespread trend.

In the work of Rico we encounter a formal abandonment of all

[3] Rico, *Lectura,* pp. 477–479, 494.
[4] Ibid., p. 470 and passim.
[5] Ibid., p. 456.

questions regarding the state of the *Secretum* text before 1353. After much emphasis on what he calls our "inability to recover any particulars of the texts of 1347 and 1349"[6] Rico presents the thesis that in 1353 Petrarch completely rejected the two preceding drafts of his work and wrote a new one. "Without doubt," he admits, "orientaciones y elementos" of the earlier stages would persist in Petrarch's final reworking, just as others would disappear. But the persistent factors have been so intimately assimilated into the "rifacimento" of 1353 that they have lost much of their individuality, "and there is no way to distinguish them."[7] This is a fanciful web spun over the presumed gap in our knowledge, not insight gained from an actual analysis of the *Secretum*. In the same vein we are told how to hypothesize the appearance of the *Secretum* in 1347: "It is valid to conjecture that the *Secretum* [of 1347] would have contained (God knows in what form) a good number of the traits that connect the present text with the *De Vita Solitaria* and *De Otio Religioso* [of 1346 and 1347]" and with some of the early *familiares*. "Therefore, it is valid to think that the original *Secretum* was already conceived as an explication of Petrarch's *nuova maniera*, [namely] of the convergence of classicism and Christianity, of the marriage of the ethical with the aesthetic, of the great increment in reflection and subjectivity — in favor of *philosophia* at the expense of *eloquentia*. *To desire to prove more is for the present to condemn ourselves to frustration* [my emphasis]."[8]

It has seemed fit to assemble these quotations, because nothing else could equally well illustrate the point that, as in earlier *Secretum* scholarship, the newly offered picture suffers from blind spots. In years past we accepted verbatim what we were told in the *Secretum* about the date of arrival of a visitor from the hereafter (St. Augustine), neglecting our critical duty to look beyond the text to see whether allegations made in the fictive dialogue were confirmed by outside sources. Now, since no manuscripts of 1347 and 1349 are available, we are expected to be satisfied as a matter of course with what the transmitted text tells us (or seems to tell us); we should again forsake our obligation to ascertain whether any sources outside the text might enlighten us about the *Secretum*'s physical and intellec-

---

[6] Ibid., pp. 469–470. See also p. 455.
[7] Ibid., p. 470.
[8] Ibid., p. 497.

tual growth. In effect, we are being asked to forgo as impossible the very thing required for understanding the *Secretum*'s history: the reconstruction, as far as possible, of the work as it was during the 1340s. There is no doubt that this neglect could be as harmful as the unthinking use to which the "visit" of the long-dead saint has been put in the past.

(2) Consecutive Layers in the Text of Books I and II, and Petrarch's Personal Experiences during the Late 1340s

I

I propose to turn to the second book of the *Secretum* first, because unlike Book I its exploration of Petrarch's guilt and innocence against the backdrop of the medieval Seven Deadly Sins provides an opportunity to consult an objective source outside the *Secretum*.

In the section on Petrarch's concupiscence — the sin of *luxuria* in the terminology of the Scholastics and medieval father confessors — we find a Franciscus who has "relapsed" into sin after having overcome *luxuria* and kept free of it for some time.[9] As the *Secretum* tells us, he had managed for a time to stay chaste with the help of Plato's philosophical instruction, according to which nothing impairs our vision of the divinity more "quam appetitus carnales et . . . inflammata libido." "At times I raised myself up," Franciscus says, "thanks to the hand of God stretched out to me, as I recognized with incredible and immense joy. . . . Now that I have once again fallen into my old misery because of my heaviness, I feel with a keen sense of bitterness that failing which has again undone me."[10] To this Augustine replies: "Indeed, I do not think it so strange, for I have witnessed your conflict; I have seen you fall and once more rise up, and now that you are down again I have decided out of pity to help you, prostrate as you are" (. . . *et cadentem et resurgentem vidi, et nunc prostratum miseratus*

---

[9] Carrara, pp. 98–104.

[10] "Ita enim interdum, Deo manum porrigente, surrexi ut incredibili quadam et immensa cum dulcedine . . . agnoscerem; et nunc meo pondere in antiquas miserias relapsus, quid me iterum perdiderit cum amarissimo gustu mentis experior" (ibid., p. 100).

opem ferre disposui).[11] "Cadentem," "resurgentem," "et nunc prostratum" (or "nunc in antiquas miserias relapsus"): one wonders what personal experience could have inspired the joy and then the misery displayed in these statements.

Earlier readers of the *Secretum* recalled the sexual relationship which resulted in the birth of Petrarch's daughter, Francesca, in 1343 [12] and suggested that this was the source of Petrarch's distress. But there is nothing to prove or disprove such a conjecture, and his despair seems to have had deeper emotional roots than the impending birth of an illegitimate child, to whom he was to be a loving father. That guess was appropriate as long as it accompanied the belief that the first draft of the *Secretum* was written as early as 1342–43. But now that it has been shown that no part of the *Secretum* was conceived before 1347, it no longer seems likely that Petrarch was thinking of events of 1342 and 1343, although this cannot be excluded from the outset in view of the fact that the Franciscus of the dialogue occasionally shows the mark of the year to which the "visit" of Augustine is attributed. This matter cannot be decided unless we find reliable information about Petrarch's private life during the period between 1342–43 and the second half of the 1340s.

In the case of Petrarch's *luxuria,* such information exists in an almost documentary form. When Petrarch (born on July 20, 1304) was approaching his fortieth birthday — that is, the symbolic date by which he hoped to be free from carnal sin because Augustine had experienced his conversion before he turned forty [13] — he decided to drive himself to still greater efforts to lead a chaste life by carefully recording his lapses. This unique diary of a sort runs from April 21, 1344, to August 2, 1349; that is, it includes the period of the first two drafts of the *Secretum*.[14] For five and a half years Petrarch faithfully noted the exact time when he, a cleric who had taken the lower

[11] Ibid.

[12] See Baron, *From Petrarch to Leonardo Bruni,* p. 60.

[13] We will deal with this problem in detail in Chap. 7 (4).

[14] It has been known and accessible since Pierre de Nolhac discovered and published it from the endpapers of a manuscript in Petrarch's library containing the correspondence between Abélard and Héloïse and a number of other medieval writings (Ms. Paris lat. 2923). See Pierre de Nolhac, "Excursus VI: Les mémoriaux intimes de Pétrarque," in *Pétrarque et l'humanisme* (Paris, 1892; 2nd ed., 1907).

orders, fell into carnal sin, mixing factual accounts with laments and indications of when he felt the need for, and consulted, a father confessor. These entries allow us to draw a curve of Petrarch's actual defeats and victories. From April 1344 to October 1345 he was in sin; subsequently, for more than two and a half years, he was victor over himself. From May 30, 1348, to August 2, 1349, he was again in sin, the record ending about a year before his pilgrimage to Rome on the occasion of the jubilee of 1350, the event he later remembered as having put an end to his carnal desire.

The failure of Petrarch students to use this unique document for the interpretation of the *Secretum*, as long as its earliest draft was assumed to have been written in 1342–43, is easily explained: it must have seemed that Petrarch's "cadere" and "resurgere" followed by a relapse, as set forth in the *luxuria* section of the *Secretum*, had occurred much earlier than the time recorded in the diary. Not until the earliest *Secretum* draft is redated to 1347 can it be seen that the dialogue and the diary are contemporaneous and the dated entries of the diary can provide a key to the date of the *luxuria* discussion found in the dialogue. This unparalleled opportunity for verifying a portion of Book II makes it necessary to go into what may perhaps seem to be tedious detail.

There is no reason to believe that the opening entry of the diary, dated April 21, 1344, records the first time Petrarch "fell." The fact that Francesca was born in 1343 makes it probable that he had been engaging in carnal intercourse for some time. Remembering, furthermore, that in April 1344 he was nearing his forties, we shall not be wrong in assuming that his entries were begun in that April because the approaching end of his fortieth year was causing him increasing restlessness, and that the merciless recording of his transgressions was a semi-monastic, psychological device for intensifying his own distress and shame.

A perusal of the diary assures us that it took Petrarch a long time before he could feel he had begun a spiritual "resurgence." According to his entries, May was the only month in 1344 in which he was free of carnal desire, and although he may have thought after August 23 that he had attained his goal, the summer and autumn of the following year (1345) proved that nothing had changed. In July and October of that year the old type of entry reappears, along with what must

be a reference to confessional aid: "Hinc fr[ater] celitus adhib[itus] et
cet" — a sign that he still felt the invincibility of his appetites.

After October 1345, however, he at long last overcame his desires
and was delivered from *luxuria* for more than two and a half years. It
is easy to see the cause of this change: shortly after that date Petrarch
returned to Provence from northern Italy for the happy solitary stay
in the Vaucluse during which the *De Vita Solitaria* and *De Otio Religioso*
were composed. In November 1347 he returned for another limited
period to the cities of northern Italy. After spending half a year there
(from November 1347 to late May 1348), he fell back into *luxuria*. His
first confession of this relapse was entered in his diary on May 30, a
week and a half after learning about Laura's death. This is not the
place to weigh what Laura's disappearance from the world and his
return to the Italian milieu, as well as the deaths of many of his most
intimate friends during the Black Death, might have done to his
inner stability; but the obvious conclusion is that it was this profound
upheaval in his life — and not any occurrence of preceding years —
that brought about the relapse in his bitter struggle against temptation. Not only do we find him in September 1348 again having re-
course to the confessional, but when he began to slip he filled the
space preceding his May 30, 1348, entry with lamentations. From
then until August 2, 1349, every month, with the exception only of
March and April 1349, shows record of cohabitation, resulting in a
list almost twice as long as that of 1344–45.

At the same time it should be stressed that this relapse was not
followed by another, big or small, and that the confession in his diary
of August 2, 1349, seems to mark the last time that Petrarch was
unable to conquer his desire. The following year, 1350, was the year
of the Roman jubilee, and in October he set out on his pilgrimage to
Rome. As will be discussed more fully in a later chapter, his correspondence reveals that in future years he was to regard that event as
the turning point in the history of his carnal vexations.[15] He was
then forty-six and three months old.

The surviving version of the *luxuria* section, because it exactly
parallels the record in his diary, must have been written in 1349 —
or at any rate before Petrarch felt the beneficial influence of the 1350
pilgrimage. Thus not merely a line or two of a version earlier than

[15] Below, p. 212.

1353 has been preserved but an entire section of the second book, which, in conception and form, is still what it must have been in 1349.

Given the fundamental importance of the *luxuria* section for our knowledge of the early *Secretum,* it is worth anticipating some possible doubts regarding this account. One of them might issue from a hypothesis already mentioned near the start of this section, namely, that in part the *Secretum* may not record Petrarch's introspection at the time of his writing but instead refer to conditions prevailing in the period presupposed in the conversation, the winter of 1342–43. Since Petrarch had been in sin during that period as well, as Francesca's birth in 1343 indicates, might it not be conjectured that the *luxuria* section reflects Petrarch's suffering in 1342–43?

The answer is that such an assumption would present us with an utterly implausible situation. For since the "relapse" described in the *luxuria* section was preceded by a period of sin that was followed by a temporary victory, the identification of the relapse with events in 1342–43 would only be possible if we assumed that the very same cycle had also occurred in the late 1330s and early 1340s: sin and temporary victory followed by a relapse. In that case we would have a first occurrence of the three-stage cycle during the late 1330s and early 1340s, described in the *luxuria* section, and a recurrence of the same cycle during the middle and late 1340s, described in Petrarch's diary. But as soon as we identify the "relapse" of the *luxuria* section not with the year Francesca was born but with the relapse of 1348–49 so much deplored in the diary, everything becomes simple and natural; we see that no repetition of the cycle is needed. In such a situation one should recall an old rule of criticism: if there is an alternative between a simple and a complicated explanation, we may expect simplicity to point to the correct solution.

A second hypothesis which, if correct, would seem to contradict the facts emerging from our analysis of the *luxuria* section is that the *Secretum* was "recast" as a whole in 1353. If Petrarch wrote a virtually new text in that year, the *luxuria* section as we have it cannot have been composed in 1349, and one might then argue as follows: the fact that Petrarch was already free of *luxuria* in 1353 is not an insurmountable obstacle to the assumption that he wrote the *luxuria* section at that time. He must have rewritten the *Secretum* text — perhaps even twice (not only in 1353 but also in 1349), according to Rico — at least partly for artistic reasons; for why should he have rewritten it in its entirety unless he was concerned with its literary balance and effectiveness? Perhaps he wished to present the misery of his past *luxuria* in a dramatic way, and in that case it might be rash to conclude that he could not in 1353 have depicted the sin committed and the misery suffered in 1348–49 as if they were a present evil. This extravagant hypothesis — that the extant *luxuria* text with its despair and lamentations might have been composed after Petrarch's inner peace was restored in 1350 — can be definitively excluded only by refuting the assumption that the *Secretum* was completely rewritten in 1353. Such a refutation will be the main objective of Chapter 4.

Finally, to anticipate a third possible scruple: one might ask whether the relatively short *luxuria* section does not offer too narrow a base for judging the second book in general. Is it not possible that the discussion of *luxuria* is, after all, an exception? Why should we think that other sections dealing with the deadly sins were also in place by 1349? The obvious answer is that *luxuria* appears in Book II only as one link in the traditional chain of sins upon which Petrarch is being spiritually examined. The discussion must from the outset have included all seven of the deadly sins in order to establish which of them might have created obstacles to Petrarch's spiritual strivings. Accordingly, although we possess the badly needed chronological evidence only for *luxuria,* we may assume that all the sins were being treated in Book II when *luxuria* was first discussed. There is no guarantee, of course, that just because the *luxuria* section remained unchanged in 1353, vital new experiences did not induce Petrarch in that year to make changes or additions in sections devoted to other sins. Quite to the contrary; it will be a burden of Chapter 6 to prove that at least two of those sections — those on *avaritia* and *accidia* — were indeed enlarged and changed in 1353 by crucial interpolations. But this should not cause us to forget that by 1349 the general content of Book II must have been a systematic scrutiny of Petrarch's behavior in regard to all seven of the deadly sins.

Only in one respect does the *luxuria* diary fail to reveal everything we would like to know about the history of the *luxuria* paragraph: it does not tell us how the original text of 1347 looked, before Petrarch's relapse into sin inspired the form of 1349 which has been handed down to us. But we happen to have another unusual source of information, one which can tell us something about the text of 1347 now that we are familiar with the vicissitudes of Petrarch's sexual desires.

The source I have in mind is *Fam.* X 5, a letter in which Petrarch reminds his brother Gherardo, the Carthusian monk, that he had admonished Petrarch to give up carnal intercourse when they had last met. He has been following this advice, Petrarch says in the letter, and "more than death itself, I now fear cohabitation with a woman, without which I sometimes believed I could not live."

When Gherardo joined the charterhouse of Montrieux in 1342, his close relationship with Francesco ended suddenly, and thereafter the meetings of the two brothers were few and far between. Petrarch visited Montrieux twice, in the spring of 1347 and in April 1353, and thus the year in which Gherardo gave his oral advice must have been either 1342 or 1347. Petrarch scholars have accordingly split into two groups, one maintaining that *Fam.* X 5 was written in 1347 and contains a reference to Petrarch's meeting with Gherardo in 1342,[16] the other and larger one maintaining that it was written in 1352 and contains a reference to their meeting in 1347.[17] But in light of what we know about the pattern of Petrarch's sexual behavior, this choice between alternative dates no longer exists. He could not have believed in 1347 that he could not live without a woman, for he was chaste during the early part of that year and continued to be so for another year and a half.[18] Gherardo could not therefore have admonished him in 1347 to shun "cohabitation with a woman."[19]

The other alternative must be the correct one. Gherardo's oral counsel was given in 1342, and *Fam.* X 5 was written sometime during the two and a half years between October 1345 and May 1348 in which Petrarch was free from desire — basically, that is, at the time of the first drafting of the *Secretum.* Everything agrees with this conclusion, and it can be relied upon that Petrarch was confiding essen-

[16] Thus Salvatore Maugeri, *Ricostruzione storica della conversione morale del Petrarca* (Catania, 1932), p. 44 (cited in Ernest H. Wilkins, *Petrarch's Correspondence* [Padua, 1960], pp. 38, 66).

[17] From Giuseppe Fracassetti, ed., *Francisci Petrarchae epistolae de rebus familiaribus et variae* (Florence, 1859–63), and Henry Cochin, *Le frère de Pétrarque* (Paris, 1903), pp. 53, 81, to Morris Bishop, *Letters from Petrarch* (London, 1966), and Rico, *Lectura,* p. 194, n.230.

[18] See p. 26, above.

[19] This also nullifies Wilkins' and Constable's educated guess, 1352 (Ernest H. Wilkins, *Life of Petrarch* [Chicago, 1961], p. 117, and Giles Constable, "Petrarch and Monasticism," in *Francesco Petrarca: Citizen of the World,* ed. Aldo S. Bernardo, Proceedings of the World Petrarch Congress, Washington, D.C., 1974 [Padua and Albany, N.Y., 1980], p. 74, n.102).

tially the same feelings to his brother that were in the analysis of his *luxuria* in the original, 1347 draft of the *Secretum*. We may even go so far as to speculate that what follows in the letter also had a parallel in the original *Secretum* text, before it was replaced by a revision in 1349: "though I am often bewildered by painful temptations, when I recall what a woman really is, every temptation quickly vanishes and I regain my freedom and peace."[20]

It is another question whether the altered conduct with regard to *luxuria* was the only change reflected in the 1349 text of Book II or whether Petrarch's conduct with regard to other sins also changed between 1347 and 1349. The most profound alterations in the second book were not made until 1353, as we shall learn in Chapter 6; but there is at least one other sign that serious changes in Petrarch's manner of living left their mark on Book II in 1349. We must say a word about this before turning to the more complicated situation in Book I.

The sin of *ambitio* in the second book is not usually included in the canon of the Seven Deadly Sins, and it is treated by Petrarch as an annex to *avaritia*. In the *avaritia* paragraph, Augustine accuses Franciscus of being tainted with political and social *ambitio* as well as avarice, an accusation the truth of which Franciscus vehemently denies. An intimation of a recent change in his life is embedded in Franciscus' self-defense. "Then it has been of no help to me that I fled from cities as long as I was at liberty to do so [*dum licuit*]. It has been of no help that I have scorned crowds and public life, have settled down in the midst of woods and in rural silence, and have shown my hatred for empty honors. For I am still accused of having been ambitious my entire life!"[21] Under no circumstances can Petrarch have written this in 1347, when he was living in the "silvarum recessus et silentia rura" of the Vaucluse and felt he was free of ambition. But in the period between his temporary move to Italy late in 1347 and his return to the Vaucluse in mid-1351 — the period which he spent

---

[20]". . . quod consortium femine, sine quo interdum extimaveram non posse vivere, morte nunc gravius pertimesco, et quanquam sepe tentationibus turber acerrimis, tamen dum in animum redit quid est femina, omnis tentatio confestim avolat et ego ad libertatem et ad pacem meam redeo" (*Fam.* X 5 [29]).

[21]"Nichil ergo michi profuit urbes fugisse, dum licuit, populosque et actus publicos despexisse, silvarum recessus et silentia rura secutum odium ventosis honoribus indixisse: adhuc ambitionis insimulor!" (Carrara, p. 94).

mostly as a denizen of Parma and Padua in close connection with the
courts of these two cities — he could no longer hide the truth from
himself that he had developed a sense of ambition. We may say,
therefore, that we have a situation here which parallels that of the
luxuria paragraph in 1349: sudden changes in Petrarch's external life
caused him to introduce the idea of "curae" into a paragraph of the
second book for which there had been no need in 1347.

But can we be sure that the addition to the original text was made
in 1349 and not later, in 1353, since Petrarch also spent the second
half of the latter year in northern Italy? At that time he was similarly
connected with a princely court, that of the Visconti in Milan. There
is a clear difference in tone, however, between the changes made in
1349 and those made in 1353. Petrarch's attitude toward city life in
the *ambitio* paragraph is wholly positive, and the abandonment of
rural life stirs up no regrets, whereas the turn to city life in 1353 is the
last great "cura" added to the *Secretum*. There will be much to say
about this contrast in the course of our study.[22]

II

Let us now turn our attention to the genesis of Book I. Among the
reasons for transferring the origin of the *Secretum* from 1342–43 to
1347 is Petrarch's statement that by the time he composed Book I,
Augustine's *De Vera Religione* had become for him one of the most beloved and intensely studied writings of the church father. This did
not fully happen, as Rico has proven, until Petrarch wrote his *De
Otio Religioso* (about March 1347), in which the *De Vera Religione* is
given a place of honor similar to that in the *Secretum*.[23]

Do not the pages of Book I which thus exclude a time of origin
much earlier than 1347 also exclude any time much after the moment
of Petrarch's greatest enthusiasm for the *De Vera Religione*, when he
filled the margins of his copy with admiring annotations? As the
Franciscus of the *Secretum* describes the role played by the *De Vera
Religione* for his spiritual development: "It was not so long ago [*nuper*]
that I came across that work of yours in one of my digressions from

---

[22] In particular in Chap. 6 (1) and 8 (2). The above interpretation of the *ambitio*
paragraph corrects my earlier, erroneous statement that possibly only the words
"dum licuit" were written in 1349 (Baron, *From Petrarch to Leonardo Bruni*, p. 63).

[23] See p. 5f., above.

the study of philosophy and poetry, and it was with very great eagerness that I perused it in its entirety [*perlegi*]. Indeed, I was like a person setting out from his own country to see the world and coming to
the gate of some famous city quite new to him, where, charmed by the
novelty of everything around him, he stops now here, now there, and
looks intently at all that meets his gaze."[24] Now, it is true that Rico,
not without reason, found fault with this dramatic over-simplification
of Petrarch's, because in fact Petrarch had become familiar with the
De Vera Religione more gradually. Nevertheless, these vivid pages can
serve as guidance in another respect; for whether literally true or
not,[25] the phrase "nuper incidi" and the rejoicing in a work that eventually seemed to him to have unlocked a new spiritual world set the
tone for the entire paragraph in Book I. Since we find that the exceptional importance the *De Vera Religione* had for Petrarch about 1347 is
also evident in the *De Otio Religioso* — whereas the *De Vera Religione*
had lost its novelty for him by 1353 — it seems natural to conclude
that these pages in Book I were inspired by Petrarch's experiences
around 1347.

The correctness of this interpretation is supported by the context
in which the discussion of the *De Vera Religione* takes place in the *Secretum*. It appears on the last pages of Book I and thus leads directly to
the analysis in Book II of Petrarch's life and state of mind with respect to the Seven Deadly Sins. It is, indeed, in this conclusion to
Book I that Augustine is made to formulate the ultimate objective of
the soul searching pursued in the subsequent books. Here he points
out the dangers of entanglement in secular interests and pursuits.
When the "imagines rerum visibilium" crowd in upon the soul, it
grows heavy and confused, because it is not made for them. "Hence
that disease of confusing delusions . . . damages the thinking faculty
of the soul, and with its fatal, distracting complexity bars the way to
clear meditation, by which it would mount to the threshold of the
one supreme illuminator of the world."[26] To Petrarch at that time,
this dualistic picture of the world and human life was nowhere more

---

[24]"In quem librum nuper incidi, a philosophorum et poetarum lectione digre-
diens, itaque cupidissime perlegi: haud aliter quam qui videndi studio peregrinatur
a patria, ubi ignotum famose cuiuspiam urbis limen ingreditur, nova captus locorum dulcedine passimque subsistens, obvia queque circumspicit" (Carrara, p. 66).
[25]This will be discussed in Chap. 7 (3).
[26]"Hinc pestis illa fantasmatum vestros discerpens laceransque cogitatus, medita-

forcefully expressed than in the *De Vera Religione*. It is the "varietas mortifera," the over-abundance of interests and passions, that gives rise to "illa intestina discordia," as it is called in the last paragraph of Book I. In Book II, Augustine will try to discover the root of such distractions by examining the marks left on Petrarch's life and thought by the deadly sins. In Book III he will make an (only half successful) attempt to deliver Petrarch from his "two adamantine chains";[27] that is, the two fetters from which Petrarch is unable to free himself: his love for Laura and his thirst for glory.

This, then, is the spiritual concatenation between the final pages of Book I and Books II and III. The end of Book I, in fact, formally defines the central point of Petrarch's entire "secretus conflictus curarum mearum": "This," says Augustine, "is the disease that has harmed you. . . . Overwhelmed by too many diverse impressions made on it, and forever struggling with its own cares, your weak spirit is crushed, so that it has no strength to judge."[28]

Viewed against this over-all structure of the *Secretum,* it is safe to say that Book II can never have existed alone, that is, without the preparation and introduction given it at the end of Book I. This is not the same as saying that the first two books in their entirety must have formed part of the *Secretum* during the 1340s; for it is possible, of course, that those final programmatic pages of the first book might originally have opened Book II and that the rest of Book I might not yet have existed. Indeed, this cannot be excluded unless we can convince ourselves that the concluding pages of Book I are in clear correlation with the preceding sections of the book. A structural analysis of Book I is thus a necessary part of our effort to reconstruct the original *Secretum.*

III

Does the conversation throughout the first book pave the way for the Augustinian finale? According to Rico, the key to the train of thought

---

tionibusque clarificis, quibus ad unum solum summumque lumen ascenditur, iter obstruens varietate mortifera" (Carrara, pp. 64–66).

[27] As Augustine calls them near the beginning of Book III: "Duabus adhuc adamantinis dextra levaque premeris cathenis, que nec de morte neque de vita sinunt cogitare" (ibid., p. 130).

[28] Ibid., pp. 66–68.

characteristic of Book I is to be found in its stoic ideas, which also
dominate many of Petrarch's *familiares* from the early 1350s onward.
The opening pages of Book I, Rico says, "unfold from the nucleus of
an initial syllogism," which the Franciscus of the *Secretum* "does not
hesitate to identify . . . as 'stoic,'" and "the stoic premise of the 'opi-
nionum perversitas' systematically reappears to explain the great
questions of the debate" and "is, clearly, a key to the first book."[29]
While acknowledging the importance of the stoic element for Book I,
we ought to bear in mind that the extent of the stoic ideas in the debate, which reminds us of the *familiares* of the early 1350s, need not
necessarily have been the same in the original *Secretum*. It is easily
possible that stoic motives and definitions were inserted when Petrarch's stoic tendencies were growing particularly strong in his *familiares*. We shall have to keep this possibility in mind regarding the
origin of the *Secretum's* Stoicism.

But let us return to the original question, whether Petrarch's
praise of Augustine's *De Vera Religione* is an organic outgrowth of the
preceding discussion. After the unmistakably stoic hue of the first
four or five pages of Book I (about which we shall have more to say
presently), the emphasis changes, and Augustine emerges not as a
semi-stoic philosopher but as a religious and thoroughly medieval
teacher. Moreover, from here on, the conversation with Augustine
becomes a critical examination of Petrarch's own spiritual experience
and needs. Augustine must be aware, says Franciscus, "how often I
have pondered over my *miseria* and the subject of death"; but such
meditation has always been helpful only for a short time. This is the
reason, he declares, why he resists Augustine's assertion "that no one
has ever fallen into misery except of his own free will, or remained
miserable except by his own consent; the exact opposite of what my
own sad experience has proved." The first break in Franciscus' defense comes when Augustine reminds him that without sin there is no
miseria, and without freedom of will there is no sin. "I am compelled
to acknowledge that my *miseria* began through my own will," replies
Franciscus. "I feel it is true of myself, and I conjecture the same to be
true of others." But just "as it is true that no man ever fell involuntarily, so it is true that countless numbers of those who have thus fallen
voluntarily nevertheless do not voluntarily remain so. I affirm this

---

[29]"Es, claro, una llave del libro primero" (Rico, *Lectura,* p. 459).

confidently of myself."[30] With this the debate turns to the question whether Franciscus has had the right sort of "will," and the answer comes not from any philosophy but from the example set by Augustine, who during his days on earth likewise "filled the air with the bitterest sighs." At the end "I remained what I was until deep meditation at last showed me the root of my *miseria*. . . . And after that my will became fully changed"; weakness turned to strength and "I was transformed instantly and became another man, another Augustine altogether."[31]

This recollection of Augustine's conversion has the strongest effect on the Franciscus of Book I. From it emerges the crucial question which he puts to Augustine: how can it be that "until now I have not wanted what I have always believed I wanted?" The answer Augustine gives is that wishes and desires remain powerless until they shape man's entire being. "Such a desire can grow fully in no one who has not extinguished all other desires. You know how many different things one longs for in life. You must first learn to count all these as nothing before you can rise to the desire for the highest felicity."[32]

The first step in this self-education, Augustine goes on to say, is continuously to think of oneself as a mortal being. He draws a frightening picture of death, bodily decomposition, and putrefaction — the nearest literary counterpart to the awesome fresco in the *camposanto* of Pisa[33] — only to hear from Franciscus that he had indeed long been accustomed "to lay down my body at night as do those who die, and my shrinking mind imagines that the hour itself, with all its horrors, is at hand. I conceive it all so intently, as if I were in the very agony of dying."[34] And yet, after such violent emotion, "we return to what we were before. . . . What, then, is it, I ask, that holds me back? What hidden obstacle is there which makes it come about that hitherto all these meditations have availed nothing . . . and I continue to be the same person I have always been?"[35] The cause cannot be an inclination to look upon one's death as something still far in the future,

[30] Carrara, pp. 36–38.
[31] Ibid., p. 40.
[32] Ibid., pp. 44–46.
[33] Ibid., p. 54.
[34] Ibid., p. 58.
[35] Ibid.

though Augustine suggests this, because Franciscus feels certain that no one else has tended so much from early youth to make death the very center of his thinking. And so, he eventually exclaims, "the question remains: what is it that holds me back?" Whereupon Augustine finally tries to find out "what stands in the way of your efforts."[36] He now emerges — on those concluding pages of Book I — as the writer of the *De Vera Religione*.

The first, strong impression left by this reading is of a logical, continuous train of thought, almost throughout the first book, that ultimately culminates in the praise of the *De Vera Religione*. And since the pages containing that praise stem, as we have seen, from the period around 1347, there can be little doubt that virtually everything we recognize as Augustinian in Book I must have been part of the original *Secretum*. If anything can serve as a "key" to Book I, it must indeed be this persistent component, not Stoicism. But persistent does not mean ubiquitous, and there is some justification for Rico's comment that from the very beginning of the book, pages can be found with unquestionably stoic flavor, such as is also found in some of the *familiares* of the early 1350s.

We have already intimated what the reason for this might be: the Augustinian overtones, which must have been characteristic of the first, 1347 draft of Book I, may in certain places have been given a new veneer of stoic reasoning during the early 1350s, when Petrarch showed a strong preference for stoic attitudes. This would, of course, remain a mere hypothesis if we were unable to recognize the fractures where the original Augustinian context was interrupted and later resumed. But we are far from such a state of ignorance, as the ease with which we can recognize the Stoicism of the first four or five pages of the book already indicates. We will see presently that there are only one or two other basically stoic sections in the text of the first book. There is, of course, no guarantee that more minor alterations were not also made when Petrarch revised at least a few portions of his work in 1349 and 1353; in fact, there ought to be such changes in the text. But this is a different matter from those substantial, uninterrupted sections whose signs of composition during the 1350s — stoic ideas and formulations as well as the use of the term "stoic phi-

---

[36] Ibid., pp. 62–64.

losophers" — are so prevalent that no one can doubt their late origin. If we are able to delineate the boundaries of these major groups of stoic-sounding pages, we shall have isolated the substantial additions to the text and be justified in thinking that whatever is left of the first book is fundamentally the text composed in 1347.

Let us try to define those islands of Stoicism in a primarily Augustinian context.

IV

I have been talking cautiously about "one or two" stoic sections in Book I, aside from the stoic part at the beginning of the book, because one of those sections is not clearly marked by an assemblage of stoic dicta; and yet it does contain an intimation of stoic ethics and psychology.

This intimation is given at the crucial point where Augustine is at last ready to counsel Franciscus concerning the causes of his lack of spiritual earnestness — just before Franciscus commends Augustine's *De Vera Religione* for having given him the greatest help. Augustine refers to Virgil's famous verses on the divine human semen, which the dullness of the body constantly suppresses:

> . . . hence spring fears,
> Desire, and grief, and pleasures of the world,
> And so, in darkness prisoned, they no more
> Look upward to heaven's face.[37]

"Do you not discern in the poet's words that four-headed monster so deadly to man's nature?" Augustine asks Franciscus. "I clearly discern the fourfold passion of our nature," Franciscus replies, and then analyzes this perilous human passion: "First, we divide it in two with respect to past and future, and then subdivide it with respect to good and evil. And so, distracted by these four winds, the quietness of the human soul perishes."[38]

This, of course, is the language of the Stoic school; two pairs of

---

[37]"Hinc metuunt cupiuntque dolent gaudentque, neque auras / respiciunt, clause tenebris et carcere ceco" (*Aeneid* VI, verses 730–734). I am following William H. Draper's translation in his *Petrarch's Secret* (London, 1911), p. 42.

[38]Carrara, p. 64.

principal human passions had in fact been distinguished by Stoics since Zeno.[39] The conclusion thus seems to suggest itself that we have found a case where the "stoic" Petrarch of the 1350s expanded and modified his Augustinian reasoning. But we find these same Virgilian verses already quoted in Augustine's *De Civitate Dei* XIV 3 with precisely the same interpretation, including the reference to the stoic "quattuor animi perturbationes: cupiditatem, timorem, laetitiam, tristitiam."[40] Given Petrarch's life-long esteem for this work of Augustine's, the stoic comments on the Virgilian verses reproduced in the *Secretum* appear in a different light. Once we recognize that Petrarch merely adopted a stoic interpretation contained in one of Augustine's works, we must admit that he could have done this as easily in 1347 as in 1353; and the apparent exception to the rule that stoic-sounding passages in the first book of the *Secretum* are collected in special pockets of the text turns out not to be an exception after all. The real stoic commentator in this case is not the Petrarch of the *Secretum* but the Augustine of the *De Civitate Dei*. So this ambiguous case has to be ruled out, but our analysis of the two remaining stoic areas in the first book — one of them the introductory pages at the beginning of the book — stands manifestly on safer ground. It will be best to begin with the second, since its boundaries are evident and, when sufficiently analyzed, beyond dispute.

This area is found at the very center of Augustine's admonition to Franciscus to base all serious spiritual aspirations on the meditation of death. After Augustine's complaint that "you will find few people who give serious consideration to the fact that they will die,"[41] it takes several pages before Franciscus' claim to be one of those few is refuted by Augustine's accusation that his way of meditating does little good, that he must let it "sink into his heart"[42] by imagining the agony of death and the macabre decomposition of each organ of the body.[43] On the intervening pages[44] — at a quite unlikely spot, that is

[39] See Wilhelm Windelband, *Geschichte der abendländischen Philosophie im Altertum* (Munich, 1923), p. 233.

[40] See Carrara, p. 64, n.1.

[41] Ibid., p. 50.

[42] "Et ego quidem non ambigo . . . crebras cogitationes mortis occurrere, sed que nec satis alte descendant . . ." (ibid., p. 54).

[43] Ibid. See paraphrase, p. 35, above.

[44] Carrara, pp. 52–54.

— we are confronted by a discussion of whether everyone may not be expected to be conscious of his mortality, because the generally accepted "definition" of man implies that he is an "animal" equipped with reason and subject to death. This "definition" is subsequently used by Augustine to depict the role played by reason in the thinking of an ideal human being: "of someone so governed by reason that all his conduct is regulated by it, all his appetites subject to it alone; someone who has so mastered every motion of his spirit through reason that he knows it alone distinguishes him from the savagery of the brute, and that it is only by submission to its guidance that he deserves the name of human"; a sage "so convinced of his own mortality as to have it always before his eyes." This is the tone of some of the *familiares* of the early 1350s, and the entire paragraph looks like a paradigm of the manner in which Petrarch might be expected to "stoicize" his originally Augustinian discussion in 1353.

This glorification of reason appears together with a topic that even more clearly cannot have been treated earlier than 1353. When Franciscus refers to the definition of man that emphasizes his mortality, Augustine inveighs against the craze found among modern schoolmen for defining everything: "This prattling of the dialecticians will never cease; it throws up summaries and definitions like bubbles, matter indeed for endless controversy, but for the most part they know nothing of the real truth of the things they talk about. So if you ask one of this school for the definition of a human being . . . , he has his answer down pat, as the saying goes. . . . The best way to deal with this brood . . . is to launch at their heads some such invective as this: You wretched creatures, why this everlasting labor for nothing . . . ? Heaven grant that your foolishness . . . does as little harm as possible to the excellent minds and capacities of the young!"[45]

This is an exact counterpart to Petrarch's well-known controversy — unparalleled in his earlier years — with the "dialecticians" pilloried in his *Invective Contra Medicum* (composed in 1352–53); and since the topic appears quite unconnected with the basic theme of Petrarch's striving for spirituality in the first book of the *Secretum,* one cannot doubt that these ideas must have been placed in the *Secretum* at about the time when Petrarch composed the *Invective.*

[45] Ibid., p. 52.

The consequences for our understanding of the origin of the area we are analyzing, and of the genesis of the first book in general, are so obvious that they need hardly be spelled out. But a final appraisal should not be undertaken without an experimental rereading: let us see what Petrarch's text would be like if we skipped the stoic part of suspected late origin and read the remaining text.

> Aug. to Fr.: "You will find few people who give serious consideration to the fact that they will die. . . ."
>
> Fr.: "Until now I have believed myself to be one of that number."
>
> Aug.: "I do not doubt, since in your life experience has served you so often as a teacher and you so often remember what you read in books, that the thought of death has more than once entered your head. But still it has not sunk into your heart as deeply as it ought to."
>
> Fr.: "What do you call sinking into my heart? Though I think I understand, I should like you to explain it more clearly."

Then Augustine explains by unveiling the full, macabre picture of dying and death.[46]

The reader who recalls the circuitous route of Petrarch's argument will be struck by the natural simplicity in the flow of thought and expression when the suspect passages (amounting to more than a page) are thus removed. As the traditional text stands, a strange detour takes us from the accusation that there are few human beings who think earnestly enough of death, to the discussion of the definition of man as mortal, to the "garrulitas dialecticorum" in the universities, to the ideal image of a man ruled by reason alone, back to the initial accusation that only rare people are capable of such earnest thought, and finally, to Petrarch's long-delayed response to Augustine: "Until now I have believed myself to be one of that number."

The evidence that this suspect paragraph is indeed an insertion satisfies all three criteria required for discovering interpolations in a text. First, the style of expression and direction of thought in the suspect area ought to be different from those in the body of the work in

---

[46] Aug.: ". . . paucos invenies sat profunde cogitantes esse sibi necessario moriendum" (ibid., p. 50). Fr.: "Ego me hactenus ex paucis rebar." Aug.: "Et ego quidem non ambigo tibi tam multa . . . ex librorum lectione repetenti, crebras cogitationes mortis occurrere, sed que nec satis alte descendant nec satis tenaciter hereant" (ibid., p. 54).

question; as we have seen, in this case they are strikingly different.[47] Second, there should be at least one line or paragraph in the insertion that points clearly to a specific date; there is a paragraph pointing to 1352–53.[48] Finally, if the suspect area is a true insertion, the text preceding and following should connect coherently and stand on its own when the interpolation is removed; this, too, has been demonstrated in the case under review. Even if there were no second "stoic pocket" within Book I, therefore, we would now be in a position to argue that since Petrarch inserted at least one paragraph based on Stoicism during the early 1350s, an older text must have existed into which the "stoicizing" paragraph was incorporated.

But this interpolation in the body of the discussion on the meditation of death is not the only evidence of later interference; we have already mentioned that Rico drew attention to the fact that Book I opens with a number of stoic-sounding pages.[49] A scrutiny of those first pages, in my judgment, yields results no less definitive than the exploration of the area just discussed, although the structure of the introductory pages is more complicated and consequently requires a greater critical effort. However, an additional reward will be a more detailed view of the working methods used by Petrarch as he gradually corrected some of his pages.

V

At the beginning of Book I, Augustine's diagnosis of Petrarch's chief psychological problem — the inability of his "will" to overcome the distraction of countless worldly pursuits — is almost immediately followed by a discussion (comprising several pages) of the stoic doctrine that no true sage can be unhappy ("miser") against his will. Augustine here appears as a teacher of stoic wisdom, and Franciscus' natural inclination chafes against his teacher's stoic bent — "You ask me to return to the precepts of the Stoics, which are remote from the opinions of the people and nearer to truth than to usage"[50] — until

[47] See esp. p. 39, above.
[48] Ibid.
[49] See pp. 33f., above.
[50] "... ad stoicorum precepta me revocas, populorum opinionibus aversa et veritati propinquiora quam usui" (Carrara, p. 34).

finally Franciscus admits that he does not "doubt that the Stoics' rules are far wiser than the blunders of the crowd." Yet he continues to lament: "Even though the maxim of the Stoics holds good, one can concede that many people [like myself] are very unhappy in spite of themselves and even though they deplore it."[51] In these pages, where Augustine has almost become a Stoic, we are again, as we shall see, looking over the shoulder of the half-stoic Petrarch of 1353.

Our understanding of the scene and its chronology is enhanced by a rather surprising aspect: the "stoic" intermezzo is sandwiched between an analysis by Augustine of the incentives of an efficient human will (on the first page) and a reiteration of this analysis a few pages later. The latter is introduced by Augustine's remark, at the conclusion of his appeal to stoic authority, that "we have wandered somewhat from our course, but we are slowly working back to our starting point. Or have you forgotten whence we set out?"[52] To which Franciscus replies: "I had begun to lose sight of it, but it is coming back to me now." Then Augustine refreshes Franciscus' memory by ostensibly repeating the advice he gives on the first page for the strengthening of Franciscus' will.[53]

Now, this reiteration need not in itself raise suspicions regarding the unity of composition in this part of the dialogue. Nevertheless, we should carefully examine the context in which the conversation begins and the manner in which the reiteration takes place; for it is not really true that Augustine repeats his advice to Franciscus. A comparison shows that the two suggestions for hardening the will in three successive steps are by no means identical. On the first page of the book, the presentation stresses that "just as he who becomes aware of his *miseria* by deep and continual meditation will ardently wish to leave it behind, and he who begins to have such a wish will strive for its realization, so he who strives for this realization will be able to attain his goal. Indeed, it is clear that the third step cannot be impeded except by a deficiency of the second, nor the second except by a deficiency of the first. One must acknowledge, therefore, that the first is, so to speak, the root of man's salvation."[54] However, *after*

[51] Ibid.

[52] "Aliquantulum evagati sumus, sed iam sensim ad primordia nostra revertimur . . ." (ibid.)

[53] Ibid.

[54] "Ut, sicut qui se miserum alta et fixa meditatione cognoverit cupiat esse non

the section in which the references to stoic doctrine and Franciscus' protests against it occur, Augustine asserts that he had previously advised Franciscus "to make clear that the first step in avoiding the distress of mortal life and raising the soul to higher things is to practice meditation on death and on man's *miseria,* and that the second is to develop a vehement desire and zeal to rise. Once these two steps were taken toward the place to which your strivings aspired, I promised an easy ascent."[55]

At first glance the variation may seem trivial, but the longer one considers it the more it points to a basic difference in plan, even though both formulations depict a triad of necessary psychic stages. It is, in fact, only in the second analysis that "meditatio mortis" appears at all. Confronted with this discrepancy one recalls that throughout Book I meditation on man's mortality — and on the decomposition of the body after death — is the most essential educational expedient in the plan devised for Franciscus.[56] Even *before* the first analysis, on page one of Book I, we encounter a passage marked by the role of "meditatio mortis." For in the few introductory lines preceding the analysis of the three stages, Augustine admonishes Franciscus not to forgo "memoriam proprie miserie et meditationem mortis assiduam." Following the several stoically oriented pages, "meditatio mortis" reappears, not only in the context of the second triad but also immediately afterward when Franciscus calls on Augustine and Lady Truth to bear witness to the veracity of his outcry: "How often have I pondered over my *miseria* and the subject of death!"[57]

In view of this clear incongruity, we are obliged to look attentively at the strange double presentation. All the cited facts could be brought

---

miser, et qui id optare ceperit sectetur, sic et qui id sectatus fuerit, possit etiam adipisci. Enimvero tertium huiusmodi sicut nonnisi ex secundi, sic secundum nonnisi ex primi defectu prepediri posse compertum est; ita primum illud ceu radix humane salutis subsistat oportet" (ibid., pp. 28–30).

[55]"Id agere tecum institueram, ut ostenderem, ad evadendum huius nostre mortalitatis angustias ad tollendumque se se altius, primum veluti gradum obtinere meditationem mortis humaneque miserie; secundum vero desiderium vehemens studiumque surgendi; quibus exactis ad id, quo vestra suspirat intentio, ascensum facilem pollicebar . . ." (ibid., p. 34).

[56]Ibid., pp. 32–33.

[57]" . . . quotiens ad conditionis mee miseriam mortemque respexerim . . ." (ibid., p. 36).

into harmony by accepting the major elements of the following hypothesis. First, the strongly stoic-oriented section, which includes, on the first page of Book I, the analysis that omits "meditatio mortis," may have to be considered part of Petrarch's work on the *Secretum* in 1353. Second, in that year the *original* form — the one that begins "primum veluti gradum obtinere meditationem mortis humaneque miserie" — was made to *follow* the stoic section.[58] Finally, this displaced analysis of the efficiency of the will was given a sort of introduction in 1353, when Petrarch added the apology that the discussion had deviated a little but was now returning to its starting point.

I have called these conclusions a hypothesis, but if it could be shown conclusively that the triad lacking the reference to "meditatio mortis" on the first page of Book I is indeed the later of the two formulations, we would be justified in calling our hypothesis proved. It is possible, it seems to me, to establish the chronological order of the two forms empirically through a comparison of the crucial passages. The construction of the form which includes "meditatio mortis" may be characterized by using a simple metaphor: a ladder with several rungs. If you wish to rise high above the limitations of your mortal life, the relevant sentence suggests, you must know "primum veluti gradum obtinere meditationem mortis humaneque miserie; secundum vero desiderium vehemens studiumque surgendi." Once these two rungs have been climbed, the further ascent will be easy. But in the analysis on the first page, which lacks the reference to "meditatio mortis," the mechanism of ascent is profoundly different. For here a dynamic psychological process is revealed, one marked by inevitability. It starts with certain axioms regarding human nature: no sick person can be found who does not fervently desire the restitution of his health, and no one is so indolent and negligent "that he would not eagerly try to achieve what his heart greatly desires." So once the first step has been taken, all consequences are unavoidable. True understanding (through philosophical *meditatio*) generates a wish; the wish generates eager aspiration; aspiration generates the ability to reach one's goal. "It is thus clear that the third step cannot be im-

---

[58] Ibid., p. 34. Incidentally, not only the original triad was relocated but also the several pages that in the initial text of Book I had followed the triad recommending "meditatio mortis."

peded except by a deficiency of the second, nor the second except by a deficiency of the first."

This is certainly a much more maturely elaborated causal analysis than the simple enumeration of ladderlike rungs to be climbed in the version that succeeds the stoic section. We now begin to understand that the strange absence of "meditatio mortis" in the formulation on the first page cannot be a casual omission. In a psycho-philosophical scheme meant to make intelligible the emergence of strong wishes from philosophical meditation, of new aspirations from these wishes, and of new strength in conduct from these aspirations, there is no need for "meditatio mortis" in the harsh medieval sense. This does not mean, however, that in 1353 Petrarch no longer put emphasis on the medieval philosophy of death the way he had in 1347. By the device of making Augustine declare the two successive definitions identical ("iam sensim ad primordia nostra revertimur, nisi forte unde discesseramus oblitus es"), Petrarch successfully managed to incorporate the causal scheme within a context that stressed "meditatio mortis" as an indispensable step toward self-education. In 1353 he must have split the text of 1347 immediately after Augustine's introductory admonition (that is, after ". . . nichil efficacius reperiri quam memoriam proprie miserie et meditationem mortis assiduam"), thus inserting stoic material in the same way that he was forming a stoic pocket in the second half of Book I. For by the 1350s he was persuaded that reasoned stoic arguments should not be weakened by emotional elements, and hence he omitted references to the philosophy of death from his additions.

Let us conclude by describing the pocket thus created at the opening of the first book. It comprises the following. (1) An introductory admonition is provided by Augustine in the high-sounding style of some of the stoic *familiares* of the early 1350s: "Atqui omnibus ex conditionibus vestris, o mortales, nullam magis admiror, nullam magis exhorreo, quam quod miseriis vestris ex industria favetis et impendens periculum dissimulatis agnoscere, considerationemque illam, si ingeratur, excluditis." This is followed by (2) an analysis of the three stages of the will, with no reference to "meditatio mortis," which opens the way to (3) the psychological debate whether one can fall into *miseria* against one's will, to (4) Petrarch's mention that all this is "stoic" teaching, and, finally, to (5) the bridging passage leading the discussion back to its starting point, that is, from a stoic discussion to the Augustinian ideas of the year 1347.[59]

Judged in general, therefore, it is not very difficult in the first two books to separate the original text from elements added in Petrarch's later years — in other words, to distinguish what goes back to either 1347 or 1349 and what must be additions of 1353. But matters are much more complex where the third book is concerned. What are we able to find out about the presence of Book III during the 1340s?

[59] Ibid., pp. 28–34.

CHAPTER THREE

Book III in the Light of Two Petrarchan Poems in the Volgare

(1) "I'vo pensando" as a Guide to the *Secretum:* The Date of This Canzone

I

In one respect the conditions for studying the genesis of Books II and III are somewhat similar. In both cases, data from outside sources assist us in establishing that certain paragraphs in the *Secretum* fit the conditions of the late 1340s rather than those of 1353.

But to proceed from this to a synoptic view of what the third book was like during the 1340s is a much more complicated task than it is for the second book. Whereas in Book II, owing to Petrarch's employment of the traditional system of the Seven Deadly Sins, there is no doubt how the *Secretum* conversation was structured in the 1340s, in the case of Book III we need first of all to discover evidence outside the *Secretum* that might help to show whether Book III included in the 1340s what it does today — whether, that is, it contained the account of Petrarch's struggle with his two "adamantine chains": his love for Laura and his desire for glory.

It has often been thought that the canzone "I'vo pensando" (no. 264 in Petrarch's *Canzoniere*) can play this role, since it sets forth a psychological analysis of Petrarch's two dominant passions in a way very similar to that given in the third book. "I'vo pensando" has, indeed, been regarded as a counterpart to Book III and in recent years has been described as "born in the wake of the *Secretum*" and as "the poetic equivalent of the third book."[1] In the words of Ernest H. Wilkins, the heart of Book III is "Petrarch's love for Laura and his desire for fame . . . in conflict with his hope for eternal salvation. This

---

[1] "Nata sulla scia del *Secretum*" (Adelia Noferi, *L'esperienza poetica del Petrarca* [Florence, 1962], p. 247). "Poetic equivalent" was used by Ernest H. Wilkins, *Life of Petrarch* (Chicago, 1961), p. 47.

same . . . conflict . . . finds lyric utterance in . . . 'I'vo pensando.'" [2]
Mere parallelism between the two works is not enough, however; we
must be sure that the poem was composed after the first or second
Secretum draft of the 1340s, and not very long afterward at that. For
only in this event could the canzone be looked upon as a reflection of
Book III during the 1340s.

What reliable knowledge do we have concerning the date of the
canzone? No one, so far as I know, has ever seriously doubted that
this poem, which delves relentlessly into the circumstances of Petrarch's captivity by his love, was written *before* he was told that
Laura had died of the plague, that is, before May 19, 1348. On the
other hand, there has been a complete lack of agreement about the
poem's *terminus post quem*. There is not a single year between 1340 and
1348 to which it has not been assigned at one time or another. [3] But
we no longer need to be troubled by this uncertainty now that the *terminus post quem* has changed for the *Secretum*. None of the scholars
who studied the canzone in the past would ever have suggested the
early 1340s but for the purpose of making its date conform to that of
the *Secretum*. The early datings were always proposed under the assumption that 1342–43 was the year when the *Secretum* was first
drafted; presumably none of the older scholars would have hesitated
to transfer the date of the canzone's composition to 1347 or a little
later if he had thought that the original *Secretum* was composed in
that year.

II

There are elements in "I'vo pensando" that have long puzzled readers.
The canzone is complicated by its opening lines, in which Petrarch
confesses that in writing his poem he is, as he puts it, weeping in a
way he had never wept in his earlier poems: thoughts of his pitiful
inner state have carried him "spesso ad altro lagrimar ch' i'non
soleva." For, "seeing the end draw nearer every day, I have asked
God a thousand times for those wings with which our intellect raises

---

[2] Ernest H. Wilkins, "On Petrarch's *Accidia* and His Adamantine Chains," *Speculum* XXXVII (1962), p. 593.

[3] See the long list of chronological propositions compiled by Ernest H. Wilkins,
"On Petrarch's *Ad Seipsum* and *I'vo Pensando*," *Speculum* XXXII (1957), pp. 90–91.
Wilkins himself finally suggested 1344 in *Life of Petrarch*, p. 47.

itself from this mortal prison to heaven" — and yet all his tears have not affected his conduct. This, of course, is precisely his lament and the psychological description he gives of himself in Book III. But why had the tone of his lyric poetry changed, as he maintains, and what caused him now to feel that his end was approaching and made him care more deeply for his salvation? Modern commentators on the canzone and the words "ad altro lagrimar" were first inclined to think of the Black Death of 1348, thus dating the canzone to the first few months of that year (before Petrarch heard of Laura's death). But why, then, do we not find a hint of the terrors of 1348? In his copy of the *Canzoniere,* Boccaccio identifies Petrarch's expectation of death with a more ordinary epidemic in 1340, and this date has therefore been preferred by some scholars. Obstacles remain, however; nothing we know of the year 1340 makes Petrarch's deep inner crisis understandable, and (still worse now that the first *Secretum* draft has been redated) this dating would make "I'vo pensando" long precede the crisis of the *Secretum.*

A way of escape from this impossible alternative, which dominated scholarly debate during the 1920s, was pointed out by Arnaldo Foresti (in his *Aneddoti della vita di Francesco Petrarca,* 1928); it has remained the most widely accepted one. According to Foresti, the agitating event reflected in the introductory verses of "I'vo pensando" need not, after all, have been an epidemic (none is referred to in the poem). It should be recalled, rather, that shortly after the *Secretum* was drafted (in 1342–43, Foresti still believed), another event was to "pervaderne le più intime fibre" of Petrarch's view of life: in April 1343 his beloved brother, Gherardo, decided to become a Carthusian monk. As Foresti puts it in a psychological reconstruction: "He was gravely agitated by his humble brother, who was about to climb to his charterhouse and disappear from the world's stage. And he in turn? Would he continue to be a ship lost in a storm, thrown by the waves against the rocks, in danger of losing himself forever?"[4] If Foresti were correct, the date of "I'vo pensando" would have to be about 1344; and although there is nothing to demonstrate that Gherardo's monastic seclusion was indeed the event that caused Petrarch's agitation, nothing occurred for fifty years after Foresti to prompt a reexamination of his argument.

[4] Arnaldo Foresti, *Aneddoti della vita di Francesco Petrarca* (Brescia, 1928), p. 115.

There is no better illustration of the predominance of Foresti's hypothesis — and of the difficulties produced by it — than its effect on the most clear-headed Petrarch scholar of the half century following its publication. When Ernest H. Wilkins first concluded, in his *The Making of the Canzoniere* (1951), that the successive versions of the collection of Petrarch's poems prove that "I'vo pensando" was incorporated in the *Canzoniere* between 1347 and 1350, he judged that the poem "was written at Vaucluse in 1347"[5] and that this could be relied upon all the more firmly because it was in accord with the findings of what he called a recent "excellent study," namely, the article "La cronologia della canzone I'vo pensando" by G. A. Levi.[6] Yet a few years later Wilkins reversed himself by stating that the inclusion of "I'vo pensando" in the *Canzoniere* in 1347, or not much later, did not exclude the possibility that it had already existed a few years earlier as a separate poem.[7] He therefore reverted to Foresti's argument, reasoning that "the *Secretum* was written in Provence in the years 1342–43. . . . The canzone may well have been written either in Provence in 1343 or in Parma in 1344–45. . . . I conclude, therefore, that *I'vo pensando* was probably written in the period 1343–47, and more probably in the period 1343–45 than later."[8] In his *Life of Petrarch* (1961), Wilkins finally decided that "I'vo pensando" was "probably written" during "the first nine months of 1344."[9]

These rather convoluted attempts to date "I'vo pensando" clearly depended on the traditional acceptance of 1342–43 as the date of the original *Secretum*. The shift to 1347 has as its consequence that all those former proposals are now seen to suffer from the same mistake made in the chronology of the *Secretum:* a predating by about five years. This includes Foresti's and Wilkins' attempts to bring the canzone closer in time to the *Secretum* by dating it 1343–44. As a result, we must ascribe a new significance to another aspect of Wilkins' *The Making of the Canzoniere*. For in this early work he had demonstrated

[5] Ernest H. Wilkins, *The Making of the Canzoniere and Other Petrarchan Studies* (Rome, 1951), pp. 152–153.

[6] *Giornale Storico della Letteratura Italiana* CXI (1938), pp. 255–268.

[7] "This discussion," Wilkins added, "supersedes the discussion . . . in *The Making of the Canzoniere*" ("On Petrarch's *Ad Seipsum* and *I'vo Pensando*," p. 91).

[8] Ibid.

[9] P. 47. Citing Foresti, Adelia Noferi similarly dated the canzone "probabilmente intorno al 1345" (*L'esperienza poetica del Petrarca*, p. 247).

that after a desultory start at gathering some of his earliest *rime* in the early 1340s, Petrarch did not add to his book of poems until 1347 when its present form in two "parts" emerged, the first introduced by no. 1, "Voi ch'ascoltate," and the second by no. 264, "I'vo pensando." Thanks to Wilkins' use of Petrarch's autographic manuscript, Vat. Lat. 3196, where some of the selected pieces were first copied and then revised before being entered in the final collection in Vat. Lat. 3195, we can establish that no. 265 was composed in September 1350 and no. 268 was being worked on from November 1349 to April 1351. As Wilkins summed it up at that time: nos. 264–270 were "composed by 1351" in their "final form."[10] Does this not make it very probable that no. 264, too, was given its present shape some time between 1347 and 1351?

After so much vacillation in the past, the transfer of the date of the original *Secretum* draft from 1342–43 to 1347 has now brought the dates of composition of the two works so close together that "I'vo pensando" can finally perform the function for the study of the *Secretum*'s third book which had long been envisaged for it. At the same time, it is remarkable how fully Wilkins' original views are confirmed once the time of the *Secretum*'s genesis has been changed. Since Petrarch did not begin serious work on his collection of poems before 1347, and since the division of the *Canzoniere* into two parts and the arrangement of the opening section of Part II (where "I'vo pensando" appears) were carried out no later than 1351, it seems impossible to believe that this canzone can have succeeded the 1347 draft of the *Secretum* by many years. Presumably the poem followed closely upon the *Secretum* during the year that passed before Laura's death became known to Petrarch on May 19, 1348.

It might nevertheless be asked: how certain can we be that "I'vo pensando" was composed before Petrarch heard of Laura's death? Nothing in the canzone reveals his knowledge of it, yet the position of the poem in the *Canzoniere* is bound to raise suspicion. Whereas all 263 poems of Part I were written *in vita di Laura*, 101 of the 103 in Part II were clearly written during the period *in morte*. So the accommodation of "I'vo pensando" in Part II leads one to wonder whether, despite appearances, the poem does not belong for some obscure reason to the period after Laura had died.

---

[10] Wilkins, *The Making of the Canzoniere,* pp. 150–153.

The contradiction between its general tone and content and its placement in the *in morte* part of the *Canzoniere* is convincingly removed through an ingenious explanation given by Wilkins. He suggested that under the new spiritual influence hinted at in the first few lines of "I'vo pensando" Petrarch devised a second part for the *Canzoniere* — and placed "I'vo pensando" in it — prior to May 19, 1348. This plan was soon "too firmly fixed in Petrarch's mind to be altered even by the death of Laura." Thus "I'vo pensando" remained the introductory piece of the second part when the latter grew into a collection of poems not with a new spiritual orientation but rather *in morte di Madonna Laura.* [11]

In light of present knowledge about the genesis of the *Secretum,* we may argue: Foresti erred in his inference that Gherardo's entrance into the Carthusian order in 1343 was what transformed Petrarch spiritually. If "I'vo pensando" was written as late as 1347 or early 1348 — as we have found — Gherardo's vows of 1343 cannot have been the causative event. The crisis that made Petrarch feel in 1347 that he was entering a new period in his inner life must be identified with the "curae" to which he gave literary expression in the *Secretum.*

III

Another problem of particular significance for the *Secretum* still remains unsolved, however. Can we indeed feel confident that "I'vo pensando" was written not only near in time to the *Secretum* draft of 1347 but *after* it and consequently reflects some of the early features of Book III? We have no direct evidence for the exact order in which the two works were composed, and any inference regarding the sequence of the poem and the dialogue must, therefore, be carefully considered. Actually, the signs all point in one direction; but the reader must judge for himself whether they seem strong enough.

Since Wilkins once asked himself the same question — namely, whether Petrarch's philosophical inquiry into the values defended in Book III did not precede their lyrical expression — we would do well to start by looking at his reasoning. As he saw it, the "much more probable sequence" is that Petrarch "formulated his concept of his triple conflict [the clash between salvation, love, and glory] while he was working on his complete and detailed self-analysis [in the

[11] Ibid., pp. 192–193.

Secretum]; gave that conflict the commanding place in that analysis; and later on, led either by irrepressible continuance of the actual conflict or by purely artistic judgment or by both causes, decided to give it lyric treatment, and told of it in the compact and highly artistic canzone."[12] It seems to me that we should keep the argument of this experienced Petrarch scholar in mind.

Moving on to some related observations of our own, we find an enlightening image near the beginning of "I'vo pensando": "Until now no prayer or sigh or weeping has helped me; and that is fair, for he who has fallen along the way though able to stand deserves to lie on the ground against his will." Readers of the *Secretum* may recall the corresponding discussion in Book I, where a broader exposition of the same notion is set forth. There Franciscus admits to Augustine, for the first time in the *Secretum* controversy, that his feeling of having fallen into *miseria* and sin against his will may not have been entirely correct. Now "I perceive," he tells Augustine, "that the beginning of my *miseria* did arise from my own will. I feel it is true of me and guess it to be true of others; provided, however, that you, too, acknowledge a truth. . . . Namely, as it is true that no man ever fell involuntarily, it is also true that countless numbers of those who have fallen by their own will do not remain on the ground voluntarily. I say this confidently of myself. And I believe that this has happened to me as a punishment: because I would not stand when I could, I cannot now rise when I would."[13] This calls forth a sequence of experiences and conclusions which the poet is able to summarize in "I'vo pensando" in the concise notion that "he who has fallen along the way though able to stand deserves to lie on the ground against his will." Psychologically, the phase which necessarily had to come first was a false feeling of innocence, followed by the two other stages described in the *Secretum:* falling into sin voluntarily and being unable to forswear it once it has been committed. In other words, just as

---

[12] Wilkins, "On Petrarch's *Ad Seipsum* and *I'vo Pensando*," pp. 90–91.

[13] Fr.: "Video me paulatim de proposito excidere, et fateri cogor, quod initium miserie mee ex proprio processit arbitrio; hoc in me sentio in aliisque conicio. Modo tu michi quoque verum fateare." Aug.: "Quid me fateri postulas?" Fr.: "Ut sicut verum est neminem nisi sponte corruere, sic etiam illud verum sit: innumerabiles sponte prolapsos non sua tamen sponte iacere; quod de me ipso fidenter affirmem. Idque michi datum arbitror in penam ut, quia dum stare possem nolui, assurgere nequeam dum velim" (Carrara, p. 38).

Wilkins envisaged it, the analysis in the *Secretum* appears to be the necessary preparation for the mature idea employed by the poet of the canzone; and although we are concerned here with a passage in the first book and not the third, this does not change the conclusion that the canzone presupposes the self-analysis of the *Secretum*.

We arrive at a similar conclusion when we try to interpret an evident oddity in the structure of "I'vo pensando." Notwithstanding its great beauty and psychological penetration, there is an imbalance between the intimated plan of the poem and its actual execution. At the beginning of the second half of the canzone (verses 81–87 of 136 verses altogether), Petrarch asks in despair how he can navigate his boat through life when it is held back among the rocks by "two knots" (*da . . . duo nodi*), two passions: *amor* and *gloria*. But in the actual structure of the poem, these passions are not on a par; the emphasis is clearly on *amor*. Having devoted nearly half the canzone exclusively to the sweetness and perils of his love, Petrarch adds eighteen verses (55–72) recalling that in his heart there is "d'altra parte un pensier dolce et agro," his burning desire for "fama gloriosa et alma," which has been growing in him "since I slept in swaddling clothes," even though he knows that fame is wind and shadow and wishes "to embrace the truth." Yet he does not state this without qualification: "But that other desire with which I am filled [i.e., *amor*] seems to cast a shadow over all others born beside it" (v. 73f.); and after acknowledging the "duo nodi," he shows a still more surprising partiality by completely omitting *gloria* when he points the moral of his canzone: "I see what I am doing, and I am not deceived by an imperfect knowledge of the truth; rather, it is Amor who forces me, he who never lets anyone follow the path of honor who believes in him too much."[14] From these verses on, "fame" and "glory" are not mentioned again in the canzone.

How can we account for this imbalance? Why was Petrarch not content to speak solely of his *amor* — "that other desire with which I am filled, [which] seems to cast a shadow over all others born beside it" — as he did in so many of his vernacular poems? It is difficult to

---

[14]"Quel ch'i' fo veggio, et non m'inganna il vero / mal conosciuto, anzi me sforza Amore, / che la strada d'onore / mai nol lassa seguir, chi troppo il crede; /" ("I'vo pensando," in Francesco Petrarca, *Canzoniere*, ed. Gianfranco Contini [Turin, 1964], verses 91–94).

find another explanation except that at the time the canzone was composed he was guided by a statement he had made elsewhere: namely, that the driving force in his life was not *amor* alone but a dual passion. This may be put another way: if Book III had not already been in existence and fresh in Petrarch's memory, "I'vo pensando" would hardly have referred to the longing for fame as his second, still indomitable passion. Under the circumstances it is understandable that for once Petrarch tried in a vernacular poem to give a more complex psychological picture than is usual in his love lyrics.[15]

When these conjectures regarding the chronological sequence of the dialogue and the poem are joined in the testimony showing that "I'vo pensando" appeared in the *Canzoniere* between 1347 and 1351, one need not hesitate to use the canzone as a reflection of the *Secretum* in the years preceding the changes of 1353.

IV

What can be learned from "I'vo pensando" about the function of Book III in the *Secretum* of the 1340s? In the version of the *Secretum* that has come down to us, the demonstration in Book II that Petrarch's lapses with respect to the Seven Deadly Sins cannot be the major cause of his lack of spiritual vigor is followed in Book III by the argument that he is held back strongly by two other "fetters" (*catenae*): his love for Laura and his thirst for fame; even Augustine's wisdom and indignation are insufficient to extinguish these burning emotions. Every essential element in this link between Books II and III is also found in the poetic vision of the canzone of 1347–48: "What does it profit me to grease my little bark, since it is held among the rocks by two such knots [*nodi*, which, like *catenae*, means *fetters*]. You, my Lord, who have freed me completely from the other fetters that bind the world in various ways, why do you not now take

---

[15] The systematic argument I have just presented was first suggested to me by a sagacious *obiter dictum* of G. A. Levi in his study "La cronologia della canzone *I'vo pensando,*" *Giornale Storico della Letteratura Italiana* CXI (1938), p. 260: ". . . leggendola [la canzone *I'vo pensando*] attentamente è facile avvertire in essa uno squilibrio: dopo avere parlato . . . del desiderio di fama, si dimentica, e fino alla fine . . . non parla più se non dell'amore di Laura. . . . io credo che l'impressione schietta di ognuno sia che il tormento di cui [Petrarca] avrebbe voluto liberarsi fosse propriamente l'amore di Laura. Se non si fosse ricordato del *Secretum* probabilmènte di quell'altra passione non avrebbe parlato."

this shame from my brow [i.e., his passion for *amor* and *gloria*]? ...
I want to defend myself but have no weapons."[16] This, to repeat, is
exactly the link that connects Books II and III in the surviving text of
the *Secretum*.

"I'vo pensando" is less informative about the specific subjects of
the debate that were already present in Book III during the 1340s.
But it at least offers clues for the identification of certain details.
When we read in the canzone that "the more someone longs for real
merit, the more he is forbidden to love a mortal thing with the faith
that belongs to God alone,"[17] we recall that in Book III of the *Secretum*
this is precisely the argument that silences Petrarch's defense of his
love for Laura. In the text handed down to us, the heart of Augustine's
dispute with Franciscus is undoubtedly the stern claim that passionate love for a human being is bound to weaken man's love of God.
Laura, "to whom you profess to owe everything, has been your ruin,"
Augustine argues when nothing else has proved strong enough to
convince Petrarch. "She has inclined your heart to love a creature
more than the Creator; and that is the path which, sooner than any
other, leads to death." When Petrarch protests that "the love I feel for
her has most certainly led me to love God," Augustine rejoins: "This
is an inversion of the true order. ... All creatures should be dear
to us because of our love for the Creator," and not the other way
around. "Nothing causes man to forget or despise God so much as
the love of things temporal, and above all else the passion which we
call love." What finally makes Petrarch admit that he is "beaten" is
Augustine's verdict that the greatest of all the evils caused by worldly
love is "that it engenders forgetfulness of God."[18]

There is another homology which shows that Book III was in Petrarch's mind when he wrote the canzone of 1347–48. In the *gloria*
section of Book III, one of Augustine's major accusations is that Franciscus, by putting his time and energy into the preparation of two

[16]"Che giova dunque perché tutta spalme / la mia barchetta, poi che 'nfra li
scogli / è ritenuta anchor da ta' duo nodi? / Tu che dagli altri, che 'n diversi modi /
legano 'l mondo, in tutto mi disciogli, / signor mio, ché non togli / omai dal volto
mio questa vergogna? / ... e vorrei far difesa, e non ò l'arme" ("I'vo pensando,"
verses 81–90).

[17]"Ché mortal cosa amar con tanta fede / quanta a Dio sol per debito convensi, /
piú si disdice a chi piú pregio brama" ("I'vo pensando," verses 99–101).

[18]Carrara, pp. 154, 156, 160.

historically oriented works (the *Africa* and *De Viris*), was in danger "of forgetting himself while writing about others."[19] Since *gloria* is only a limited concern of the canzone, one looks in vain for this motif in the few verses on "fama gloriosa et alma." But it does re-emerge in the canzone, expressed in nearly the same words though transferred from "fama" to a condemnation of Petrarch's writing poems about Laura: "and time flies while I write of someone else, not caring about myself."[20]

Our principal interest in these homologies lies in the assurance they give us of an actual connection between the *Secretum* and "I'vo pensando," thereby endorsing the correctness of the assumptions that the *Secretum* was drafted early in 1347 and the canzone composed before Petrarch heard of Laura's death in May 1348. Vice versa, we would be moving in a wrong direction, to say the least, if we continued to believe that "I'vo pensando" was composed as early as 1344.

(2) Petrarch's Reconsideration of a Theme in Book III: His Canzone "Quel'antiquo mio dolce empio signore"

I

Is "I'vo pensando" (no. 264 of the *Canzoniere*) the only one of Petrarch's poems to shed light on Book III of the *Secretum* during the 1340s? Scholars have long believed that another poem in the *Canzoniere* in important respects complements the reflection of the *Secretum* discernible in "I'vo pensando." Are they right?

Poem no. 360 — "Quel'antiquo mio dolce empio signore [Amore]" — though separated from no. 264 by almost all of Part II of the *Canzoniere*, looks indeed like a close relative of "I'vo pensando," although it is not at all concerned with Petrarch's striving for *gloria-fama;* instead, it reproduces almost every turn of the debate in *Secretum* III on Petrarch's *amor*.

There is one major difference between no. 360 of the *Canzoniere* and Book III of the *Secretum:* the former is not a debate in which traditional values triumph over Petrarch's passion but an altercation —

---

[19]"... deque aliis scribens, tui ipsius oblivisceris" (ibid., p. 192).

[20]"... il tempo fugge / che, scrivendo d'altrui, di me non calme; /" ("I'vo pensando," verses 75–76).

a formal litigation before a law court presided over by the symbolic
figure of *Giudizia-Ragione*. Both sides — the value as well as the danger
of Petrarch's love — here have their day in court. The speakers in the
canzone are not Franciscus and Augustine but Petrarch and Amore,
the mythical originator of Petrarch's love. The consequent change in
the structure of the argument — from Franciscus defending his love
against Augustine's accusations in Book III, to the father of all love,
Amore, defending Petrarch's love against Petrarch's own regrets and
fears in the canzone — does not in itself alter the nature of the conflict, in as much as the praises and complaints in both disputes are
expressions of the same clash of opinions. In both poem no. 360 and
Book III, the accusations against *amor* are ultimately based on the
charge that earthly love "has made me [Petrarch] love God less than
I ought to and less concerned about myself," as the canzone puts it.[21]
In Book III, Augustine depicts the pernicious effects of Petrarch's
love: "Remember now," he says, "how from the moment this sickness
took hold of your mind you suddenly fell to lamenting and were
brought to such a pitch of wretchedness that with morbid pleasure
you fed on tears and sighs, passing sleepless nights, . . . scorning
everything, hating life, and longing for death; conceiving a melancholy love for solitude and avoiding your fellow men; so that one
might well apply to you . . . what Homer said of Bellerophon: 'There
in the alien fields he wandered sad, / Eating his heart out, far from
the ways of men.'"[22] Although the details are not always identical,
Petrarch's lamentation in "Quel'antiquo mio dolce" similarly fuses a
debate about the hierarchy of values with the psychology of a restless
lover: since my love began "I have felt nothing but sorrow and scorn,
and I have suffered so many and such strange torments that in the
end . . . I have come to hate life." Thus, inner unrest "has made me
search in wildernesses. . . . Since I have been his [Amore's] I have not
had a tranquil hour, nor do I expect any, and my nights have ban-
ished sleep. . . . Hence come the tears and suffering, the words and
sighs which are wearing me out. . . ."

The near identity of the two disputes is also evident in the defense
of Petrarch's love. Franciscus asserts in the *Secretum* that "what I am,

---

[21] "... m'à fatto men amare Dio / ch'i' non deveva, et men curar me stesso: /"
("Quel'antiquo mio dolce," verses 31–32).
[22] Carrara, p. 156.

I owe to her [Laura], and I should never have obtained what little fame and glory I have, had she not by the power of this love quickened into life the feeble germ of virtue that nature had sown in my heart. It was she who turned my youthful soul away from all that was base, who . . . forced me to look upwards. . . . It is a certain truth that by love we grow like what we love. . . . It is no wonder, then, that such renown as hers should have . . . sweetened the toil that I had to endure to attain what I desired."[23] In "Quel'antiquo mio dolce," Amore argues against scorning love and accuses Petrarch of ingratitude: He has "risen to some fame only through me. . . . And my greatest service has been that I have pulled him back from a thousand vicious acts. For low things could never please him . . . once he became the vassal of her [Laura] who . . . made him like herself. Whatever is exceptional or noble in him, he has from her and from me, of whom he complains. . . . Again, I gave him wings to fly above the heavens by way of mortal things, which are a ladder to the Creator if one judges them rightly; for looking fixedly at the many great virtues in that hope of his, he could have risen from one likeness [of Creation] to the next, up to the high First Cause."[24]

We see clearly from this comparison that even in the fine details of the dispute concerning the rights and wrongs of Petrarch's love, the poem and the self-analysis in the third book of the *Secretum* are alike in all fundamental respects. Although the accuser and defender are different in accordance with the way Petrarch imagines each scene, "the cause of the debate remains the same, and so do the reasons adduced by both sides," as a perceptive student of both the "Quel'antiquo mio dolce" and the *Secretum* once defined the relationship between the two disputations.[25]

Does the poem at the end of Part II of the *Canzoniere*, then, bear a similar relationship to Book III of the *Secretum* as "I'vo pensando"? It should give one pause that, even though "Quel'antiquo mio dolce" gives no hint anywhere in the course of the litigation that Laura is dead, at the end — after Amore boasts that *he* gave Laura to him "as a support for his frail life" — Petrarch "raises the tearful cry: He [Amore] gave her to me, indeed, but he soon took her back!" To

---

[23] Ibid., p. 144.
[24] "Quel'antiquo mio dolce," verses 88ff., 121–143.
[25] Foresti, *Aneddoti*, p. 116.

which Amore replies: "Not I, but One who desired her for Himself,"
namely God.

How can this blatant discrepancy in the poem be explained?

II

As in the case of "I'vo pensando," it was Foresti who offered the interpretation accepted by most Petrarch students until very recently. As
he argued in 1928, the allusion to Laura's death is not made until just
before the end of the poem. "If the last few verses are removed, a
reader . . . will not hesitate to assume that the canzone was composed
while Laura was still alive." Verses 61–75 make it certain, Foresti
said, that the body of the poem cannot be from a later period.
"Amore is not accused here as an old, past evil; he is brought to trial
for the evil he is causing currently"; and Petrarch "clearly speaks
about present conditions, not a situation already past." In particular,
"the poet would not be able to say 'né cangiar posso l'ostinata voglia,'
nor speak of having been deprived of his liberty if Laura were not
still living and he were not still trying to conquer his passion. The
canzone was resumed [and its ending adapted] later, perhaps not
many years after Laura's death, when the author was enriching the
Secretum with additions."[26]

In 1951, Wilkins, in his *The Making of the Canzoniere,* likewise claimed
that "Quel'antiquo mio dolce" was "written before the death of
Laura, though retouched afterward,"[27] and he defended the correctness of Foresti's interpretation by explaining that this canzone,
"written before the death of Laura and before any other assignable
poem of Part II (except perhaps no. 266), was completed or revised
in its last stanzas during the last period of Petrarch's work, in such a
way as to include a few references to the death of Laura."[28] But
when, specifically, is "Quel'antiquo mio dolce" supposed to have
been retouched? In the "Chronological Conspectus" of *The Making of
the Canzoniere,* the date of the final version is ascribed to Petrarch's
Milanese period (1353–61),[29] presumably for no other reason than
that Wilkins had Foresti's suggestion in mind: no. 360 "was resumed

---

[26] Ibid., pp. 116–118.
[27] Wilkins, *The Making of the Canzoniere,* p. 188.
[28] Ibid., p. 368.
[29] Ibid., p. 354. Poem "no. 356" discussed here was finally numbered 360.

later, perhaps not many years after Laura's death." Still more recently
Adelia Noferi, in her widely read *L'esperienza poetica del Petrarca* (1962),
also assumed "that *Quel'antiquo mio dolce* must have been written at a
time very near to that of the dialogues [of the *Secretum*] and that the
canzone looks like a versification of the dialogues" — adding to the
speculation by conjecturing that "incorporation in the *Canzoniere,*
with some revisions, [occurred] at the time when the last corrections
in the *Secretum* were made."[30]

Rico, on the other hand, tried to find a solution by using the opposite approach; he saw the "Quel'antiquo mio dolce" puzzle as another
occasion for skepticism regarding insertions or later changes. No.
360, he decided, "is evidently to be dated after 1348." For since "there
is no reason to assume that the reference to Laura's death is an addition," we should not speculate about later changes but conclude that
Petrarch, throughout the major part of the poem, was trying "to sus-
tain . . . the mood of the period [when Laura was still] *in vita.*" In any
case, "it is obvious that the canzone points straight to the *Secretum.*"[31]

What we can learn from this glance at past "Quel'antiquo mio
dolce" criticism is that when it comes to the question whether the
canzone should be used as a source for the 1340s or rather for a later
period, virtually nothing reliable has been provided beyond a re-
minder that it is only too easy to argue either side. A closer look at
the available information may yield more positive results.

III

The same exploration of the growth of the *Canzoniere* by which
Wilkins endeavored to secure a reliable dating for "I'vo pensando"
can yield some evidence for "Quel'antiquo mio dolce." Since Wilkins'
methodical analysis of the successive versions put it beyond doubt
that "Quel'antiquo" belongs to the group of poems inserted at the end
of Petrarch's final copy of the *Canzoniere* during the last year of his
life,[32] we may be able to answer a related question: was any other
poem in that group originally written while Laura was *in vita*?

[30] Noferi, *L'esperienza poetica del Petrarca,* p. 246.
[31] "*Quel'antiquo mio dolce* . . . se data evidentemente después de 1348 . . . ; y no hay
por qué pensar que la referencia a la muerte de Laura sea una adición." For, the
reference to the death of the lady indicates "que Petrarca . . . mantenía en el orbe
literario el talante de la época 'in vita.'" "Anterior o posterior, se diría obvio que la
canción envía derechamente al *Secretum*" (Rico, *Lectura,* p. 262 and n.40).
[32] Wilkins, *The Making of the Canzoniere,* pp. 188, 194.

The poems in question, like all in the *Canzoniere,* do not appear in strict chronological order; their sequence often depends on their content or a desire for variation. In the section concluding Part II, some poems from the time of Petrarch's first, piercing grief after Laura's death are mixed with others marked by the quite different grief of later years. Still, all the poems in this group were written *in morte di Laura:* Laura appearing to Petrarch from another life, or Petrarch dreaming of her in heaven. If no. 360 were from Laura's lifetime, it would be the only poem in the concluding section from the period before 1348 and would have been left lying far longer than any of the other poems (more than twenty-five years) before being admitted to the *Canzoniere.*

There is another, somewhat complicated consideration which ultimately leads us in the same direction. One understands readily enough that in a poem written roughly at the time of the original *Secretum* Petrarch should have pursued motifs and ideas very close to those expressed in the *Secretum.* But the further we move away from 1347–49 in our attempt to find the date of no. 360, the less understandable it becomes how Petrarch could have reiterated extensive passages of the *Secretum* debates on his *amor* in a form so similar "that [no. 360] looks like a versification of the [*Secretum*] dialogues," to quote Noferi again. Or, to phrase it somewhat differently: if we move the date of the canzone away from the pre-1348 period we turn from Scylla to Charybdis — unless we succeed in discovering in Petrarch's later years a specific circumstance leading him to revive his interest in the *Secretum* to a point where he might repeat almost exactly part of the argument of his conversation with Augustine. This, in the last analysis, is the crucial problem in any attempt to reconstruct the relationship between "Quel'antiquo mio dolce" and the *Secretum.*

We must begin by pointing to the well-known fact that Petrarch implanted a kind of rudimentary chronology in his *Canzoniere* through a number of so-called anniversary or self-dating poems — poems which indicate in plain words that a certain number of years has passed since an earlier event, usually the beginning of Petrarch's love and, later, Laura's death. These signals occur infrequently and certainly should not be considered a substitute for documentary information; they tell us, though, what chronological impressions the author wanted his readers to form.

The following will give some idea of these chronological intimations. By the middle of Part I it has become clear from various hints that the poet has been moving primarily in the atmosphere of the early 1340s; in no. 118 it is stated that sixteen full years of his love have passed ("Rimansi a dietro il sestodecimo anno de' miei sospiri"), that is, the poet is presumably writing in 1343. Near the end of Part I (no. 221) we read that Petrarch has been burning with love for twenty years, which means that the poet is writing in 1347. At the beginning of Part II Laura is still *in vita,* because "I'vo pensando" (no. 264) is closely followed by indications (in no. 266) that eighteen years have gone by since the beginning of Petrarch's love (in 1327) and fifteen years since he first met his friend Giovanni Colonna (in 1330). The next poem (no. 267) speaks of Laura's death, and from then on the reader knows that he is reading poems *in morte di Laura.* In what way is he expected to count the years passing *in morte*? He is given two hints. According to no. 287, a friend, Sennuccio del Bene, had just died — about a year and a half after Petrarch had learned about Laura's death in May 1348; and in no. 364, closely following "Quel'antiquo mio dolce" (no. 360), we read that "love kept me twenty-one years aflame / happy in the fire and full of hope amid sorrow; / since my lady and my heart with her / rose to heaven, ten years longer crying."[33]

It is obvious that Petrarch wanted his readers to understand by way of this calendar that he was giving them an approximation of the period to which his preceding poems belonged. This gives us some idea of the date of "Quel'antiquo mio dolce"; but there is more to guide us. That the canzone belongs to the group for which no. 364 provides the chronological clue is confirmed by information we have about the incorporation of the individual poems in the successive collections of the *Canzoniere.* Neither no. 360 nor no. 364 was added during the earlier periods that Petrarch's clues identify as the 1340s or the period *in vita di Laura.* No. 364 was included only after 1367 and may easily have been added as late as 1372; no. 360 was added in 1373–74.[34] In Petrarch's final copy of the *Canzoniere* (Ms. Vat. Lat. 3195) both poems are found on the sheets inserted just before the end of the manuscript to provide space for the last group of poems. But the most interesting bit of information comes from the chronological

---

[33]"Tennemi Amor anni ventuno ardendo, / lieto nel foco, et nel duol pien di speme; / poi che madonna e 'l mio cor seco inseme / saliro al ciel, dieci altri anni piangendo" (canzone no. 364, verses 1–4).

[34]Wilkins, *The Making of the Canzoniere,* p. 194.

clue in no. 364, which allows us to calculate the following: 1327 (the year Petrarch met Laura), plus twenty-one years *in vita,* plus ten years after Laura's death equals 1358. This is the year in which Petrarch reread the *Secretum,* apparently after a considerable interval of time, and wrote the marginal notes in his final autograph. And now it also appears to be the year — or at least the period — to which we may date Petrarch's renewed interest in the *Secretum* that gave rise to the canzone "Quel'antiquo mio dolce."

IV

Seen from this perspective, "Quel'antiquo mio dolce" acquires a new and unexpected importance for the history of the *Secretum.* For one now wonders whether, when rereading his dialogue with Augustine in 1358, Petrarch still viewed that autobiographical dispute entirely in its initial light; whether "Quel'antiquo mio dolce" may not reveal a change in his values during the ten years that had passed since the composition of the original *Secretum,* and if it does, how such a change might have affected the canzone.

Of course, little such effect could be expected if the canzone were really nothing but "una versificazione" in the vernacular of the *Secretum* debate on Petrarch's love. But this is far from being the case. Though the particular topics of the debate have remained the same, the setting, personae, and the very outcome have been so changed that a greater contrast between the *forma mentis* of the conversation with Augustine and that presented in the canzone can hardly be imagined. In the dialogue, Franciscus pleads that he owes all the higher forces of his mind, and the ideals that have kept him upright, to his love; earthly love has even facilitated love of God. But the church father tells him that to think thus is a perversion of nature and the world created by God, that nothing is deadlier to salvation than the dream of a ladder leading man from earthly values to heaven, from the love of a creature to the love of God. Because this is self-evident to Franciscus once it is pointed out to him, he finally submits to every condemnation uttered by Augustine; there can be but one teacher and one doctrine. In the canzone there are two parties, each pleading its own case. Petrarch, obedient, reiterates almost literally what Augustine teaches him in the *Secretum;* but now it is left to Amore himself to lay before an impartial judge what Franciscus is incapable of defending against Augustine. In the end the judge shows two reactions: "It pleases me to have heard both pleas," *Giudizia-Ragione* says "with a smile"; but this is "so great a lawsuit" that an immediate decision is impossible, "more time is needed."[35]

It would be wrong to object against this interpretation that nothing can be found elsewhere in the *Canzoniere* to harmonize with the outlook and values expressed in the canzone. For an essential corollary of our interpretation is that "Quel'antiquo mio dolce" is not a regular canzone among those of the *Canzoniere*. It is in various respects a frank paradox, and an evaluation of it must acknowledge its paradoxical character, both within the *Canzoniere* and in its internal construction. What is perhaps most striking is the very appearance of Amore's plea for the value of earthly love among the last, quite differently attuned poems. We have already referred to the climax, Amore's proud claim concerning his gifts to Petrarch: "Whatever is exceptional or noble in him, he has from her [Laura] and me, of whom he complains. . . . I gave him wings to fly above the heavens by way of mortal things, which are a ladder to the Creator if one judges them rightly." When the canzone containing these lines was added to the *Canzoniere* as no. 360 during the last year of Petrarch's life, the two concluding poems (no. 365 and the appeal to the Virgin Mary) were already in place, incorporated four years or so before[36] and expressing, as it were, Petrarch's farewell to his collection of poems in the typical language and tone of the latter part of the *Canzoniere:* "I go weeping," no. 365 begins, "for my past time / which I spent in loving a mortal thing / without lifting myself in flight, though I had wings / to make of myself perhaps a not base example."[37] What is surprising is not so much that it took Petrarch so long to decide to incorporate no. 360 — longer, apparently, than it did any other of his poems — as that he ever made up his mind at all to set it into such an alien context.

We have already pointed out some of the discrepancies that were bound to develop when a poem that, except for its last few lines,

[35]"Ella allor sorridendo: /'Piacemi aver vostre questioni udite, / ma piú tempo bisogna a tanta lite'" ("Quel'antiquo mio dolce," verses 155–157).

[36]See Wilkins, *The Making of the Canzoniere,* pp. 188, 194.

[37]"I'vo piangendo i miei passati tempi / i quai posi in amar cosa mortale, / senza levarmi a volo, abbiend'io l'ale, / per dar forse di me non bassi exempi" (canzone no. 365, verses 1–4).

gives the impression of having been written *in vita di Laura* was placed among the poems in which Laura is seen in heaven or coming down to Petrarch on earth. This dissonance bears further illustration. Petrarch, we find, has not made the slightest effort to mitigate the contradictions between the poem and the surrounding context of the *Canzoniere*. Everything in poem no. 360 tends to create the illusion that Petrarch is dealing with a living person. "Until now [*enfin qui*] my time has been passed in flame and suffering," he complains, with an accusing finger pointed toward Amore. Though "my hair is turning, I cannot change my obstinate will: thus this cruel one whom I accuse [i.e., Amore] deprives me of all my liberty." "Hence come the tears and suffering . . . that are wearing me out." Applying his complaints to Laura directly, Petrarch speaks of her as "that other enemy of mine whom I shun" (*quell'altra mia nemica ch'i' fuggia*). This creates a clear dissonance in a section of the *Canzoniere* otherwise occupied by poems whose tone is best described by Petrarch's own words in no. 362: "I fly to heaven so often on the wings of thought that I almost seem to be one of those who possess their treasure there, leaving on earth their rent veils." Then Laura "leads me to her Lord; I incline myself, humbly begging that He permit me to stay and look upon both their faces." Within no. 360 itself, of course, the reader is equally taken aback by the almost offensive carelessness with which the foregoing references to Laura *in vita* are suddenly followed by Petrarch's tearful outcry against Amore's proud contention that it was he who "gave" him Laura: "He gave her to me, indeed, but he soon took her back." To which Amore answers unequivocally (that is, with respect to the fact that Laura has died): "Not I, but One who desired her for Himself."

It is this twofold lack of cohesion that is so puzzling for the reader of no. 360, especially since it comes from a supreme master in the art of incorporating interpolations into a text. Only the following assumption, it seems to me, is able to give meaning and compatibility to all the observations we have made. When — to begin with — Petrarch reread the third book of the *Secretum* in 1358, he must have felt unhappy about the unjust outcome of the debate, which, in the framework of Augustine's all-out attack, had quite ungratefully made Laura appear almost like Petrarch's enemy and the destroyer of his spiritual calm. Moreover, at the time of his rereading he was already composing those many poems *in morte di Laura* that depict a saintly Laura in heaven, full of tenderness and love for him. Thus the idea came to him to establish a better balance than Augustine's insensitive condemnation in the *Secretum* had achieved by imagining an impartial, not easily decided litigation before the court of *Guidizia-Ragione*. Though composed a decade after Laura's death, it yet allowed the tensions of Laura's lifetime to become real once more with the vividness of the past. The balance was now redressed, but what issued was inevitably a poem with so many embarrassing features, especially when it became part of the entirely dissimilar concluding section of the *Canzoniere*, that Petrarch did not put his finishing touches to the powerful canzone until it was finally incorporated into the collection with the last batch of appended poems — presumably more or less in its original state.

Assuming that this interpretation of "Quel'antiquo mio dolce" and its genesis is fundamentally valid, we will better understand how it happens that the poem so closely reflects the third book of the *Secretum,* down to the details of diction, without belonging to the period in which Book III was composed. Furthermore, as a text that reveals the growth in Petrarch's mind of a more critical attitude toward a central theme of Book III, it can be used as a source of information on Petrarch's thinking in the late 1350s, that is, during his years in Milan. In some of the chapters that follow, "Quel'antiquo mio dolce" will in fact serve us in this capacity.[38]

[38]After I had finished this chapter, I came upon Bernardo's discussion of the chronology of the last poems in the *Canzoniere* (see Aldo S. Bernardo, *Petrarch, Laura, and the Triumphs* [Albany, N.Y., 1974], pp. 158–161 and 193–196). Bernardo pays little attention to the time and circumstances of the genesis of canzone 360. He has more to say about the observation that Petrarch's indecision whether to repent and renounce his love plays an important role in the last poems and that his rearrangement of them suggested that he was moving toward "unequivocal repentance and a turning away from Laura." In such a context, the strangeness of what I have called the paradoxical character of canzone 360 becomes even more marked. The two approaches supplement each other and are both needed.

CHAPTER FOUR

Book III and the Theory That the *Secretum*
Was Totally Recast in Early 1353:
Its Incongruity with Petrarch's
Work Habits and Life

(1) An Introductory Consideration

The main attempt so far in this study has been to reconstruct the lost drafts of the *Secretum* from the late 1340s in as much detail as possible. The next task should logically be to distinguish the various groups of elements in the *Secretum* text pointing respectively to the late 1340s and 1353. But this cannot be done as easily as we might wish, primarily because Petrarch, who was ultimately a poet, was extraordinarily sensitive to his changing environment — as he himself was very much aware — and his views were consequently apt to fluctuate. Whenever he returned to earlier surroundings, the emotions and aspirations he had experienced in them came back to him and were frequently expressed in a form difficult to distinguish from statements made in former years. This phenomenon has so vexed Petrarch's biographers that at one time it was claimed that Petrarch's thinking had no "history" or development at all.[1]

When considering the *Secretum*, a work clearly marked by the ideal of "solitudo,"[2] we must never lose sight of the frequent changes in Petrarch's environment. Until he finally settled in northern Italy in the summer of 1353, his dwelling place alternated every few years, not only between the Vaucluse and Avignon, but between Provence and Italy. The sojourn in the Vaucluse during which the first draft of the *Secretum* was written came to an end in November 1347. Subsequently he lived for three and a half years (November 1347 to June 1351) in

---

[1] Claimed, that is, by Umberto Bosco, in *Petrarca* (Turin, 1946) and subsequently by many others. See Baron, *From Petrarch to Leonardo Bruni,* pp. 11–13.

[2] Baron, *From Petrarch to Leonardo Bruni,* pp. 62–64, and Rico, *Lectura,* passim.

various middle-sized cities of northern Italy, where he was not un-
affected by urban influences, and in the summer of 1351 he returned
to Provence for two more years. His decision to remain for that
length of time was largely motivated by a desire to complete in the
familiar surroundings of the Vaucluse some of the works originally
inspired by his life there. The scene was thus set in the early 1350s
for a softening of any differences in conduct, feeling, and expression
that might have existed between the 1351–53 and the 1345–47 dweller
in the Vaucluse and lover of solitude.

A similar mitigation of differences emerges when we concentrate
on the two passions discussed in Book III: Petrarch's love for Laura
and the "desiderium gloriae" which drove him to dedicate his life to
the two works written in praise of ancient Rome, the *Africa* and the
De Viris Illustribus. In the discussion of his passions, too, the dividing
line between reactions in 1347 and 1353 is often blurred. For instance,
though Laura died in May 1348, the love poetry devoted to her did
not cease in the 1350s but came to express a transformed love for her
in morte. She was now visualized as looking down upon Petrarch and
caring for his salvation from her place near God. The love sonnets
and canzones were gradually collected by Petrarch in a single book
of lyric poetry devoted to his one love and its spiritualization. We
have already touched upon the perplexity one sometimes feels when
trying to decide whether certain expressions of Petrarch's relationship to Laura *in vita* may not have been written during the 1350s,
when his poetic imagination recalled the love and suffering of earlier
days.

Petrarch's dedication to the *Africa* and *De Viris Illustribus,* it is true,
increasingly gave way to new literary endeavors; beginning in the
late 1340s, both were even set aside for extended periods. Still, Petrarch never entirely abandoned those two early works. At the beginning of the 1350s he looked for ways to adapt them to his changing
values, most strikingly by expanding the *De Viris Illustribus* — originally planned to span Roman history from Romulus to Titus — into
a project "bringing together illustrious men from all countries and
ages" (*ex omnibus terris ac seculis illustres viros in unum contrahendi*). Precisely during the years 1351–53, this change resulted in the addition
of twelve biblical and other pre-Romulean figures to the older Rome-
oriented work, after which Petrarch set the *De Viris* aside for a long

period of time.³ Taken all in all, even during the 1350s Petrarch refused to abandon the conviction, or hope, that his fame would principally depend on the *Africa* and *De Viris,* in spite of his increasing doubt that he would ever be able to finish them.

Once this characteristic fluctuation of Petrarch's guiding interests is given adequate weight, it becomes obvious that if we had to rely solely on a comparison of his thinking in 1347, 1349, and 1353, we would draw few conclusions with any power to convince — except perhaps for Book I, where, as we have observed, the juxtaposition of Augustinian motifs, which guided Petrarch in 1347, with a number of "stoicizing" pages pointing to the early 1350s is so evident that the parts can be clearly distinguished. In the last two books, the structure of the text is more complicated, particularly in Book III where the conclusion that certain passages in Petrarch's discussion of his *amor* and *desiderium gloriae* betray feelings or experiences later than 1347 is in need of some outside support. Book II is less confusing, but still in need of additional support, because we know that Petrarch's feelings of guilt or innocence with respect to the Seven Deadly Sins must have changed between 1347 and 1353, especially since the paragraph on the sin of *luxuria* was indeed adapted to new conditions in 1349.

Thus, in addition to the attempts to reconstruct the *Secretum* texts of 1347 and 1349 and to compare Petrarch's opinions in 1347, 1349, and 1353, a third procedure is necessary: the examination of a more factual kind of evidence regarding Petrarch's actual work on the *Secretum.* For if it could be shown beyond a doubt that Petrarch wrote his final autograph toward the end of his time in Provence, and that in the same period he was intensely occupied with recasting his text — two main theses of Rico — the conjecture that essential parts of Book III reflect Petrarch's thinking in early 1353 would be strengthened. Conversely, if it could be demonstrated that the facts of Petrarch's life make it unlikely that he was occupied with the *Secretum* in that period, this conjecture would be weakened.

Before we attempt to come to grips with the problem thus posed, let us look at the external form in which the text of the *Secretum* has come down to us.

³ See Baron, *From Petrarch to Leonardo Bruni,* pp. 23ff. I shall say more about these matters concerning the *De Viris* in Chap. 5.

(2) Petrarch's Autograph and His Own Dating of the *Secretum* "1353. 1349. 1347"

I

Although Petrarch's final autograph has not been preserved, we know from its transcription by the Florentine Franciscan friar Te-daldo della Casa after Petrarch's death that it contained two notes, one opposite the title, the other at the end of the text. The first — directly or indirectly — provides clues to the time when the autograph was written; the second tells us something about the years in which the *Secretum* was worked on. They are not easy to understand and may even be termed enigmatic. But since they represent what amounts to the only fragments of documentary evidence concerning the date of the autograph and the periods of Petrarch's occupation with the *Secretum*, their interpretation must precede any analysis of the ideas expressed in the work. The marginal notes have been the subject of discussion in recent times, but although increasing light has been shed on their meaning, they remain controversial.

The first of these two notes must be read in conjunction with the title line: "De secreto conflictu curarum mearum liber primus incipit, facturus totidem libros de secreta pace animi, si pax erit." Marginal note: "Fac de secreta pace animi totidem, si pax sit usquam. 1358."[4] In view of this comment of Petrarch's, scholars were long inclined, beginning with Sabbadini's study of 1917, to date the period in which the final autograph was written somewhat loosely as shortly before or in 1358, the consensus being that Petrarch put his final touches to the *Secretum* between the middle of 1353 and 1358.[5]

This long-standing general agreement was in its nature not too

---

[4] See Rico, *Lectura*, p. 10, and Baron, *From Petrarch to Leonardo Bruni*, p. 52, n.3.

[5] "La nota marginale ... significa che egli nel 1358 si ricopiava la redazione definitiva dei tre libri del *Secretus conflictus curarum*" (Remigio Sabbadini, "Note filologiche sul 'Secretum' del Petrarca," *Rivista di Filologia e di Istruzione Classica* XLV [1917], p. 27). "Il *Secretum* fu ... ritoccato tra il 1353 e il '58" (*Prose*, p. 1162). During the summer of 1358 Petrarch "made some revisions in the *Secretum*" (Ernest H. Wilkins, *Life of Petrarch* [Chicago, 1961], p. 162). "... it was only in 1358 that Petrarch had the final copy made, and since even at that time he considered the possibility of resuming the work [by adding three other books 'de secreta pace animi'], the conflicts and anxieties underlying the *Secretum* had probably remained vital issues until not long before 1358" (Baron, *From Petrarch to Leonardo Bruni*, p. 52).

dissimilar from the long-held consensus on the 1342–43 origin of the original *Secretum*, which ignored the possibility that Petrarch used the vague term "nuper" with various meanings. Rico insists that the note of 1358 does not tell us anything about the date or circumstances in which the final autograph was written but simply conveys the information that Petrarch, on the occasion of a "rereading" in 1358, made a note "to exhort himself to persevere in his plan,"[6] namely, to add to the *Secretum* — as promised in the title opposite the note — three books "de secreta pace animi, si pax erit"; or, as the note puts it, "si pax sit usquam." In other words, just as in his reexamination of the term "nuper," Rico has opened the way for rethinking an important aspect of the *Secretum* chronology. In the case of the 1358 note, we are told that since we do not actually learn anything about the autograph from it, and since, therefore, the earlier assumptions about Petrarch's occupation with the autograph in Milan remain unsupported, its preparation could conceivably go back as far as the last months of Petrarch's stay in Provence. Not only does the 1358 note *permit* such conjectures, it encourages and even *requires* them, Rico provocatively concludes.

II

A number of observations, according to Rico, bear out this illation. The first, which will meet with considerable doubt, is that the two references to the planned addition of three more books to the *Secretum* must have been written not only at different times but in "two distinctly different periods" (*dos épocas distintas*) of Petrarch's life.[7] Rico believes that we can infer this from a comparison of the title, "facturus totidem libros de secreta pace animi, si pax erit," with the marginal annotation, "Fac de secreta pace animi totidem, si pax sit usquam," because the first form shows a "more resolved" (*mas decidido*) tone, whereas the note is more "timid and conditional" (*timido y condicionado*); thence the conclusion that the title and note must be considerably separated in time and, since the note is dated 1358, that the autograph with the title may have preceded Petrarch's move to Milan.

---

[6]"... una nota al margen exhortándose a perseverar en el proyecto [proposed in the title line]" (Rico, *Lectura*, p. 12).

[7]For this and what follows, see ibid., pp. 11–12.

There is nothing in the two quoted passages to support such claims. Even apart from the extravagance of the speculation that the conjectured time difference allows us to place the autograph in the period of Petrarch's stay in Provence, the variance between the two passages is so fine that it can easily mislead. Both passages make Petrarch's plan to add three further books dependent on the same condition, because both say "if" (*si,* not *quando*) there should be peace. The one word added in the note is *usquam,* and this disparity does not permit any unequivocal interpretation. The change from "if there will be peace" to "if there should be peace anywhere" *could* be due to increasing skepticism regarding the desired result, but the addition of the spacial element in *usquam* might have another meaning: if Petrarch should find peace of mind "somewhere." If during his stay in Milan he indeed felt increasingly close to finding inner peace, the passage of 1358 — "if there should be peace [of mind for me] anywhere" — could be understood as the hope that such a state of mind might be attainable in Milanese surroundings or under comparable conditions "somewhere," presumably in northern Italy. This would be the very opposite of an increasing doubt whether he could eventually find inner peace at all. The correct interpretation can only be determined by looking beyond the *Secretum* — namely, to Petrarch's state of mind as it is revealed in his contemporaneous letters. In *Var.* 25 of 1360, he reminded Boccaccio that they had orally agreed in 1359 that Milan was the only good place for Petrarch to reside in, considering the state of Italy and Europe: "not only that Milan was more appropriate for me [Petrarch] and my interests than any other place, but also that no place other than Milan could be found in which it would be convenient for me to live, with the single exception of Padua."

I may perhaps be allowed to avail myself of an earlier estimate I gave of the period in question.

> Not before about 1358 was . . . [Petrarch's] inner peace restored. At that time his letters report that . . . he was beginning to find peace of mind in the city [Milan]. Although he still sighed, he said, for the "*vera solitudo*" . . . , he had now mastered the art "of being at rest in the center of the storm" and of "achieving solitude and leisure in the midst of city life [*in mediis urbibus ipse mihi solitudinem atque otium conflare didicerim*]." At that time Petrarch could believe that the "struggles of his soul" reflected in the *Secretum* had come to an end. In such circumstances he . . . added

to the title, *De secreto conflictu curarum mearum,* the cautiously hopeful note that he would write a continuation "de secreta pace animi," "si pax sit usquam."[8]

Since Petrarch did report in his correspondence, about 1358 when he wrote his note, that he felt he had learned the art "of being at rest in the center of the storm" and of finding solitude and *otium* in the midst of cities, the meaning of *usquam* in the note must be: I have hope that I will attain inner peace and, consequently, that I will be able to write three more books, perhaps in Milan, perhaps somewhere else. But then the note cannot have been a means for Petrarch "to exhort himself to persevere in his [old] project." Rather, it must be seen as one among several indications that Petrarch's concept of inner peace was changing in the atmosphere of northern Italy, now that he knew it would be his home for the future. The concept had originally taken form in connection with Petrarch's half-monastic withdrawal from the world, especially the urban world, and with his hope that he would eventually find the strength to emulate Augustine's conversion. But now it gained a more secular hue, becoming an expectation that he would find solitude and concentration of mind "in mediis urbibus." That there was a new tendency in Petrarch's thinking about 1358 to harmonize his "conflictus curarum suarum" we already know from what we have observed of his reaction in the canzone "Quel'antiquo mio dolce" to the stern condemnation of his love in Book III of the *Secretum.* There, too, an Augustinian devaluation of a secular pursuit gives way to a more balanced attitude toward conflicting values.

Although a fuller appreciation of this background to Petrarch's reactions around 1358 must be left for a later point in our discussion,[9] we can already learn from it how little the theory of the "dos épocas distintas" separating the *Secretum* from the note of 1358 can be used to gauge Petrarch's thinking at that time, or to speculate about the amount of time that passed between the autograph and the note, or even to push the composition of the autograph back to the "época" preceding Petrarch's move to Milan.

---

[8] Baron, *From Petrarch to Leonardo Bruni,* pp. 80–81. On *Ep. Var.* 25, see Ernest H. Wilkins, *Petrarch's Eight Years in Milan* (Cambridge, Mass., 1958), p. 182.

[9] Below, pp. 230ff.

III

Whereas this argument of Rico's appears to be mistaken from the outset, another line of reasoning proposed by him as evidence for the pre-Milan origin of Petrarch's autograph — and consequently of the *Secretum* as handed down to us — might at first glance seem to be more promising. This argument is based on the external appearance of Tedaldo's transcript. The copyist Tedaldo is well known for his fidelity in transcribing, which extends to pointing out erasures and interpolations in the text and to indicating whether changes were made between the lines, in the margin, or on attached slips of paper. Tedaldo's copy of the autograph includes the two marginal notes at the beginning and end but fails to indicate any other additions or irregularities in the autograph. How can we explain this, since there is no reason to suspect that Tedaldo was less exact than usual when he copied the *Secretum*? To Rico, the only possible explanation is that after a "complete reworking" (*una refundición íntegra*) of the *Secretum* in the early spring of 1353, "Petrarca no lo revisó posteriormente." "If . . . Tedaldo merely transcribed the introductory and concluding notes, it was because there were no others." In other words, no changes or additions of any sort were made by Petrarch in Milan.[10] There are many claims in Rico's book, therefore, that Petrarch's autograph (with the exception of those two marginal notes) was composed in its entirety during his sojourn in Provence.

Several points should be emphasized in connection with this theory. Even though we can assume on the authority of Petrarch's chronological note ("1353. 1349. 1347") that substantial changes were made in the *Secretum* in 1353, nothing favors the first six months of the year, when Petrarch was in Provence, over the latter six months, when he was in Milan. Which part of the year we consider most probable must depend on what we can learn from evidence outside the *Secretum;* and we shall see in Chapter 6 that a reliable claim can be made for the second (Milanese) half of 1353.

Another point is that we must distinguish between the procedure of adding elements to the text in 1353 — largely due to new impressions in Petrarch's life — and the ultimate retouching and recopying of his much-corrected working copy. The latter might take us well

----

[10] Rico, *Lectura,* pp. 470–471.

beyond 1353, for nothing is known that prevents the fair copy from having been made a few years later. If it was made only shortly before the note of 1358 was added, Petrarch could still have jotted down "1353. 1349. 1347" to record the years in which the work was *composed*, without having intended to say that 1353 represents the year of the final fair copy. Thus, if Tedaldo failed to indicate any corrections in the manuscript he copied, a very likely explanation is that whatever changes were prompted by Petrarch's Milanese environment were entered shortly after his arrival in Milan, during the second half of 1353, and were, therefore, already incorporated in the final autograph and not visible to Tedaldo when he made his transcription after Petrarch's death.

I cannot see any reason why this natural alternative should appear less acceptable than the idea of a fair copy written immediately before Petrarch's departure from Provence, at the very time of major worry and uncertainty about his future life. There is an air of unreality in the notion that Petrarch used his last hectic weeks in the Vaucluse to rewrite the *Secretum* from scratch, refusing to avail himself of its previous versions and, under the most adverse conditions, composing a basically new work with such sureness of touch that Tedaldo later found an autographic fair copy written without any corrections or changes.

Before reconciling ourselves to such an implausible picture, we ought to look at it far more closely. First, we need to see whether Petrarch's work habits as we know them from other writings do not make the assumption of a "recasting" (or even of two, one in 1349 and one in 1353) extremely improbable. Second, we should examine more skeptically the premise that, if we accept the "1353. 1349. 1347" note as documentary evidence of Petrarch's engagement on the *Secretum* in 1353, we have to conclude that it was completed during his sojourn in Provence. Since some of the reasons for doubt on the latter point have already been touched upon, it will be best to explore them first.

IV

A discussion of Petrarch's reference to the periods when he worked on the *Secretum* should begin with a consideration of some reservations recently expressed by Guido Martellotti. In a review of Rico's work, Martellotti declared himself unconvinced by the theory "that the three dates [in Petrarch's chronological note] refer to three successive recastings [*rifacimenti*] of the entire work." His general conclusion was: "Devo confessare che la cosa mi lascia perplesso"; Petrarch's note, "nel suo insieme, rimane per me alquanto misteriosa." For one must take into consideration not only the three dates but the entire note, "Modo 3. 1353. 1349. 1347." Seen as a whole, Martellotti says, the note has "the look of a subjective remark: a brief, sad statement that there are only three books at present [not yet those to be written *de secreta pace animi*] and that Petrarch has so far not found peace of mind; one fails to understand why Petrarch felt it necessary to add that the situation had been the same in preceding years [by also referring to 1349 and 1347], since his remark [that only three books have been completed] is dated 1353."[11]

Martellotti's point is well taken. It is important for the reader to realize that in the form in which we have it in Fra Tedaldo's transcript, Petrarch's note simply makes no sense. Since we have only Tedaldo's copy of the note, Martellotti suggests, "it may be necessary to suppose that Tedaldo's much praised accuracy in reproducing everything exactly may have faltered at this point by misrepresenting, if nothing else, the position of the note."[12] This observation seems to point to the real problem: when read as a whole, the note indeed appears "alquanto misteriosa," and the high esteem in which Tedaldo's reliability is held is not sufficient assurance that he did not for some reason change its position and external appearance. This means, however, that we also cannot take it for granted that its five components originally formed a unit; with their ambiguous telegraphic style, they may not have been intended to convey a single, coherent message.

To all appearances, "modo 3" answers the question implied in Petrarch's note opposite the beginning of the work, "Fac de secreta pace animi totidem [libros] si pax sit usquam . . ."; "only 3" must mean that these intended books, 4–6, were never written, and this is how Tedaldo understood it when he stated in his *explicit* ". . . et sic liber de secreto conflictu continet 3 libros." On the other hand, "1353. 1349.

---

[11] *Annali della Scuola Normale Superiore di Pisa,* Classe di Lettere, ser. 3, VI (1976), pp. 1395–1396.

[12] Ibid., p. 1396.

1347" is to all appearances a reference to the years in which Petrarch was working on the *Secretum*, whatever the inverse order of the dates may signify. So the question that quite naturally arises from Martellotti's premises is whether there is any reason to think that Tedaldo might himself have brought the two portions of the note together.

In any event, Tedaldo added the *explicit* at the end of his transcript: "Explicit liber III domini Francisci Petrarche de secreto conflictu *curarum suarum* [my emphasis], et sic liber de secreto conflictu continet 3 libros." That this was not written by Petrarch is self-evident and is confirmed by the difference in form of Petrarch's *incipit:* "De secreto conflictu *curarum mearum* liber primus incipit, facturus totidem libros de secreta pace animi si pax erit." Tedaldo's reason for adding an *explicit* of his own is obvious: since the autograph began with ". . . facturus totidem libros de secreta pace animi si pax erit" and thus left open the question of what Petrarch might finally have done, Tedaldo wanted to assure future Florentine readers that those other three books were not included in the text he had been copying in Padua. Obviously, Petrarch's enigmatic "modo 3" in the margin was not in itself clear enough for contemporary readers, just as it is not clear enough for modern readers; so Tedaldo had to testify in an *explicit* that he had found no more than three books. But the proper place for such an *explicit* was very probably occupied in the autograph by Petrarch's chronological note, "1353. 1349. 1347." Such chronological annotations are usually found below the finished work, not in the margin, and Petrarch's autographs are no exception. If this was the case in the *Secretum* autograph, what could Tedaldo do? He could not copy "1353. 1349. 1347" first and then add "Explicit liber III Domini Francisci Petrarche . . . ," because this would have made Petrarch's notation appear to be a part of *Liber* III, which it was not. It would have been even more confusing for him to put Petrarch's autographic note *after* his own *explicit*. The only other alternative was to put it in the margin, that is, to make it follow the note Petrarch had written there, so that the marginal annotation would read "Modo 3. 1353. 1349. 1347."

The correctness of such a reconstruction cannot, of course, ever be proven. We can only draw attention to the probability that Tedaldo found himself in this predicament and reacted in the manner described. Given this likelihood, we should not insist on trying to understand the marginal note as a unit. On the contrary, we have every right to use its two parts as separate messages, regardless of whether the puzzling note was contrived in the suspected manner or Petrarch himself combined two unconnected statements.

V

The three unexplained dates in Petrarch's note have frequently caused error and confusion, even apart from their connection with the phrase "modo 3." Lorenzo Mehus in the eighteenth century and Georg Voigt in the nineteenth assumed from Petrarch's data that Book I originated in 1353, Book II in 1349, and Book III in 1347.[13] Rico's interpretation of the triad of years as the dates when the work was written and rewritten is a step in the right direction, especially because it forces attention to the fact that the year 1342–43 fails to appear in Petrarch's list.[14] But Rico tries to extract more evidence from our source than it contains. He argues that, since Petrarch began his list with 1353, the text of that year must have been more than an adaptation and enlargement of the preceding text; it must have been a full "recasting" of the work. Moreover, since Petrarch listed 1349 and 1347 alongside and on a par with 1353, each of the three years must have seen a rewriting (practically a new autograph).

This is a lot to deduce from such a narrow premise; we must look more closely at Rico's line of reasoning and imaginative reconstruction:[15]

> Let us try to reconstruct what could have passed through the mind of Petrarch . . . when he wrote in the margin: "Modo 3. 1353. 1349. 1347." We can understand the significance of these figures. 1353 comes first . . . because the author saw 1353 as the essential year of the elaboration. . . . It comes first because in 1353 there were not merely retouchings and disconnected additions, but the entire work was rewritten. To Petrarch, the *Secretum* was substantially a product of 1353. . . . Next, presumably while still in the act, he considered that the book had passed through two previous stages, which were annulled by the *remaniement* of 1353. . . . The three figures refer, then, not to insertions and retouchings but to redac-

---

[13] See p. 22, above.

[14] Summarized by Rico as an "originale" and two "rimaneggiamenti," in Francisco Rico, "Precisazioni di cronologia petrarchesca: Le 'Familiares' VIII 2–5, e i rifacimenti del 'Secretum,'" *Giornale Storico della Letteratura Italiana* CLV (1978), p. 489.

[15] What follows is a potpourri of citations from Rico, *Lectura*, pp. 14–16, 454–455.

tions and recastings of the work in its entirety [*redacciones y refundiciones cabales, de cuerpo entero*]. Only if this is the case does the inverse order of the dates become understandable. . . . At first Petrarch surely did not intend to give more references [than 1353]. But being a meticulous man he had doubts: the work had undergone an initial redaction and a reworking, and it was worth the trouble to note it. . . . In accordance with the degree of importance, he went from major to minor: 1349, 1347. That he first thought of 1353 indicates that in that year he did not limit himself to a partial effort of inserting and rephrasing, but instead completely rewrote the work. And since [his work in] 1353 cannot be seen as something fragmentary, 1349 and 1347 . . . must refer to comparable [completely new] versions.

I think that most of Rico's readers are likely to agree with me that a more probable explanation for the inverse order of Petrarch's three dates is simply that he first wanted to jot down only "1353" as the year in which the work was finally completed but then felt that the other two years also deserved to be mentioned. There is no need to believe that the initial reference to 1353 means that Petrarch considered the text of that year to be a total recasting, or that the order of the references corresponds to a regression in significance, "from major to minor," in Petrarch's eyes. But if this explanation is to be more than just possible, we need additional concrete information.

Chapter 2 established that the relapse into *luxuria* deplored in Book II occurred in 1349 and that by 1353 Petrarch had long been free of this sin. What this means is that, in the one instance where we have access to information approaching the certainty of documentary evidence, we find that in 1353 Petrarch simply carried over a portion of his older text, even though it was a self-incriminating one. Is it plausible that the old, outdated text on *luxuria* would have been retained in 1353 if Petrarch had wanted to write virtually a new book rather than merely emending and complementing an older one? The sole reasonable inference seems to be that he meant to preserve the original text — which naturally would in some respects not fit the circumstances of 1353 — except where he decided that certain experiences and events that had occurred in his life between 1347 and 1353 had to be incorporated. This also seems to be the more natural assumption for the reason observed in Chapters 2 and 3: that the first draft of 1347 already had the basic structure of the final autograph — a division into three books fulfilling the functions and covering the major topics of the present three books.

It is true that certain facts at first appear to contradict these conclusions. Literary critics of the *Canzoniere* have become increasingly aware that Petrarch was in the habit of recasting his poems. Many of them have experienced no end of changes made over the course of years not only in single words and verses but also in their entire structure.[16] Aldo Scaglione, in a persuasive article, has described the "open form" of Petrarch's sonnets and his reluctance to look upon any of them as final and permanent as long as he was alive.[17] There were similar recastings in the much longer triumphs, especially in the successive versions of the *triumphus Fame;* and Enrico Fenzi has emphasized that to understand the gradual growth of the *Africa,* we must recognize that many of the changes made in it were not mere "aggiunte" to the text but part of an "organic growth that organizes and reconstructs all data on a higher level."[18]

Rico's thesis that the growth of the *Secretum,* too, was a matter not of making additions but of rewriting and recasting an entire text must be viewed in the light of this trend in the study of Petrarch's poetry.[19] Ultimately, this is again a case of comparing unlike models. As I pointed out once before in this study,[20] there is great danger in this method, for there are crucial differences between a poem or an *epistola familiaris* and a work like the *Secretum.* The continuous recasting of Petrarch's poems clearly has artistic roots; the innumerable changes were mostly intended to perfect the over-all aesthetic form.

[16] See Dennis Dutschke, *F. Petrarca: Canzone XXIII from First to Final Version* (Ravenna, 1977).

[17] Aldo Scaglione, "The Structure of the *Canzoniere* and Petrarch's Method of Composition," in *Francesco Petrarca: Citizen of the World,* ed. Aldo S. Bernardo, Proceedings of the World Petrarch Congress, Washington, D.C., 1974 (Padua and Albany, N.Y., 1980), pp. 301–313. See in particular: "His method [as a poet] can be described specifically as open-ended rather than as one clearly tending to end in a final static product" (p. 301); "Literature and poetry are, throughout the poet's career, an ideal of never-ending, infinite perfectibility. The author is not really interested in 'publication' because his real deadline can only be set by death" (p. 311).

[18] "La continuazione del lavoro non è quella delle aggiunte, ma quella, appunto, organica, che investe e ricompone tutti i dati a un livello più alto" (Enrico Fenzi, "Dall'*Africa* al *Secretum,*" in *Il Petrarca ad Arquà,* Atti del Convegno di Studi nel VI Centenario, ed. Giuseppe Billanovich and Giuseppe Frasso [Padua, 1975], p. 108). On Fenzi see p. 124f., below.

[19] This is one of the cardinal points of Rico's approach according to his "Precisazioni," esp. pp. 518, 522f., where he insists that the changes in the *Secretum* were not "interpolazioni" or "addizioni occasionali" but "un processo . . . di rimaneggiamento globale" and "un rifacimento nel senso più stretto della parola."

[20] See p. 15, above.

Why should the method needed to achieve artistic perfection have been used for philosophical and psychological writings like the *Secretum*?

It would be unfair not to add that Rico has drawn one of Petrarch's Latin prose works into the range of his comparisons. The procedure followed in the *Secretum*, he maintains, was also followed in the *Vita Scipionis* (in the *De Viris Illustribus*). It, too, was written in three successive versions, the second following the first after only a few years, and the third and final one at a later time. Thus the *Vita*, he says, represents a counterpart to Petrarch's twofold rewriting of the *Secretum*, and in this case all three versions have been preserved.[21]

Now if the three-stage evolution of the *Vita Scipionis* is to be compared with that of the *Secretum*, it must not be forgotten that as a piece of historical writing the *Vita* is not necessarily subject to the same rules of composition as a text of philosophical and psychological analysis. Historical biographies tend to increase considerably in volume from edition to edition as more knowledge is gained from historical sources. This is especially true of Petrarch's *De Viris Illustribus*, the first humanistic effort to master some of the high points of Roman history. In the specific case of the *Vita* of Scipio — the hero of the *Africa* epic and the center of Petrarch's entire early historiographic activity — the biography, initially part of the *De Viris*, grew from a chapter of about 30 pages into a historical narrative of about 130 pages. There was a special reason, therefore, for the two recastings of this biography.

Moreover, it is significant for the comparison with the *Secretum* that despite its enormous expansion and unusually long period of maturation — from the early 1340s to the late 1350s — the *Vita Scipionis* was never completely rewritten, as Rico has suggested for the 1349 and 1353 versions of the *Secretum*. Page after page of the three consecutive stages of the *Vita Scipionis* demonstrates that the original text was by no means replaced but changed sporadically through selective corrections, stylistic alterations, and interpolations, in the very manner which Rico rejects for the *Secretum*. It is only in places where Petrarch was faced with too many new questions or facts that whole pages were rewritten.[22]

[21] See Rico, "Precisazioni," p. 489, n.21.
[22] See Martellotti's comparison of the three versions of the *Vita Scipionis* in Francesco Petrarca, *La vita di Scipione l'africano,* ed. Guido Martellotti (Milan, 1954), pp.

However, it is from Petrarch's philosophical Latin writings — for the *Secretum* is basically a philosophical work — that one must determine whether his work habits show a tendency to repeatedly recast entire works. Since the *De Vita Solitaria* and the *De Otio Religioso* were composed close to the time of the original *Secretum*, anything we can learn about their literary development should be especially helpful in judging the history of the *Secretum*. In both the *De Vita* and the *De Otio* the original texts were subjected to repeated changes, especially during the ten years or so after their initial composition. The original text of the *De Vita*, like that of the *Secretum*, has apparently not been preserved; but again in parallel with the *Secretum*, we have proof outside the text that all known *libri* (only two in this case) formed part of the original version.[23] The work was not recast but transformed through small corrections and sometimes extensive interpolations. As B. L. Ullman writes in his study of the genesis of the *De Vita Solitaria*, we should not talk of "first and second editions" at all but rather say that "the first draft underwent changes from time to time."[24] In the *De Otio* the transformed text contains about a hundred additions, mostly small, but among them "vaste giunte che ne accrescono notabilmente l'estensione." In spite of these, it is described by its editor in La Letteratura Italiana: Storia e Testi as "un organico rimaneggiamento" (that is, a rearrangement or readjustment), not a recasting.[25]

12-13; and esp. his comments on the various transformations: "Le varianti sono da principio di assai poco rilievo, per lo più semplici ritocchi che potevano essere operati agevolmente nel margine o nell'interlinea; da un terzo in poi le differenze si fanno più apprezzabili per l'aggiunta di interi episodi, quali l'incontro di Massinissa con Sofonisba. . . ." "Mentre dunque nella prima parte il testo fu sottoposto a una semplice revisione, nella seconda invero fu riscritto con altri criteri, in parte almeno su fogli a sé." See also Aldo S. Bernardo's synopsis of Martellotti's conclusions, in *Petrarca, Scipio, and the Africa* (Baltimore, 1962), pp. 104–110, and esp.: ". . . the Beta version consists, for the most part, of insertions and elaborations to the original text" (p. 107); in Alpha "there is hardly a page which does not have at least grammatical or syntactical changes when compared to the corresponding section of the Beta form" (p. 108).

[23] We know this because, only one year later, the *De Otio* referred to Liber II of the *De Vita Solitaria* and because *Sen.* XIII 1 specifically stated that both books of the *De Vita* were composed in the Vaucluse *at one time*. See B. L. Ullman, "The Composition of Petrarch's *De Vita Solitaria*," in *Miscellanea Giovanni Mercati*, vol. IV, Studi e Testi 124 (Vatican City, 1946), pp. 122–123.

[24] Ibid., p. 122.

[25] *Prose*, p. 1168.

Perhaps the most instructive parallel is to be found in Petrarch's *De Sui Ipsius et Multorum Ignorantia,* written shortly before 1370. Here we encounter the unique situation of two preserved autograph copies of the same philosophical work, separated from each other by only about two years — approximately the amount of time separating the 1347 and 1349 versions of the *Secretum*. When, at the end of 1367, the first autograph, which was intended as the dedication copy, was completed, Petrarch did not at once send it to the addressee but let it lie while its pages and margins were subjected to the usual treatment. In June 1370, he completed another fair copy, incorporating all the changes he had made up to that time; but no sooner had he finished it than he again began making changes. The entire process is summarized in the "nota critica ai testi" in La Letteratura Italiana:[26] "To the first form of his work Petrarch added substantial complements, which found their places in the margins of the [autograph] manuscript until there was opportunity for a new transcription in another manuscript — a complete, fair copy. Then, however, the new text in turn received numerous marginal additions, fruits of the unceasing corrective activity of the author; and he took care to enter them in the older manuscript as well, with the effect that the two autographs today present a nearly identical text."[27]

The idea that Petrarch abruptly discarded the first draft of the *Secretum* and replaced it with two successive rewritings *ab ovo* without retaining a single page older than 1353 thus not only appears improbable but does not take due account of his actual work habits. It is misleading in view of the fact that the mature versions of virtually all of Petrarch's comparable Latin works — wherever we can sufficiently reconstruct the history of their genesis — show the survival of their author's original inspiration. All in all, they conform to the type

---

[26] Ibid., p. 1174.

[27] The genesis of the *De Remediis Utriusque Fortunae* was no different from that of the earlier philosophical works. Its growth in two stages did not involve a rewriting but rather an amendment of the text by means of additions. As Klaus Heitmann concludes in his "La genesi del *De remediis utriusque fortune* del Petrarca," *Convivium* XXV (1957), p. 25, the *De Remediis* "venne redatto in due tappe. Il primo 85 per cento (molto probabilmente fino al cap. II 93 inclusivamente) fu scritto fra la fine del 1356 e la metà del 1357. L'opera giunse allora ad un pieno compimento.... Nell'autunno ... del 1366 fu ampliata, con l'aggiunta dell'ultimo 15 per cento. Molti indizi ci fanno credere che allo stesso tempo l'umanista ritoccò lievemente anche quello che aveva scritto nel 1356-57." See also p. 167, n.38, below.

of gradually expanding texts and manuscripts, full of marginal and other interpolations that develop or transform the initial draft at certain points. This, as we have seen, is how the *De Vita Solitaria* and *De Otio Religioso* were changed between 1346, the year preceding the *Secretum,* and 1347 — after they had both been conceived with striking rapidity during the forty days of Lent between Ash Wednesday and Easter. In both cases, the existing evidence forces us to conclude that their general structure and all their organically important parts were already in place at the time the works were conceived.

In short, what we have learned in the preceding analysis about the gradual accretion of the *Secretum* is in full accord with Petrarch's usual method of working, whereas the proposed scheme of several successive "rifacimenti" of whole works is contrary to everything he did elsewhere in his prose writings.

(3) The False Hypothesis That the *Secretum* Was Hastily Rewritten before Petrarch's Move from Provence to Northern Italy in Mid-1353

I

Next to cutting the ties between the *Secretum* and the alleged crisis of 1342–43, the greatest change in the recent perspective of the *Secretum* has been the proposed ascription of the traditional text in toto to 1353. In Rico's eyes, there is no difference in the reliability of these two major aspects of his basic thesis, and in view of the apparent abundance of information to which he refers it is no wonder that there have been few objections. But there are disquieting points in his argument, and these will be systematically examined in what remains of this chapter.

Some of the most provoking pages of Rico's description of the role of the year 1353 for the *Secretum* are encountered at the point where it is reported how Augustine, near the end of the discussion of Petrarch's love for Laura in Book III, advises Franciscus to leave Provence and seek inner peace by traveling in Italy — advice wholeheartedly accepted by Franciscus. At precisely that point in Book III, Rico says, one encounters a noticeable change in the text: "Up to our page [p.

172 of the edition by Enrico Carrara] there are no signs [*segnales*] of hurry; after it, there are many."[28]

Two questions of considerable methodological interest posed by Rico in this context are whether Petrarch may not himself have been on the verge of leaving Provence for Italy in the spring of 1353 when he made Augustine propose such a move to Franciscus, and whether the remainder of the book does not reveal a "hurried composition, explainable by Petrarch's desire to finish a text in the process of being written in a limited time," namely, during his last few weeks in Provence. After all, the argument runs, we have precise information that, after a period of hesitation, Petrarch suddenly decided in the early spring of 1353 to leave for Italy. We know this, we are told, from a letter Petrarch wrote to Zanobi da Strada on April 28, in which he says that although few roads in Italy are yet safe, his disgust for Avignon is such that anything he might encounter while traveling would be better than staying on, and that he has therefore decided to leave as soon as he can manage it, "in great haste, like one fleeing from a prison" (*velut is qui carcerem fugit, festinabundus*) — after returning to the Vaucluse for a final visit of no more than eight days.[29] And although Petrarch could not leave for Italy quite as soon as he had planned, he was indeed on his way there by late May or early June.

Most probably, Rico comments, Petrarch had resolved to leave with as little delay as possible somewhat earlier than April 28, namely, in the middle of April, when he visited the monastery of Montrieux to bid his brother farewell. Between that visit and the end of May, there would have been ample time to write the last twenty pages of Book III. "Hence, our page and all that follows brings us to the beginning of the spring of 1353. Likewise, *rebus sic stantibus,* everything preceding [page 172] ought to be dated immediately prior." And so "the trend of the argument [*las pistas*] and the evidence converge: a recasting of the *Secretum,* intensive and decisive, from the *incipit* to the *explicit,* was done in Provence during the winter and in the days before the beginning of the spring of 1353. This, I believe, can be concluded with certainty."[30]

[28] Rico, *Lectura,* p. 468.
[29] *Fam.* XVI 10.
[30] Rico, *Lectura,* p. 468.

Why necessarily in Provence and not in Milan, after Petrarch's return to Italy? Because "in Milan . . . there was no reason to hurry; instead, everything [there] invited Petrarch to engage in long-term projects such as the *De Remediis*."[31] The facts speak against such confidence. There are indications pointing in both directions, Rico admits.[32] On the other hand, it does not seem to be "comprehensible that Petrarch, just when he was pressed for time, would hastily attempt to complete a work that had been neglected for years. On the other, it is quite logical that before entering upon a vital new period [in Italy] he would want to finish a well advanced project of *rewriting* [*sic*], the plan of which was clear in his mind."[33]

Whatever one may think of the tight-rope walking inherent in such speculations, some doubts immediately intrude. A certain hastiness in the latter portions of a literary work is not an altogether rare occurrence, and one can think of many reasons why Petrarch might have become less careful, other than his decision finally to leave Provence as he did in the middle of 1353. For instance, we have learned from Guido Martellotti that something similar to what Rico believes happened at the end of the *Secretum* did in fact occur during preparation of the second version of Petrarch's *Vita Scipionis*, written in 1341–43. Martellotti thought that it "betrays a certain haste" (*tradisca una certa fretta*), which led to repetition and sometimes imperfect integration.[34] Does this observation also demand the conclusion that the text of the *Vita Scipionis* was completed in August 1343 before Petrarch left for Italy, and that the "hastily" written autograph of the second version of the *Vita* cannot have undergone substantial change in later years?

Before the slackening of the author's attention in the third book of the *Secretum* can be used to argue in favor of the period in 1353 preceding his move to Italy, we have to be certain that the alleged signs of haste cannot be traced to 1347 or 1349, the other two years in which Petrarch was — or may have been — occupied with the formulation

[31] Ibid.

[32] Ibid., p. 467f.

[33] "Tampoco es comprensible que Petrarca, justamente cuando se hallaba urgido por la prisa, se pusiera a completar atropelladamente una obra arrinconada hacía años. En cambio, es bien lógico que, antes de iniciar la nueva etapa vital que avizoraba, deseara rematar una tarea de *rewriting* sumamente adelantada y cuyo esquema tenía claro en la cabeza" (ibid., p. 467).

[34] Martellotti, *La vita di Scipione*, intro. p. 12.

of Augustine's advice to travel in Italy. Rico is by no means unaware of the need for considering Petrarch's situation in those alternative years, and he would probably not have insisted so readily on 1353 if he had not been convinced that his detailed examination of Book III elsewhere in his volume eliminated 1347 and 1349 as possible choices. There is good reason, however, to question the justification for that conviction.

We shall do well to differentiate between two separate lines in Rico's argument. The first, on closer examination, turns out to be a near relation of those many hypotheses which we have already characterized as purely speculative. "It seems clear," he says, "that the passages which reflect haste . . . must pertain to the last version of the *Secretum*. For if it were not so, that is, if they had been part of the first or second redaction, they undoubtedly [*sin duda*] would have been rewritten in the final stage in order to homogenize the work."[35] What militates against the assumption that outdated statements from the earlier versions of the *Secretum* would generally have been corrected in 1353 is of course the testimony of the *luxuria* section that in its case such an eventual rewriting did not take place. Nor is the *Secretum* unique among Petrarch's writings in this respect. For in another text on which Petrarch was working during his last year in the Vaucluse (in 1352–53, that is, precisely during the period under review) there is a clear example of Petrarch's unconcern with correcting what he had imperfectly written in Provence. In this instance, he found himself unable to say why Aristotle had reproached the ancient poets, "because I lack fresh recollection of the relevant passage [in Aristotle's *Metaphysics*], and there is no copy of the *Metaphysics* in these mountains." When he came to reorganize the *Invective* in Milan, he left the quoted sentence with its reference to mountains unchanged.[36] Applied to the *Secretum*, this is an effective warning against any expectation that passages of early versions must necessarily "have been rewritten in the final stage in order to homogenize the work."

[35] Rico, *Lectura,* p. 375.

[36] "Quenam . . . poetarum culpa, rem veram, si intelligatur, salubremque narrantium? Aut quenam aristotelica illa reprehensio? Si tamen ita est; neque enim michi nunc aut eius loci memoria recens, aut inter hos montes liber ipse methaphisicus est presens" (*Invective Contra Medicum,* Liber tertius, ed. P. G. Ricci [Rome, 1950], p. 72. In *Prose,* p. 676).

The other line in Rico's argument for 1353 is his emphasis on our need to date Augustine's advice that Franciscus should undertake a "peregrinatio" to Italy. Augustine's counsel is intended to free Petrarch from his love. Accordingly, its purpose is psychological: the prescribed cure is distraction through travel. "Italy, then, would be my choice for you. . . . I would not, however, wish to confine you only to one corner of the land. Go under good auspices wherever inclination may lead you; go without fear and with a free mind. . . . See how long you have been a stranger to your own country and your own self. It is time to return."[37]

As early as 1963, I attempted to show that the first of the three years of work on the *Secretum* — 1347 — can be excluded as the date of Augustine's advice to travel. Petrarch's return to Italy in November 1347 did not take place until half a year after the completion of the 1347 draft, nor did his departure from Provence in that year mean anything to him but a return to the house he had owned in Parma since 1344. He certainly was not planning to travel freely in 1347. Not until he accepted a canonry in Padua in March 1349, after a rift with the residing bishop of Parma caused him to rule out a future in that city and look for possibilities elsewhere in northern Italy, did he begin a life that was not confined to a single corner.[38] We are also directed to 1349 when we consider that Augustine's praise of Italy as the goal for Petrarch's "peregrinatio" refers to Petrarch's glorification of the peninsula in his *Metrica* III 25, a poem written in 1349.[39]

But let us look at the particular reasons which Rico believes exclude 1349 and favor 1353. One cannot claim, he concedes, that Petrarch was confined to Parma in 1349, yet he was then in a situation not at all conducive to the carefree traveling recommended by Augustine in Book III, even though during the spring of 1349 he "enjoyed spending time in Padua and making short excursions." His "headquarters [*centro*] continued to be Parma," and when in May he made plans to lead a communal life with Luca Cristiani and two other

---

[37]"Italiam igitur suadeo, quod moribus incolarum celoque et circumfusi maris ambitu et intersecantis horas Apennini collibus et omni locorum situ, nulla usquam statio curis tuis oportunior futura sit. Ad unum vero eius angulum, te arctare noluerim. I modo felix, quocunque te fert animus. I securus et propera. . . . Nimis diu iam et a patria et a te ipso exulasti. Tempus est revertendi . . ." (Carrara, p. 172).

[38]Baron, *From Petrarch to Leonardo Bruni,* pp. 89–90.

[39]Ibid., pp. 57, 90.

friends, "he enthusiastically leaned toward Parma as his perfect base." Therefore, the section of Book III that begins with Augustine's advice to travel "can only with great difficulty be harmonized with the circumstances of 1349 and with [Petrarch's] imaginable plans for that year." On the other hand, "Augustine's curious exhortation and several related events become as clear as day if we assume that they were written during a clearly definable part of 1353." "Everything," Rico insists, "concurs in favor of this period. Over the Franciscus of the *Secretum* and the Petrarch of the last months in Provence there hangs the same fear of not being able to escape, and the same determination to return to Italy triumphs in the end."[40]

How does Rico support these claims? For one, he compares a number of presumed homologies in the concluding section of Book III and in some of the *familiares* of 1352–53, where, he thinks, strikingly similar expressions, moods, and opinions are found. He proffers five such comparisons as his basis for favoring the year 1353 over 1349. What follows is a list and systematic reevaluation of the supposed homologies. (The key words in the comparisons are italicized for clarity.)

II

(1) Franciscus in the *Secretum:* "Fugamque [away from Provence] iam meditor, sed *quo potissimum cursum dirigam incertus* sum." This is compared with Petrarch in *Fam.* XV 8 (April 24, 1352): "*incertus quo potissimum vela dem.*"

Comment: The "uncertainty" mentioned in the letter does not mean that Petrarch is trying to decide where he might best settle down. On the contrary, the gist of his letter is an ordering of his priorities: he will not accept invitations from the kings of Naples and France or go to the Curia in Avignon; nor does he wish to stay indefinitely in the Vaucluse, in spite of his enjoyment of its solitude, for there he would degenerate into a backwoodsman, a *silvanus*. He longs for Rome, and if he could once settle in the *sancta civitas* he would not leave it again. If Lelius, the Roman recipient of this request for advice, should nonetheless discourage him from coming to Rome, his second choice would be that part of northern Italy where he was happy for so many years. He is afraid, however, that civil war (which had driven him out of Parma in 1345) might frustrate any plans to return there. In that case he would look upon his life like a shipwrecked man and accept the safety and peace of the Vaucluse, giving up all thought of the world outside, "nil

---

[40] Rico, *Lectura*, pp. 344, 346.

usquam preter Sorgiam cogitabo, inter agrestes victurus." Meanwhile, "incertus quo potissimum vela dem," he is anxiously awaiting Fortuna's decision. Quite apart from the not insignificant fact that this letter was written more than a year before Petrarch left Provence in May–June 1353 (it is dated April 24, 1352), the situation presupposed in the letter is wholly different from that presupposed in the *Secretum,* where Franciscus is resolved to leave Provence but is "incertus" which country to go to until he hears Augustine's counsel to return to his native land; to go not to some narrow "corner" (*angulus*) but to travel wherever his mood and inclination may lead him. If anything can be learned from this comparison, it is that *Fam.* XV 8 and the pages in the *Secretum* have nothing in common and must have been written at different times in Petrarch's life; that there is no reason why the pages in the *Secretum* could not have been written as early as 1349 if this should be suggested by other evidence.

(2) Augustine to Franciscus in the *Secretum:* "*undique patent vie, multi portus in circuitu*"; but you should go to your native land, Italy. This is again compared with *Fam.* XV 8: according to Rico, "Petrarch contemplates many possibilities (Florence,[41] Naples, Paris, Rome, *interque Alpes et Apenninum*)."

Comment: There is no meaningful concordance here. The advice in the *Secretum* is: of all countries on earth, go to Italy! The statement in *Fam.* XV 8 says: I truly desire only Rome or the familiar land between the Alps and the Apennines. Nothing but the preference for Italy is common to the compared passages; the decisive question — what should be done when he is in Italy — is not the same. No words or phrases are identical. This example does not belong in Rico's list at all.

(3) The advice in the *Secretum,* to go "*quocumque te fert animus,*" reveals (according to Rico) that "Francesco no tiene ninguna seguridad de adónde irá." This is compared with *Fam.* XVI 10 (April 28, 1353): "Petrarca solo sabe que se consolerá '*quocunque caput hoc sors imperiosa rotaverit.*'"

Comment: As in (1), the two quotations refer to different situations: in the *Secretum,* Petrarch, who is uncertain, is directed by Augustine to go to Italy and travel freely. In April 1353, his priorities were firmly established; he wondered only which of them fortune ("sors") would permit him to realize. The selected passages show no similarity whatever, except for the one word *quocunque.*

---

[41] This is not true. Petrarch says at one point in *Fam.* XV 8 (Rossi's ed., vol. III, p. 157) that, living on the Sorge in the Vaucluse, he still often remembers the Tiber, Po, Arno, Adige, and Ticino, whereas as a "silvanus" he will eventually think only of the Sorge. This is not the same as "contemplating" Florence as a "possibility" for his future, a thought which does not appear in the letter.

(4) Augustine in the *Secretum:* "*Nimis diu iam et a patria et a te ipso exulasti. Tempus est revertendi, 'advesperascit enim et nox est amica predonibus.'*" This is compared with Petrarch in *Fam.* XV 8 (April 24, 1352): "*Satis diu peregrinati ne dicam iactati sumus; tempus est ad vesperam subsistendi figendique anchoram, ne nox deprehendat errantes.*"

Comment: Although in atmosphere and form of expression these two paragraphs are indeed similar enough to make one wonder whether they might not have originated at the same time, they may just as readily belong to two separate years in which Petrarch was anxious to begin a new life in his native land. In 1349 he would have had good reason to make Augustine rationalize — and apologize for — his lingering in northern Italy (where he had gone late in 1347). If, in spite of this consideration, one were to persist in arguing that the *Secretum* passage is contemporaneous with the letter of 1352, one would have to explain a connected chronological fact. "Advesperascit enim et nox est amica predonibus," the key words in the comparison with the letter of 1352, come from the earlier period, not from 1352; they are a quotation from Petrarch's *Psalmi Penitentiales* of about 1348. Given the choice, is it not more likely that the prayers occasioned by Petrarch's personal experience at the time of the plague were cited when they were still fresh in his mind, that is, in the *Secretum* of 1349, rather than four years later? This is a weak comparison, therefore. Indeed, it is nothing but a formal parallel, for the letter speaks of "satis diu peregrinati . . . sumus" and "figendique anchoram," whereas Augustine advises Franciscus: "Ad unum . . . angulum te arctare noluerim. I modo felix, quocunque te fert animus." The point in the one case is that it is high time to "cast anchor"; in the other, that Petrarch should not confine himself to "one corner." The situations could not be more different.

(5) Augustine's advice in the *Secretum,* shortly before page 172 in the Carrara edition: "Hoc igitur moneo, hoc suadeo, hoc iubeo: . . . ita, *sine spe reditus,* abeundum. . . . Quod si locum corpori tuo gravem pestilentemque sortitus, . . . nonne *irrediturus* effugeres?"[42] This is compared with *Metr.* III 24 (1353): return to Italy as "*incola perpetuus*"; and with *Fam.* XVI 10 (April 28, 1353): Petrarch has returned to the Vaucluse from Avignon, "ut *irrediturus* abeam."

Comment: It should be observed at once that *irrediturus* is one of Petrarch's favorite words and is used by him in many different ways. Accordingly, the inference that two passages which include this word or concept reflect the same situation or date ought to be made with the utmost caution. The comparison is no more persuasive than the parallel given in (4): although the

[42] Carrara, p. 166.

expression *irrediturus* is identical, it is used in different contexts.[43] In the second half of Book III, *irrediturus* is explained as meaning "without hope for a return" (*sine spe reditus*): that is, the context is an admonition addressed to a still vacillating Franciscus, who must be cut off psychologically from any thought of return. In the two epistolary passages unquestionably originating in 1353, on the other hand, we are shown a Petrarch who feels certain that he will soon be an Italian again on his native soil. There is nothing in the comparison of these quotations to prevent us from assuming that what we read in the *Secretum* on and around page 172 was written in 1349, when Petrarch, speaking through Augustine, had reason to justify to himself his increasingly prolonged stay in northern Italy, away from the Vaucluse. This is in contrast to the situation in 1353, when his decision to return to Italy with his indispensable books was final and an exhortation to a still wavering Petrarch would make no sense.

In summary: Considering the fragility of Rico's comparisons, it is surprising to find him concluding that "in my opinion, these [comparisons] give solid evidence [*la pura evidencia*] that our passage [page 172 in Carrara's edition] and all the passages related to it are incomprehensible unless they were composed during the final stage of Petrarch's stay in Provence. During that essentially homogeneous period, Petrarch must have produced the *Secretum*'s final recasting [*refundición*]." It is due to the basic importance of this conclusion for Rico's thesis — namely, that the work was recast in 1353 — that I have thought it necessary to try to convince the reader that the alleged bridge to the *familiares* of the 1350s is constructed on sand.[44]

III

Having gained a better perspective on the mistaken parallels between the *Secretum* and the letters of the 1350s, we must now consider the alternative — 1347 or 1349 — for the date of the concluding section of Book III.

There is nothing wrong with assuming that the *Secretum* is basically akin to some of the fictitious *familiares* in content and time of composition. But we should be on our guard against overlooking the

[43] E.g., often in connection with the inconstancy of human life: whereas in nature the seasons return annually, man leaves without returning, "irrediturus." See Giuseppe Velli, "La memoria poetica del Petrarca," in *Italia Medioevale e Umanistica* XIX (1976), esp. pp. 178-179.

[44] See Rico, *Lectura*, p. 347. Since a second volume of Rico's work has been promised, dealing in particular with the *Familiares*, it is only fair to add that other observations may be made in the future on the relationship between Book III and the *familiares* of the early 1350s.

obvious distinctions. What matters for the correct understanding of Augustine's peculiar counsel — "I would not wish to confine you to one corner of Italy. Go . . . wherever inclination may lead you; go without fear and with a free mind" — is not, after all, the (ultimately irrelevant) question whether there was a city in 1349, such as Parma, which Petrarch continued to regard and use as his headquarters in Italy. What matters is whether Petrarch was traveling frequently in 1349, driven by a desire to explore Italy and leading the kind of life for which Augustine's words could serve as an apology. This is a simple biographical question, which can be answered by a look at Petrarch's life at the time. We lose sight of the dominant tendency of that year through the shift in emphasis that results from Rico's saying "from spring on, Petrarch enjoyed spending time in Padua and making short excursions, but his headquarters continued to be Parma" or again, regarding the plan Petrarch conceived in May to live together with three friends, "he did not shun the idea of living elsewhere; however, he enthusiastically leaned toward Parma as the perfect base."

A less oblique description of Petrarch's life in 1349 gives an entirely different picture. Ever since Petrarch had come to Italy via Verona at the end of 1347, he had lived in Parma. Then in early March of 1349, through the initiative of Jacopo da Carrara, Lord of Padua, he received a second ecclesiastical office by virtue of an appointment as a canon at the Cathedral of Padua. For the first time, he no longer lived only "in one corner" of Italy. After some weeks at the Paduan court and solemn instalment in his new office, he traveled to Venice and Treviso and paid another visit to Verona; he did not return to Parma until May. During the autumn of that year, this itinerant mode of life was resumed. In September he was a guest of the ruling Pio family in Carpi in the Apennine Mountains east of Parma, and probably in the same year he paid his first visit to Ferrara as a guest of the Este. Beginning in November he lived in Padua again for several months and did not return to Parma until May 1350.

I have ventured to speak of an "itinerant mode of life," but can we be sure that this was Petrarch's own perception of his activities when he made the first major revisions in the *Secretum*, probably in the autumn of 1349? In this connection, the proposal to share a dwelling with his three friends, which Petrarch made toward the end of May — that is, in the interval between his two extended periods of travel — is

of decisive help. For it testifies to a spirit of exploration — a true wan-
derlust — that took hold of him in 1349. Although he offered his friends
as a common residence the big house in Parma that he was entitled to
use in connection with his ecclesiastical office, his praise of the house
and its location was couched in terms implying that one major aim of
their proposed companionship would be to travel together. Whenever
we wish to spend some time in the environs of Parma, he told them,
we will have the opportunity to visit Bologna and Piacenza. "When we
have a mind to travel somewhat farther, we can go to Milan and
Genoa, the first the ornament of all inland cities, the second the flower
of all ports." "We will go with a free mind [*ibimus vacui curarum*] along
those shores of the Tyrrhenian Sea which I enjoy so immensely," and
we shall find on the shores of Genoa [on the Riviera] the *otium* that
Scipio and Laelius once enjoyed more to the south, in Gaeta. "But if
our desires should ever be satiated by this part of the land, another
and not less suitable home will be available to us in Padua, in the
region north of the Po"; and next to Padua lies the most marvelous
city Petrarch professes to have seen in all Europe, Venice. Beyond it,
for the summer season, he goes on, is Treviso (like Venice, visited by
Petrarch in 1349), a city of rivers and springs, "from which any kind of
melancholy is far removed. Thus, whenever monotony, the mother of
boredom, hurts us, variety, the best medicine against ennui, will be at
hand."[45] What closer concordance of sentiment, desire, and expression could we find than between this guide to lighthearted, diverting
travel and the counsel given by Augustine in the *Secretum:* "Italy then
would be my choice for you; because the ways of its people, its climate, the seas washing its shores, the Apennine Range between
them, all promise that a sojourn there would be better suited to extir-
pate your troubles than a trip to any other place in the world. I
would not, however, wish to confine you only to one corner of the
land. Go under good auspices wherever inclination may lead you."[46]

   In the interpretation of what we may call the "travel page" of Book
III, then,[47] biographical facts win out over conjectures derived from
the 1353 thesis. Not only is there an astonishing conformity between
the letter of 1349 and the travel page, but a comparison of Petrarch's

[45] From the original (γ) version of May 19, 1349, of *Fam.* VIII 2–5. See Rossi's
ed., vol. II, pp. 201–203.
[46] See p. 96 and n.37, above, for the end of this quotation and the Latin text.
[47] Carrara, p. 172.

situation in 1353 with that attested to in the letter of 1349 leaves no doubt that Augustine's psychological counsel in the third book is the very opposite of what Petrarch needed and desired in the early 1350s. His dream of a future life in Italy at that time was to settle where it would be most convenient. There is not a single hint in the letters he wrote from Provence in 1353 that when his epistolary efforts to find an "angulus" in Italy in which to live proved unsuccessful and he decided in April to leave without a specific invitation, taking his heavy manuscripts with him, he had given up the desire to settle down and was instead dreaming once more of finding distractions in the exploration of Italy — as he had explored the coast around the gulf of Naples in 1343–44 and northern Italy in 1349–50. Moreover, by the spring of 1353 Laura had been dead for about five years, so Petrarch's resolve to return to Italy at that time could hardly have had anything to do with the remedy prescribed in the *Secretum:* a cure for his passion for her. Nor in 1353 was Petrarch in need of any admonition to return. Since 1352 he had been making every possible effort to find a place in Italy where he could settle permanently; in November 1352 he had even started on his way and had returned to the Vaucluse only because torrential rains had threatened to destroy his books as they were being transported and because news about the state of the Italian roads was full of reports of highway robberies. If he left Provence in the spring of 1353 without an offer from a specific "angulus," it was not because he wanted to be free to travel about, but because he expected that it would be easier for him to find the right place when he was in Italy and no longer dependent on correspondence.

If it were important merely to establish that the travel page in Book III belongs in spirit to 1349 and is wholly out of keeping with 1353, this chapter might be terminated here, and it could be claimed that the goal has been achieved. But the above findings have further implications. To begin with, the establishment of a paragraph earlier than 1353 in Book III supplements our knowledge of the genesis of the *Secretum* at the very point where our chronological information was found wanting. For although it was possible for us to detect pages in Books I and II that must have existed in 1347 or 1349 in basically the form in which they are now known, this was not the case in Book III, because "I'vo pensando," which reflects that book prior to May 1348, reveals more about the general structure of the early *Secretum* than it does about its particular features. Furthermore, we do not have direct evidence outside the *Secretum* for the exact chronology of Book III such as we have for Book II in the *luxuria* diary. Nevertheless, the suggested relationship of the travel page to the surviving 1349 version of *Fam.* VIII 2–5 provides a kind of equivalent in Book III to the situation in Book II, and the fact that Book III, too, takes us back to a portion of the text written in 1349 should be a warning against overestimating the role of 1353.

Besides having this implication, the above findings also strongly affect the two assertions which Rico frequently makes in connection with Augustine's advice that Franciscus should travel lightheartedly through Italy. One is that before April 1353 Petrarch had not yet fully made up his mind to return to Italy for good, a claim which, if correct, would imply that all intimations in the *Secretum* of Petrarch's firm intent to return must date from 1353 and not before. The other assertion is that the travel page and many of those that follow it show signs of having been written in an extraordinary hurry, betraying the rush of the weeks in April–May 1353 when Petrarch was on the verge of leaving Provence.

These two confident claims, together with the just refuted thesis of the 1353 origin of the travel page, may have been the cause of the apparently unopposed reception of the 1353 theory;[48] but just for that reason, we should also be quick to reexamine the related theories. Like the proverbial bundle of sticks, the three parts of the argument prove to be unbreakable only so long as they remain together. Now that the date of the travel page is seen to be 1349, are the two other attributions to 1353 still defensible?

IV

Let us first consider the proposition that Petrarch did not finally resolve to return to Italy until April 1353: that is, not until the end of a long period during which he could not decide whether to leave Provence or remain there. Rico's argument runs in *extenso*:

---

[48] See Francesco Bruni's expression of trust in his review of Rico's work, in *Medioevo Romanzo* III (1976), p. 146: "Anche le ipotesi sulle parti dell'opera [the *Secretum*] presumibilmente dovute al rifacimento ultimo del 1353, se non sempre raggiungono la certezza (né vi aspirano), sono comunque sostenute da argomentazioni che, allo stato attuale delle conoscenze, appaiono solide e bene impostate."

Petrarch returned to Provence in June 1351, originally only for the summer; but pleasure, business, and general desire detained him for almost a biennium. During this time he never stopped thinking about a return to Italy; nevertheless, he knew dark moments when all hope seemed lost, and he tried to resign himself to the eventuality of remaining in Avignon and the Vaucluse [*y procuró resignarse a la eventualidad de permanecer en Avignon y Vaucluse*]. . . . In the second half of 1353, the desire to return was rekindled (to the point where in November he set out [for Italy] unsuccessfully). At the beginning of 1353, on the other hand, he suffered a kind of crisis of discouragement: he feared being confined in Provence. . . . For several months he had serious doubts about where to settle in Italy and sounded out many friends and acquaintances; the messengers brought back news that he would be welcomed wherever he went, but his hope was not realized: no invitation, no signal seemed to be final. Eventually, with the coming of spring, he decided resolutely to go to the Peninsula on chance, without knowing where he might end up, and to endure "quicquid erit." This he did.[49]

The picture this draws of Petrarch is distorted by oversights or dubious readings of the available sources. The idea that he initially went back to the Vaucluse for a summer's stay but that "pleasure, business, and general desire detained him for almost a biennium" is correct only on the surface. For there is a document written within weeks of his arrival in the Vaucluse — *Fam.* XI 12 of July 19, 1351, addressed to Olimpius and entirely neglected by Rico in this context — in which Petrarch tells of his plan to remain in the Vaucluse so that he may complete some of the works he had begun there years ago. This letter assures Olimpius that he will spend two years there for this purpose (that is, July 1351 to June 1353) and no more. He scrupulously carried out his plan, and in late May (or possibly early June) 1353, he set out for Italy, even though the desired invitations had not arrived. Now, it is true that in spite of this illuminating letter of July 1351 one might be tempted to ask whether the very fact that Petrarch returned to Provence in June 1351 and remained there for two years does not suggest that he must have been wondering if his best prospects for the future might not after all still lie in France. However, the letter to Olimpius is not our only assurance that by 1351 Petrarch was determined to move to Italy as soon as circumstances allowed, because already two years before, in 1349 (as we

[49] Rico, *Lectura*, pp. 344–345.

have seen), he had made Augustine counsel Franciscus in the *Secretum* to leave Provence, with all its memories of Laura, "irrediturus." This must have been on Petrarch's mind when he arrived in Provence in June–July 1351; and he must also have been guided by the practical consideration that he was virtually forced to revisit the Vaucluse once more before he could settle permanently in Italy. For "transalpina solitudo mea iocundissima" (in addition to the papal demand that he come to Avignon for an interview) was not his only major incentive for returning to Provence; his indispensable and irreplaceable library needed to be transported under his supervision if he wanted to carry on his work in Italy.

Rico maintains in very definite terms that Petrarch "knew dark moments during which . . . he tried to resign himself to the eventuality of remaining in Avignon and the Vaucluse." For proof we are referred to *Fam.* XV 8 (15–17) of April 24, 1352, and *Fam.* XII 11 (7–8) of May 21, 1352,[50] but we are given no indication of how these two letters are supposed to bear out the claim. We have already become familiar with the earlier letter. It contains the query sent to Lelius in Rome and provides a carefully articulated survey of Petrarch's hopes for his future residence. No detail is omitted; nothing remains obscure. Petrarch has received invitations from many great lords, but he will never settle at the Curia in Avignon, or in the Paris of the French kings, or at the court of Naples. There are only two acceptable solutions: either Rome, for which he longs with all his heart and to which he would hurry, never to leave again, if Lelius should feel he could advise him to come; or, as a second choice, the area between the Alps and the Apennines, that part of northern Italy in which some of his best years had been spent. If even this alternative should prove impossible, nothing unusual would happen to him, he says with bitterness. One would still find him in his woods, trying in solitude to forget his troubles and the cities: "vagabor solus et liber ut nunc facio." "There would be the one difference that in these surroundings I now think of the Tiber, Po, and Arno" and other rivers of Italy, "but at that time I would be thinking of nothing but the Sorgue, living among peasants until I was buried with them at the end of my days."[51] Therefore, the letter concludes, Lelius should

[50] Ibid., p. 345, nn.322 and 323.

[51] ". . . tunc nil usquam preter Sorgiam cogitabo, inter agrestes victurus humandusque ultimoque dierum omnium . . ." (*Fam.* XV 8 [17]).

quickly let him know his judgment, never forgetting "that if I have a choice, I prefer Rome to all other places. . . . Just now I feel drawn there by a desire which becomes ever more fervent the longer it endures . . . : once I have set foot in the holy city, I will never depart from it again."[52]

To conclude from all this that Petrarch "knew dark moments in which all hope seemed lost and tried to resign himself to the eventuality of remaining in Avignon and the Vaucluse" is to distort the true meaning of the April letter and the scale of priorities expressed in it. Nor does the May letter to which Rico refers — *Fam.* XII 11 — suggest that Petrarch tried to resign himself to this eventuality. Rather, it allows us to see another aspect of the circumstances in which *Fam.* XV 8 was written. In XII 11 we find Petrarch trying to obtain from the pope certain ecclesiastical benefices, on which he would be able to live in Italy. Precisely the same values and preferences are expressed here as in the more explicit and exhaustive *Fam.* XV 8. It is true that now, one month later, Petrarch says, "Nunc vero quid sit futurum nescio," but at the same time he assures his friend that if Christ were to grant his wishes "he would live and die in Italy" and would prefer "in Italia laborare quam ubi sum [Avignon] quiescere." And, he adds, if he should be successful in his quest for needed *beneficia,* the first thing the addressee would hear about him "would be the news that I had returned [to Italy], not that I was going to return" (*non ante revertentem audies quam reversum*), so quickly would he hurry home. If he should not succeed, however, the recipient knows that in summertime "I am accustomed to console myself with sighs beyond the Alps" (*ubi lenire soleam transalpina suspiria*).

Were Petrarch's priorities less firmly established during his next "crisis of discouragement"[53] in early 1353, two months before he decided (in mid-April) not to remain in Provence beyond the planned two years? This alleged crisis of uncertainty is described by Rico as follows:

> Since the end of 1352 . . . Petrarch had felt the desire to return to Italy with particular intensity; at one moment, however, he was on the point of desisting from continuing with his plan, seeing that it was hardly fea-

[52]". . . me si detur optio libera, longe Romam locis omnibus preferre. . . . Nunc ergo quo magis dilato eo magis ardenti desiderio illuc trahor . . . : si sanctam civitatem semel intravero, nunquam inde digrediar . . ." (ibid. [18–19]).

[53] As Rico called it. See p. 99, above.

sible. Thus, in February of 1353, he considered the possibility of remaining in Provence, in the Vaucluse, avoiding Avignon (although that was impossible . . .). In April, on the other hand, his resolve was firm and effective, without reservation.[54]

Rico bases his belief in a complete change in Petrarch's mood and objectives between February and April 1353 primarily on two letters sent by Petrarch during these two months to a confidant in his Florentine circle of friends, Zanobi da Strada. In *Fam.* XVI 10 of April 28, he let this circle know through Zanobi that he was finally setting out for Italy, though nothing had yet been arranged concerning his final residence. With this brief communication one must compare the long and informative letter sent by Petrarch to Zanobi two months earlier, on February 22 (*Fam.* XV 3), which described his state of mind at that time. As Rico understands this letter, Petrarch wanted to tell Zanobi then that "he was on the point of giving up his plan," that is, to move to Italy. But Petrarch's real mood is evident from the following: "I have cast anchor [in the Vaucluse] and moored my ship, battered by the storms of life, to this rocky shore *until a harbor comes into view;* I will not go back to the Curia, nor will I make for Italy *unless I hear something new* [my emphases]."[55] There is nothing in the letter to tell us that Petrarch was deeply disturbed in February or near to abandoning his Italian plan. He merely informs Zanobi that he has gone from Avignon to the Vaucluse to find a temporary haven — "temporary," because he adds "donec portus appareat." He may well have been less worried at that time than later in April, when the hoped-for news from Italy failed to arrive and he made up his mind that it would be better to set out without further delay.

I leave it to my readers to decide whether there is anything in the quoted passage to indicate that Petrarch was contemplating the abandonment of his long-held intention to return to Italy. The best way to approach the important February letter, it seems to me, is to recall Petrarch's reactions during the two years spent in Provence, including the fact that from the very first he had explained to his friends that he would stay for two years and no longer — a sign that many of his decisions in 1352–53 must have been premeditated. To

[54] Rico, *Lectura,* pp. 468–469, n.51.

[55] ". . . ieci anchoram, . . . fessamque vite turbinibus carinam, donec portus appareat, hos inter scopulos alligavi, non rediturus ad curiam, neque nisi aliud audiero, Ausoniam [i.e., Italiam] petiturus" (*Fam.* XV 3 [9]).

sum them up: When less than half of the planned twenty-four months in Provence had passed, he began to ask his friends about future prospects in Rome and northern Italy, telling them that any other place was unacceptable, and actively tried to arrange to settle in Rome through an exchange of his ecclesiastical benefices. When, during his last six months in Provence, he reluctantly dropped Rome from his plans and no final arrangement in northern Italy had materialized, he told his friends at first (in February 1353) that he would wait in the Vaucluse for the decision from northern Italy, and finally (in April) that he would no longer wait but return to Italy immediately (with his books, as it turned out) and try his luck. Moreover, we have not even considered possible changes in Petrarch's relationship to friends at the Curia in Avignon, which may at times have prevented him from making his Italian plans as if he, after all a clergyman, were his own master. We are reminded of this aspect of his life, which does not emerge very clearly from his correspondence, when we learn that in November 1352 Cardinal Gui de Boulogne, who was allegedly absent from Avignon for a short time, withdrew his permission for Petrarch to return to Italy whenever he desired, telling him by letter that he was not to move before the cardinal's return to Avignon — a command with which Petrarch was evidently bound to comply.[56]

These, then, are the determinable facts, and their implication is obvious. Because Petrarch had had the firm intention of returning to Italy after two years ever since he had arrived in Provence in June 1351, we must not attach much importance to his indecision in 1352–53 whether to stay in the Vaucluse a few months longer or return to Italy without delay. He could have made Augustine admonish Franciscus to hurry back to his native land not only as late as April 1353 but virtually any time between June 1351 and June 1353, just as, when living in Italy, he could have made Augustine rationalize and excuse the roving life Petrarch was leading at any time between late 1347 and mid-1351.

V

We turn now to consider in greater detail the last of the strands intertwined in the 1353 thesis, the contention that the concluding pages of

---

[56] See Ernest H. Wilkins, *Studies in the Life and Works of Petrarch* (Cambridge, Mass., 1955), p. 133.

the *Secretum* betray an extraordinary "haste" in their composition. Rico argues that from page 172 to the end of Book III there are so many signs — and personal admissions — of Petrarch's having hurried, that nothing can explain them but the assumption that the second half of Book III was rewritten during the final feverish weeks of his stay in Provence. Although this conjecture does not change the facts that prove the composition of parts of the text in 1349, it might conceivably lead to the skeptical conclusion that different approaches yield different results. Yet everything considered, nothing suggests that Petrarch wrote the last pages of the *Secretum* in circumstances unique to 1353.

To quote Rico's analysis: toward the end of Book III, "rapidity of composition is recognizable . . . in the scantiness of the section on *gloria*, in the less vivid conversation progressively converted into a monologue by Augustine (making it obvious that the author was searching for a conclusion by briefly summarizing the fundamental aspects)."[57] This kind of analysis necessarily leaves the diagnosis open to doubt. To other eyes, the *gloria* section may well appear to be one of the most exhaustive Petrarch devoted to his spiritual maladies. Perhaps Rico was comparing it in length with the preceding *amor* section, which is indeed twice as long. But the latter had undergone a different kind of history. Petrarch's relationship to Laura — during her life and after her death — had repeatedly changed, and thus parts of the *amor* section almost certainly contain lengthy interpolations — just as in Book II, in the discussion of the Seven Deadly Sins, the *avaritia* and *accidia* sections are longer than the rest because these sins played changing roles in Petrarch's life and therefore required an extension of the discussion, as will be seen in another context.[58] As for Augustine's role in the debate of Book III, surely many readers of the *Secretum* will not agree that the growing length of his speeches is a sign that Petrarch spent less time on this part of his work and was thereby induced to change from a dialogue to a monologue. Augustine's redoubled efforts are, rather, a necessary preparation for the dramatic concluding scene, in which the church father and beloved teacher, despite his long, almost uninterrupted speech, fails to overcome Franciscus' inner resistance and his adherence to the literary works on which he is engaged.

[57] Rico, *Lectura*, p. 466.
[58] See Chap. 6, below.

A case for unusual haste in Petrarch's work has to rely on less ambiguous evidence; even the tabulation of Petrarch's increasing mistakes in the second half of Book III — another device employed by
Rico — can lead to errors. It is a fact that there are more mistakes
in the quotations and the recitation of details in the second half of
Book III than in the preceding parts of the *Secretum;* but, as I suggested earlier, an increase in errors caused by fatigue once the major
part of an author's work has been done is nothing very rare, and there
is no need to fall back on the exceptional conditions of Petrarch's
imminent departure for Italy in the spring of 1353 to explain them in
the case of the *Secretum*. [59] Moreover, his inaccuracy in the last twenty
pages is difficult to judge, since the same kinds of mistakes are found,
though less frequently, in the first and second books. When it is
asserted in the concluding section of the *Secretum* (180), for instance,
that the Emperor Augustus was extremely afraid of lightning, a
weakness actually ascribed to Tiberius, this is no more or less a sign
of "haste" than when a phrase of Seneca's is ascribed to Cicero or
words from the *Wisdom of Solomon* to St. Paul in the first book. [60]
Again, if after page 172 Petrarch repeatedly makes mistakes in his
quotations (from Seneca, Cicero, and Horace), even though he
appears to want to quote accurately[61] — mistakes which he would
normally have corrected before the text circulated — he also mis-
quotes in other parts of the *Secretum*. [62] What all this amounts to is that
the "defects" found from page 172 onward are basically a matter of
degree only, and it is impossible to demonstrate that they could not
have occurred just as well in 1349 (or 1347) as in 1353. This route can
only lead to a dead end rather than serving as a way to confirm the
1353 theory.

Rico ultimately tries to hold together his supposed bits of evidence
for Petrarch's extraordinary hurry — inaccurate quotations, confu-
sions of historical personae, the alleged premature termination and
decreasing vivacity of the *gloria* section — by the apparently factual
observation that Petrarch himself tells us in so many words that he is

[59] I have already mentioned that, according to Martellotti, a similar decline in
carefulness is found toward the end of the second version of Petrarch's *Vita Scipionis,*
a work not written under the conditions of 1353. See n.34, above.

[60] Carrara, pp. 60, 65, 180.

[61] Ibid., pp. 184, 198.

[62] Ibid., p. 64, from Virgil; p. 84, from Horace.

working in "haste" in the last sections of his work.[63] The only way to evaluate this claim is to list and systematically reexamine the alleged admissions.

VI

(1) Rico begins his discussion on the "urgency [*premura*] evident in the second half of Book III" with the statement: ". . . one can discern that Petrarch was writing with great speed. He does not fail to admit it candidly [by saying]: 'hoc est quod . . . dicendum tempus obtulerat' ([Carrara] 184), 'pro brevitate autem temporis satis multa . . . dicta sunt' ([Carrara] 188)."[64]

Comment: Largely owing to Rico's omission of some vital words, these passages may indeed at first give the impression that when the speaker mentions "enough has been said" he is referring to some external conditions which are restricting his time. But we must bear in mind that the speaker in both cases is Augustine, not Franciscus. What is actually happening is that Augustine is passing from one item on his agenda to the next in an ordered sequence of thoughts and means to say: it is time to think of our next point. This becomes clear as soon as the blank spaces are filled in. In the first case, the complete sentence reads: "Et hoc est quod de pudore dicendum tempus obtulerat"; and with this, Augustine's counsel proceeds from the help that can be expected from "shame" to the help that can be hoped for from "reason," the strongest incentive among the "remedia amoris." Certainly this is in no sense a "confession" by Petrarch that he is writing in haste, pressed by the "brevitas" of the time available to him.

Nor does the second passage have such a connotation once it is read in toto: "Sed quoniam, tametsi pro necessitate tua pauca quidem, pro brevitate autem temporis satis multa de uno morbo dicta sunt, ad alia transeamus" — namely, by turning from Petrarch's *amor* to his *desiderium gloriae*. Again, nothing could be less an "admission" or "confession" by Petrarch than this apportioning of his teacher's (not Franciscus') time between the subjects to be covered; least of all because it had already been necessary to extend the conversation, originally thought to require two days, to a third, and *amor* had grown to be by far the most extensive subject of the conversation, so that it was indeed time to pass on to Petrarch's second "morbus," *gloria*.

(2) Rico continues: "It must also be considered a confession when he [Petrarch] explains that he has abbreviated some material,[65] contenting himself with choosing 'pauca' from 'multa' (174), not doing justice to the

---

[63] Rico, *Lectura*, pp. 465–467.

[64] ". . . se aprecia que Petrarca trabajaba a vuela pluma. No deja ello de confesarse paladinamente. . . ." (ibid., p. 465).

[65] "Por confesiones valen también explicar que se abrevia una materia . . ." (ibid.).

'rei qualitas' (204), admitting that he has improvised 'ex tempore' (210),"
and so on.

Comment: It must again be pointed out that none of these passages can
be counted as "confessions" by Petrarch, because they are integral parts of
Augustine's speeches and make sense only as contributions by him to the
conversation. This is especially striking in the last two cases. In the first, the
words stressed by Rico, "verbis ... paucioribus ... quam rei qualitas exigebat," have nothing at all to do with the speaker's lack of time, as will immediately be realized when this judgment of Augustine's is quoted in its
entirety: "Habes de gloria iudicium meum, pluribus certe quam vel me vel
te decuit verbis explicitum, paucioribus vero quam rei qualitas exigebat.
. . ." In the second case, the meaning of the words "ex tempore," used by
Augustine (not Franciscus) to end the conversation, is clearly that whereas
Franciscus might be expected to devote time to other aspects of the matter,
he (Augustine) had only entered upon those which presented themselves
to him "spontaneously."[66]

(3) Lastly, says Rico,[67] there are places where Augustine talks quite
openly of Franciscus' being in haste. For, "it cannot be by chance [casual]
that the church father underscores the image of a Franciscus who writes *fret-*
toloso ('dum ... festinas ... ,' 192), because the character [namely, Francis-
cus] wishes to 'accelerare' his unfinished works (206) and ends by recogniz-
ing: 'neque aliam ob causam propero nunc . . .' (214)."

Comment: There can be no relationship between, on the one hand, Franciscus' vow at the end of the *Secretum* not to follow Augustine's advice to forsake the *Africa* and *De Viris* but rather to speed up work on them before
obeying Augustine's demand to turn to higher things, and, on the other, an
alleged decision to hastily complete the *Secretum* during the weeks before
Petrarch's return to Italy. The only thing these two have in common is that
something would be "speeded up": work on the *Secretum* during the next few
weeks and work on the *Africa* and *De Viris* in the years to come.[68]

---

[66]"Hec igitur, fili carissime, tecum volve et, siqua huius generis occurrunt alia,
que multa esse non dubito; sed hec erant que ex tempore se se obtulerunt." There is
not even a hint that Augustine (let alone Franciscus) is holding, or abbreviating, the
conversation under pressure of time. Enrico Carrara already understood and correctly translated the passage in Augustine's speech in his Italian rendition of the
Secretum: ". . . ma queste [riflessioni] erano quelle che al proposito mi si presentarono
spontanee" (Carrara, p. 211).

[67]Rico, *Lectura,* p. 466.

[68]Petrarch names no other work in the course of the *Secretum* debate but has Augustine make the following complaint: "Ita totam vitam his duabus curis, *ut intercur-*
rentes alias innumeras sileam [my emphasis], . . . tribuis, deque aliis scribens, tui ipsius
obliviscceris" (Carrara, p. 192). The words "ut . . . sileam" could, of course, have been
interpolated in 1353, by which time so many other works of Petrarch's had been

More precisely, the acceleration of work on the two writings named in the *Secretum* is the very heart of Franciscus' ultimate resistance to Augustine and hence is one of the major themes of the concluding pages of Book III. The only reason Rico brings Franciscus' vow to speed up his future efforts on the *Africa* and *De Viris* into his argument regarding the allegedly "hasty" work on the *Secretum* in 1353 is that Franciscus uses such words as "festinare," "accelerare," and "properare." The passage to which Rico refers, "dum immodice gloriam petens . . . festinas," exclusively concerns Petrarch's continuous involvement with two major works and the dismaying probability that even if he hurries he will finish neither by the time he dies. The same is true of Franciscus' use of "accelerare" and "properare." In short, the passages in the *Secretum* that include terms for "speeding up" are used in connection with a totally different subject: his future work on the *Africa* and *De Viris* rather than something he intends to do in Provence before his imminent departure.

To recapitulate: like the other lines of argument offered for the hypothesis of a "recasting" of the *Secretum* in 1353, the supposed discovery of unusual haste in completing the *Secretum* cannot be confirmed anywhere, not even by what Rico interprets as "confessions" that Petrarch was working under the pressure of time.

VII

In addition to his three major lines of argument, Rico points to a separate and unique piece of evidence which, he thinks, will clinch the thesis that at least the last pages of the *Secretum* show clear traces of a 1353 origin. In the third book (page 210), Augustine makes what is, indeed, a curious statement. It is of considerable interest, and Rico's argument on this point should be explored carefully, even though he has failed elsewhere to support his thesis of a 1353 origin.

The statement in question is built on a quotation from Cicero's

---

started but not finished. However, such a limiting clause would also not have been entirely unjustified in 1347. The problem is that throughout the *Secretum* the "aliae innumerae curae" are passed over in silence, whereas the *Africa* and *De Viris* are mentioned. This is therefore not a basis for deciding between the claims of 1347 and 1353. Whether Petrarch was also thinking of the *Secretum* when he wrote "alias innumeras" cannot be determined, but logic is against it. For when Franciscus talks to Augustine in the *Secretum* about his "countless other occupations," his current work — the *Secretum* itself — cannot be one of the "other" occupations he is complaining about.

Tusculans, one of the classical texts used throughout the *Secretum.*[69]
Near the end of the third book, Augustine advises Franciscus always
to keep in mind Aristotle's description of certain small animals found
along the Hypanis (a river flowing into the Black Sea) that live only
a single day and thus invite thought about the relativity of human
conceptions of age and the brevity of life. I know, says Augustine to
Franciscus, how much you have always liked this "aristotelica similitudo" and that you cannot read or hear about it "sine gravi mentis
impulsu." And then he cites the literary sources from which one may
learn about this "similitudo." You will find it, he says, "expressed
with more shining eloquence and in a more persuasive form in Cicero's *Tusculans . . . ,* either in the following words or in similar ones,
for there is now no copy of that book at hand."[70] And, indeed, in his
subsequent citation from the *Tusculans,* Augustine noticeably devi-
ates from Cicero's text.

The paragraph serves Rico as a basis for a number of inferences:
"From this it is clear that in writing our page Petrarch did not have
Cicero's work accessible."[71] Furthermore, such a situation could have
occurred only during the final, rushed days of Petrarch's stay in Provence in 1353, when his manuscripts were already packed up and he
was loath to reopen his trunks to verify a quotation.[72]

If the speaker of the words "neque enim libri nunc illius copia est"
were Franciscus and not Augustine, it might be difficult to deny the
methodological appropriateness of these inferences. But it is Augustine who is speaking, and his words must make sense in the context
of the debate. Spoken by him, the "nunc" in "neque enim libri nunc

[69] Sabbadini characterized the *Secretum* outright as "quasi un centone delle *Tusculanae*" ("Note filologiche," p. 26).

[70] "Crebro ante oculos revoca aristotelicam quandam similitudinem, quam ani-
madverti tibi admodum placere, vixque unquam sine gravi mentis impulsu legi
solere vel audiri; quam clariori eloquio et ad persuadendum aptiori in *Tusculano* quidem a Cicerone relatam invenies, aut his verbis aut profecto similibus, neque enim
libri nunc illius copia est. . ." (Carrara, p. 210).

[71] "De ahí resulta claro que al escribir nuestra página no le [i.e., to Petrarch] era
accesible la obra de Cicerón . . ." (Rico, *Lectura,* p. 430, n.602). Giuseppe Billanovich
had already concluded this in 1941, when he wrote the introduction to his edition
(much used by Rico) of Petrarch's *Rerum Memorandarum Libri* (Florence, 1947), p.
CXXIV, n.1: "Mentre [Petrarca] scrive una pagina del *Secretum* gli mancano addiri-
tura le *Tusculanae.* . . ."

[72] Rico, *Lectura,* pp. 430–431, n.602.

illius [that is, the *Tusculans*] copia est" refers not to a period in Petrarch's life — neither to spring 1353 nor to any other time — but to the imaginary scene in which Augustine addresses Franciscus. The conclusion that Petrarch may have made Augustine talk about the lack of a copy of the *Tusculans* because Petrarch's personal copy was inaccessible is pure speculation. If any true solution to the problem is to be found, it can only be through a more penetrating investigation of Augustine's remark as a part of the *Secretum* debate.

It seems to me more likely that Petrarch made Augustine hint at the absence of a copy of the *Tusculans* as an excuse for changing Cicero's phrasing, perhaps in order to make it conform to the needs of the conversation being carried on. If there is substance in this hypothesis, we should expect the departures of the Petrarchan Augustine from Cicero's words to have the appearance not of mere inaccuracies or lapses of memory, but of ever so slight ameliorations or restructurings of Cicero's argument. Only a comparison of the exact wording of the Hypanis paragraphs in the *Tusculans* and in the *Secretum* will permit a reliable judgment. The following is a confrontation of the relevant phrasings of the two texts:

Secretum, ed. Carrara, p. 210:

"Apud Hypanim" inquit "fluvium, qui ab Europe parte in Pontum influit, bestiolas quasdam nasci scribit Aristotiles, que unum diem vivant; harum que oriente sole moritur, iuvenis moritur; que vero sub meridie, iam etate provectior, at que sole occidente senex abit, eoque magis si solstitiali die. Confer universam etatem nostram cum eternitate, in eadem propemodum brevitate reperiemur ac ille."

Cicero, *Tusc.* I, 39, 94 (*Scripta Omnia,* ed. C. F. W. Mueller, vol. IV I [Lipsiae, 1904], p. 315):

Apud Hypanim fluvium, qui ab Europae parte in Pontum influit, Aristoteles ait bestiolas quasdam nasci, quae unum diem vivant. Ex his igitur hora octava quae mortua est, provecta aetate mortua est; quae vero occidente sole, decrepita, eo magis, si etiam solstitiali die. Confer nostram longissimam aetatem cum aeternitate; in eadem propemodum brevitate, qua illae bestiolae, reperiemur.

Leaving the first and last sentences of Cicero's statement out of consideration for the moment, I do not see how it can be denied that in the middle sentence at least, the comparison between a human lifetime and a single day has not only been changed but been supplemented by Petrarch, both in meaning and expression. For, whereas the passage in the *Tusculans* contains nothing but the offhand remark that a "bestiola" which passes out of life in the evening or at the sunset of its one allotted day dies "provecta aetate" or "decrepita," Petrarch's reflection goes much farther by reconstructing and defining the full life cycle: "harum [bestiolarum] que oriente sole moritur, iuvenis moritur; que vero sub meridie, iam etate provectior, at que sole occidente senex abit. . . ." This pattern of change — the addition of the idea of a cyclical succession of man's "aetates" to the much less elaborate simile of the *Tusculans* — is again discernable in the final sentence, where "Confer nostram longissimam aetatem [that is, the longest human life span] cum aeternitate" becomes "Confer universam aetatem nostram [that is, the sum of the successive *aetates* of man] cum aeternitate."

There is no danger of reading a false intention into Petrarch's changes, because the same pattern appears in his later correspondence. In a letter of 1360 (*Fam.* XXIV 1), Petrarch interpreted the Hypanis "similitudo" for a second time, and the very "blemishes" (*maculas*), attributed by Rico to an alleged lapse of memory due to the absence of a copy of the *Tusculans*, form the leitmotif for a reinterpretation of the simile. Both Petrarchan writings show the same non-Tusculan emphasis on the life cycle from youth to decrepitude. But this later use of the Hypanis simile belongs to a more mature phase in Petrarch's reinterpretation of the *Tusculans* than is found in the *Secretum*. We now find a sharper distinction between Petrarch's addition to the Aristotelian-Ciceronian simile and the rest of the text, which is quite reliably quoted from the *Tusculans*, and it becomes even clearer where the intentional retouching of the Ciceronian presentation begins: "Ille quidem [the Hypanis bestiolae] ut nos, plus minus ve distinctis spatiis suis vivunt: quedam mane obeunt, he quidem iuvenes; quedam vero sub meridiem, he iuvente medio; alie inclinata ad occasum die, he iam provectiores; alie occidente sole, he demum decrepite moriuntur . . . : tota vita hominis dies unus est, . . . in quo mane alius, alius die medio, alius tardiuscule, alius autem sero moritur; hic tener ac floridus, hic durus, hic iam aridus atque consumptus."[73]

In summary, we have found a number of facts which can only with

[73] *Fam.* XXIV 1 (28–29).

enormous difficulty, if at all, be reconciled with the assumption that
Augustine's claim to be reporting Cicero's discussion of the Hypanis
analogy imperfectly, because he has no copy of the *Tusculans* on
hand, means that Petrarch was indeed quoting inaccurately because
he lacked the Ciceronian text. It is not my intention to say that this
interpretation of Augustine's words is definitively ruled out by the
discovery that the *Secretum*'s alleged "misquotation" of the *Tusculans*
recurs and evolves in Petrarch's later correspondence. But it is certainly not permissible to say that it is "clear" that when the *Secretum*
page on the Hypanis simile was composed "the *Tusculans* was inaccessible to Petrarch."[74] The above findings are enough to provide
an alternative and much more meaningful explanation, one which is
entitled to careful consideration.

Besides, there is another obvious weakness in the attribution of
the Hypanis episode and the last pages of Book III to the spring of
1353. Here as elsewhere, Rico tends to underestimate the possibility
of insertions and occasional textual changes. He never seriously considers that the phrases which could testify to a 1352–53 origin might
be interpolations in an older text, nor does he look at the chronological evidence provided by preceding or subsequent portions of the
text. Three lines before the Hypanis episode begins, we find a quotation from Petrarch's *Epistola Metrica* I 4, which was written as early as
1337 or 1339. Following the Hypanis quotation, Augustine addresses
Franciscus once more: "Even you, who at this moment, in the flower
of life and filled with pride, are spurning others, will soon be spurned
yourself."[75] These are words fittingly directed to a relatively young
man. Theoretically, of course, Petrarch might have been thinking of
the Franciscus of 1342–43 when he wrote them, but is it likely that he
would have used such words if he had written this text as late as 1353
when he was nearly fifty?

Without other evidence, it would be arbitrary to conclude that a
page containing several reminders of the Petrarch of the 1340s, and
even the 1330s, was written in 1353 rather than in 1349. Moreover, if
Augustine's words "neque enim libri nunc illius copia est" were an
insertion of 1353 in an older text, the simile would lose its value for

---

[74] See n.71, above.
[75] "Tu quoque, qui nunc etate florida superbus alios calcas, mox ipse calcaberis"
(Carrara, p. 210).

the dating of the last part of the *Secretum*. Everything considered, since those equivocal words of Augustine's no longer have only one possible interpretation, nothing seems to prevent the Hypanis page from belonging to the draft of the *Secretum* written in 1349, which after all is the version of the work to which the travel page — not very far away — belongs. In any case, nothing *forces* us to attribute the Hypanis page to 1353.[76]

Appendix
Analogies between the *Secretum* and
Epistolae Familiares VIII 2-5

I

One other argument of which Rico makes use for his idea of a complete recasting of the *Secretum* in 1353 has been excluded from our discussion. It is based on unquestionable homologies between some of Augustine's teachings in the *Secretum* and ideas expounded in *Fam.* VIII 2-5, which at certain points are formulated in nearly the same way. Since the letter (a group of four letters in Petrarch's final presentation) has been preserved in its successive versions, we are able to ascertain that the text of the *Secretum* is in a few cases homologous to the 1349 text of the letter but much more frequently to its final text. This tells us, Rico reasons, that the development of the *Secretum* followed the same rhythm as that of the *familiaris* letter: there was at least some rewriting in 1349 and a total recasting in 1353. A philological

[76] I have omitted a piece of evidence used by Rico for his hypothesis that the *Secretum* was rewritten in 1353. In its structure, he says, Book III "conforms to [Petrarch's] *Triumphs* point by point" (Rico, *Lectura,* p. 463; see also p. 467), and work on the *Triumphs* did not begin before the end of 1352. Thus Book III cannot have been written before 1353. This is basically an application to the *Secretum* of a current controversy connected chiefly with the names of Giuseppe Billanovich and Vittore Branca, who have defended the origin of the *Triumphs* in the 1350s against Ernest H. Wilkins' attempt to prove that the drafts of the first four triumphs are older. Fortunately, we need not wait for the outcome of the ongoing debate when it comes to the question of the *Secretum*. For the basic ideas of the *Triumphs* are stated so vaguely in the *Secretum* that Petrarch could in any case have written what he says in Book III even years before the triumphs were conceived as a book. A confrontation of the two works leaves little doubt about this. What unites the consecutive processions described in the *Triumphs* is the concept of a hierarchy leading from the realm of human passions upward to divine eternity. All human beings, we are told, follow the triumphant chariot of Cupidity, but some vanquish Cupidity by following an

analysis of the successive versions of the *familiaris* letter[77] proves, he says, that scarcely a sentence was left unchanged in, or about, 1353: "Con un processo simile dovette nascere il *Secretum,*" "con un processo, pertanto, di rimaneggiamento globale," with the effect that "il *Secretum* può considerarsi legittimamente prodotto del 1353."[78]

The weakness of this interpretation is easy to see. The very idea that a single *familiaris* letter (or a small group of four) might enlighten us about the genesis of an entire complex work like the *Secretum* compounds the dangers inherent in the search for homologies. Now, it is true that Rico tells us in so many words that the *Secretum* "dall'inizio alla fine" and "da un estremo all'altro" is filled with "concomitancies" with the *familiaris* letter and that "the fact that the concomitancies occur throughout the dialogue [*ocurran a todo lo largo del diálogo*] virtually precludes the possibility that they could be due to interpolations. So we are prompted," says Rico, "to think that the text in which they appear was a complete recasting [*una refundición completa*] and not the result of sporadic retouches and insertions."[79] But this judgment contains a good deal of ambiguity: the claim that analogies with *Fam.* VIII 2-5 are found in the *Secretum* "dall'inizio alla fine" hardly lets the readers expect that, in Book I of the *Secretum*, the letter is reflected in but two references[80] to the frailty of the human body and the brevity and insecurity of

---

even higher victress, Chastity (*Pudicitia*). In the same manner, all human beings succumb to the triumph of Death, yet there are some who vanquish Death by winning lasting Fame. But Time will be victorious over all earthly Fame, and even this victory will prove ephemeral: Eternity will triumph over Time. These are the categories by means of which the course of a human life, in its ascent from earth to heaven, is described in the *Triumphs*. The same categories, Rico asserts, reappear in the third book of the *Secretum:* "The driving forces in the *Triumphs* and on the last day of the *Secretum* are the same or similar and are connected by an equivalent or related form." For, the *Amor* section of the third book "presents the *triumphus Cupidinis* over Franciscus in minute detail. Nor is the *triumphus Pudicitie* lacking: the "'pudicitie ... exemplum' of Laura overcomes the dishonest desires of the poet.... The humanist [Petrarch] sighs for a *triumphus Fame* 'inter posteros'.... But on many pages we have seen and will yet see ... how fame cedes to the *triumphus Temporis*. Lastly, the *triumphus Eternitatis* is evoked repeatedly ..." (Rico, *Lectura,* p. 399). Rico gives no further delineation of the alleged correspondence of the two works and simply adds "this is not the right moment to go more deeply into the indicated homology," promising substantiation in another volume of *Vida u obra de Petrarca* on the *Triumphs*. This substantiation has not yet been supplied, and in its absence there seems to be nothing in the *Secretum* text that could not have been thought and written before the *Triumphs* was conceived.

[77] According to Aldo S. Bernardo's anatomy of *Fam.* VIII 2-5, in "Letter-Splitting in Petrarch's *Familiares,*" *Speculum* XXXIII (1958), pp. 236-241.

[78] Rico, "Precisazioni," pp. 522-524.

[79] Ibid., p. 491, and Rico, *Lectura,* p. 461.

[80] Rico, *Lectura,* p. 84, n.106, and p. 102, n.165; the same two references, in Rico, "Precisazioni," pp. 497-499, 498.

our existence. All in all, it is a tiny part of the *Secretum* — in extent as well as in significance — that is actually paralleled by the *familiaris* letter.[81]

The most substantial homologies are found in Book II, especially in the two sections that deal with Petrarch's guilt in succumbing to *avaritia* and *accidia*. In the analysis of these sins, Augustine's prescriptions show a true kinship with the letter, and Rico acknowledges that he is mostly thinking of these analogies by saying that the homologies between the two works "si concentrano inequivocabilmente in due momenti del libro secondo: da un lato, in tutto l'esame dell'avarizia di Francesco e, dall'altro, nella riflessione sul'accidia. . . ."[82] Now, the treatment of these two sections is by no means typical of that of the text of the *Secretum* in general. They are "rifacimenti" of a few pages, as will be seen in detail in Chapter 6, interpolations added in response to quite specific experiences undergone by Petrarch after he returned to Italy. They can certainly not serve as proof for the alleged re-writing of the *Secretum* as a whole in 1353.

II

The comparison of the *Secretum* with *Fam.* VIII 2–5 suggests another direction of argument, which may ultimately turn out to be of greater importance than anything touched upon in this appendix so far.

A first step toward what I have in mind was taken by Ugo Dotti, who recognized that the detailed praise of north Italian scenery contained in *Fam.* VIII 5 makes it as good as certain that Petrarch was already living in Milan when he phrased the final version of the *familiaris* letter.[83] A critical breakthrough came with Rico's discovery that this praise includes an unusual feature, the partial but precise geographical description of the environs of Como and the Lake of Como, and that this description (which was not present in the 1349 version of *Fam.* VIII 2–5) has only two counterparts in Petrarch's entire correspondence, namely, the references to Como in *Fam.* XVII 5 and 6 of late 1353 — letters which show that Petrarch was then visiting the lake and its Alpine tributaries.[84] To put it differently, the final

---

[81] I also have doubts concerning some of Rico's observations on Augustine's utterances in the third book, including the last pages of the conversation. As Rico puts it, "punto per punto, così la pagina del *Secretum* riflette tanto i materiali utilizzati per gamma [of *Fam.* VIII 2–5] nel 1349 quanto le precisazioni e i complementi introdotti in *beta* tra il 1353 e il 1356" ("Precisazioni," p. 514). I strongly question whether those who compare the texts of *Fam.* VIII 2–5 of 1349 and 1353–56 with the *Secretum* (Carrara, pp. 196–198), as Rico suggests ("Precisazioni," pp. 511, 513–514), will find any expression clearly reflecting the *Secretum* or vice versa.

[82] Rico, "Precisazioni," pp. 519–520.

[83] "Quando lavorava alla stesura definitiva [of *Fam.* VIII 5] Petrarca si trovava a Milano" (Ugo Dotti, "L'ottavo libro delle Familiari," *Belfagor* XXVIII [1973], p. 287).

[84] Rico, "Precisazioni," p. 490f., n.23.

version of *Fam.* VIII 2-5 was in all probability phrased in late 1353 or soon thereafter, and this assumption is further strengthened by what we have known since Billanovich (1947) about the growth of the eighth book of the *familiares* letters:[85] that whereas the final text of the *Familiares* was advanced only as far as the fourth book by the time Petrarch left Provence in June 1353, *Fam.* VIII 2-5 was included when the entire final text from Book I to *Fam.* VIII 9 (12) was copied about May 1356, at Petrarch's order, for Benintendi Ravagnani of Venice. Everything considered, we clearly arrive for the final version of *Fam.* VIII 2-5 at a period between mid-1353 and mid-1356.

What are we to conclude from this information? There is no escaping the inference that, since the final version of *Fam.* VIII 2-5 was composed after Petrarch's return to Italy, the third version of the *Secretum*, which contains the most important homologies with the ultimate form of *Fam.* VIII 2-5, was also a creation of that period. Despite Rico's denial that any part of the *Secretum* could have been written after Petrarch returned to Italy, no other interpretation is plausible against the background of the facts just summarized. The inevitability of this conclusion will be recalled when the last interpolations found in the *Secretum* are dealt with in Chapter 6.

---

[85] Giuseppe Billanovich, *Petrarca letterato,* vol. I, *Lo scrittoio del Petrarca,* Edizioni di "Storia e Letteratura" 16 (Rome, 1947), pp. 8-17; Rico, "Precisazioni," n.23.

CHAPTER FIVE

In What Respect Can Book III Be Judged a Reflection of Petrarch's Mind in 1353?

(1) Preliminaries to the Biographical Background of Book III

I

Up to this point, our analysis of the third book of the *Secretum* has largely focused on the critique of theories tying the surviving text to the last of the years listed in Petrarch's chronological note, 1353. Let us recall the specific claims which I have attempted to refute. One is the contention that we know virtually nothing about the *Secretum's* development before 1353. Another is the belief that the *Secretum* was totally rewritten in the first half of 1353 and completed in haste by midyear, that is, during the last hectic weeks of Petrarch's stay in Provence. Finally, since the idea of an exhaustive occupation with the *Secretum* in Provence reduces the probability of substantial interpolations after Petrarch moved to Milan, there emerged a sort of postulate that the text of the *Secretum* remained untouched after he left Provence.

Considering how important the implications of these three theses are, priority in the preceding chapters of our study had to be given to testing their validity. The outcome leaves no room for doubt: none of them survives a thorough reexamination. To the claim that we have no knowledge of the 1347 and 1349 versions of the *Secretum* there is no more convincing rebuttal than that in Book III, as well as in the first two books, we can extrapolate some of the phrasing of the 1340s and deduce from it that the three books must have had their familiar over-all appearance since at least 1349. The hypothesis that the entire surviving text of the *Secretum* was not composed until 1353 is altogether undermined by the discovery that the traces of "haste," which at first sight seem to corroborate the 1353 chronology, have nothing to do with the specific conditions of that year. And as for the contention that no changes were made in Milan, it will emerge later that some suspicious phrases in Books II and III reflect worries and dislikes characteristic of Petrarch's Milanese years.

These worries and dislikes belong to a period for which the critical analysis of the *Secretum* can and must be supplemented by biographical considerations. But before turning to Petrarch's years in Milan, we need to examine some of the biographical data relating to the preceding biennium in the Vaucluse. After all, many of Petrarch's crucial letters and Volgare poems — the richest sources of information for his life — were written, in the form in which we have them, during those last two years in Provence. In principle, Rico has not undervalued the biographical element; invariably, however, he comes to the conclusion that the facts of Petrarch's life in Provence favor the theory that the text of the *Secretum* was rewritten there in toto. As we will see, the biographical particulars of those years do not bear this out.

II

The necessity of taking both a philological and a biographical approach is exemplified by a letter that provides the most relevant evidence for the third and last of the periods in which Petrarch worked on the *Secretum*. I am alluding to *Fam.* XI 12 of July 19, 1351, written to Olimpius (that is, Luca Cristiani) soon after Petrarch's return to the Vaucluse. In this letter Petrarch voices his hope that some of the writings previously begun in the Vaucluse will be brought to completion in their old environment within the next two years, namely, between mid-1351 and mid-1353. Readers of the letter will wonder whether the *Secretum* was among these writings, since it was, after all, the fruit of an earlier sojourn in the Vaucluse.[1]

Let us read the relevant passage in *Fam.* XI 12 carefully. After enumerating some of his reasons for revisiting Provence, Petrarch continues: "Nothing . . . has moved me more passionately than the powerful hope of putting the finishing touches to certain *opuscula* of mine, so that what was begun here [in the Vaucluse] with God's protective support may also be completed here under God's guidance.

---

[1] As Francisco Rico does, in *Lectura*, p. 419, n.563: ". . . es lícito preguntarse si . . . Petrarca no pensaría también en el *Secretum* [as well as of the *Africa* and *De Viris*]. . . ." Other respects in which *Fam.* XI 12 is helpful in interpreting the *Secretum* will be taken up in section (3) of the present chapter.

. . . So far as I can calculate the future from what I know of the past, a biennium will suffice for what I have in mind."[2]

Two statements in this passage indicate that the *Secretum* was probably not among the works Petrarch was thinking of. First, he expresses the "powerful hope" that two years of uninterrupted work will allow him to complete the *opuscula* he has in mind. We will recall that Petrarch's two other semi-philosophical works produced in the Vaucluse during 1346–47 — the *De Vita Solitaria* and the *De Otio Religioso* — were quickly written down from beginning to end, and that the changes known to have been made in their texts in later years resulted from new experiences or a desire for greater completeness, not from a need to replace or add vital sections or even refashion the work as a whole.[3] The last of Petrarch's writings inspired by the environment of the Vaucluse, the *Secretum*, as we know from our analysis of the text in the form it had taken by 1349, evolved in an equally unpredictable manner, changes being made when new experiences seemed to require them. Is it conceivable that when Petrarch wrote his letter of 1351, he could have thought it would take two full years to put "the finishing touches" (*supremam . . . imponendi manum*) to any of these three works, or that he would have expressed merely a "hope," albeit a "powerful" one, that he could finish them in that time — as if they were still filled with unsolved problems or gaping lacunae?

In July 1351 there existed only two major works that had been conceived and developed in the Vaucluse and were indeed full of unsolved problems: the *Africa* and the *De Viris*. Both were then at a stage entirely consistent with the calculations and hopes set forth in the letter to Olimpius, as a glance at Petrarch's occupation with them in Provence immediately shows. Although there is no indication in the *Familiares* before February 1352 that Petrarch concerned himself with the *Africa* while he was there, the first reference is revealing: Petrarch intends to take a shortcut in his preparation of it; he will round out the design as it is, since he may have reached the limits of

---

[2] "Nichil autem me vehementius movit quam spes ingens supremam opusculis quibusdam meis imponendi manum, ut hic incepta Deo auspice, hic eodem duce finiantur. . . . Quantum ergo de preteritis futura conicio, biennii tempus ad id quod molior satis erit . . ." (*Fam.* XI 12 [6,8]).

[3] For the genesis of the *De Vita Solitaria* and *De Otio Religioso,* see above, p. 84.

the capacity granted him by God.[4] We learn from subsequent letters that even this restraint did not solve his problem. By September, his time-consuming labors on the epic had still not resulted in any major progress, and in November the work was as unfinished as it was before; if no remedy was found, there would be no rest for him.[5] One would not expect to find any comparable problem in accounts of the vicissitudes of the *De Vita Solitaria,* the *De Otio,* or the *Secretum.*

In the *De Viris,* however, a complication not unlike the one experienced in the *Africa* developed during that same year. The *De Viris* had originally been conceived as a series of biographies of great Romans from Romulus onward, but in the second half of 1351 a previously unplanned group of twelve pre-Romulean biographies, mostly of biblical personalities, was drafted — only to be suddenly broken off in the middle of one of them, after which any hope for a rapid completion of the *De Viris* was also dashed. This attempt at a fundamental remaking of the work is again consistent with the plans for the next two years as described in his letter to Olimpius, but it is a far cry from the occasional additions made to the *De Vita Solitaria* and *De Otio.*

The conclusion that *opera* other than the *Secretum* and its two companions of 1346–47 are referred to in *Fam.* XI 12 is strengthened by a second statement in the passage quoted above. As Petrarch puts it, it is his hope that during the impending two years "what was begun here [in the Vaucluse] with God's protective support may also be completed here under God's guidance." Would we expect Petrarch to use such dramatic and elevated language if he wished to say nothing more than that he believed various writings begun in his beloved solitude would mature best in their original surroundings? This would have been a rather lofty way for him to express the literary intentions of making the kind of minor additions he incorporated into the *De Vita Solitaria* and *De Otio* during the 1350s. But if he was referring to the *Africa* and *De Viris,* with which he hoped to fulfill his longstanding ambition to initiate a new period of humanistic poetry and of historical vision, and on whose success or failure he presumed his reputation among future generations would depend, he would have

[4] *Fam.* XII 7 (6), February 20, 1352.

[5] "... quod inter manus meas diutius iam pependit et quod unum, siqua spes salutis est, anheli sitim pectoris puto vel leniet vel extinguet ..." (*Fam.* XIII 7 [4], November 1352). See also *Fam.* XIII 12 (5), September 1352.

had serious enough reason to display a strong sense of mission and invoke divine "guidance."[6]

III

Besides the information contained in the letter to Olimpius, there is other evidence which diminishes, if by itself it does not exclude, the likelihood that Petrarch worked at all on the *Secretum* while in Provence. What do we know, we may ask, of the whereabouts of the *Secretum* manuscript during the periods when Petrarch was not in Italy? The original draft, written in the Vaucluse in 1347, must naturally have gone with him to Italy late that year, for otherwise he could not have made those substantial changes in 1349 of which we have become aware. But was the draft, after having been corrected and enlarged in Italy, also with him in Provence from June 1351 onward?

By the spring of 1351, only about two years had passed since he had revised portions of the *Secretum*. These changes, made in 1349, had to be substantial because they included his responses to his move from the solitude of the Vaucluse to northern Italy in late 1347 and to his loss of Laura in the spring of 1348. Nothing of comparable magnitude occurred in Petrarch's life from mid-1349 to mid-1351, years spent in Parma, Padua, and Mantua, except perhaps his pilgrimage to the jubilee in Rome during the last quarter of 1350. Thus one can presume that there was no urgent need for further changes in his text when the time came to leave for Provence in mid-1351.

---

[6] The correct interpretation of *Fam.* XI 12, namely, that Petrarch's every tone and detail of expression in the letter make it certain that he was referring to the *Africa* and *De Viris* only and to no other work begun in the Vaucluse, was already anticipated by Ernest H. Wilkins, *Studies in the Life and Works of Petrarch* (Cambridge, Mass., 1955), pp. 84–85. We also owe to Wilkins a precious list of Petrarch's references to his own works as "opuscula," including the *Africa* (ibid., p. 84f., n.4) — definite proof that the use of this disparaging term does not cast doubt on the application of the information in *Fam.* XI 12 to Petrarch's two major works. As Wilkins puts it, Petrarch's usage shows that *opuscula* "is properly to be taken simply as a deprecatory reference by Petrarch to works of his own." Wilkins' list would be even longer if other expressions of self-belittlement were included. At the end of the *De Vita Solitaria,* Petrarch classifies this capital work among his "qualibuscunque literulis," which is an even less respectable synonym for "opuscula." (See *Prose,* p. 588, and also Baron, *From Petrarch to Leonardo Bruni,* p. 43.) This makes it still more obvious that the use of such terms has nothing to do with the importance or format of the work itself.

When he departed from northern Italy in early June, Petrarch believed (as we can be sure from his intimate correspondence with Boccaccio) that he would be gone only for that summer,[7] intending to complete some business at the papal Curia in Avignon and afterwards to do some writing in the Vaucluse. Considering the small amount of time he thought he would have available in the Vaucluse and the fact that the *Secretum* had so recently been updated, is it likely that he would have taken the manuscript with him on his arduous trip across the Alps on horseback?[8]

It might be objected that if he took the *Africa* and *De Viris* with him to Provence he could just as well have taken the *Secretum*. But it is not at all necessary to assume that the *Africa* and *De Viris* accompanied him on his transalpine journey. Although it is true that he resumed his labors on the *De Viris* almost at once after arriving in the Vaucluse in June or July 1351,[9] this does not mean that he had the manuscript with him. For the work he did first (probably continuing it throughout the winter of 1351–52) amounted to writing (with the help of his library in the Vaucluse) a number of entirely new *vitae*, which were to be placed before the Roman *vitae* prepared earlier. This concentration on a wholly new and separate section of the *De*

---

[7] *Fam.* XI 6, to Boccaccio. On this letter, see below, p. 132. *Fam.* XI 6 — together with *Fam.* XI 12 — is a basic source of our information. It shows that the poetic longing for the Vaucluse which Petrarch expressed in a poem enclosed with *Fam.* XI 4 in late April or early May was forgotten by late May or early June (the date of *Fam.* XI 6) when Petrarch made his final plans for the journey to Provence. In the brief poem (eight lines) of April–May, he had adumbrated his life-long connection with the Vaucluse and closed with the verse "In my old age I desire to live out my allotted time in the Enclosed Vale and there, under thy guidance, to die" (the guidance being that of Bishop Philippe de Cabassoles; "et clausa cupio, te duce, Valle mori"). Only a month later, when Petrarch was leaving Italy, this mood had disappeared. He was now resolved to stay away merely for the summer, and a month later, that he would definitely be back after two years — the plan he followed faithfully during his sojourn in Provence.

[8] The same argument can be made for the *De Vita Solitaria* and the *De Otio Religioso:* since it is well known that Petrarch made his crossings of the Alps on horseback, he would presumably not have taken manuscripts with him unnecessarily; and it seems, indeed, that no changes were made in these two works between mid-1351 and mid-1353. See Wilkins' conclusion (*Studies in the Life,* p. 96) that "it is possible, but improbable, that he [Petrarch] worked ... on the *De vita,* or on the *De otio* during his stay in Provence." For this, Wilkins refers to two of the most careful students of the *De Vita* and *De Otio,* B. L. Ullman and Giuseppe Rotondi.

[9] This will be discussed in detail in the next section of this chapter; see pp. 126, 129.

Viris speaks rather in favor of Petrarch's having no access to the already extant parts of his work.

As for the *Africa,* all we know is that relatively late in the Provençal biennium — February–November 1352 [10] — Petrarch reconsidered the many still unsolved problems posed by the epic, decided that a curtailed plan was imperative, and at the end of the year still felt frustrated and far from any solution. We do not know whether he actually made changes in the text or added any new verses. [11]

Admittedly, we cannot prove that Petrarch did not have the manuscript of the *Secretum* with him when he wrote to Olimpius about his change in plans. Yet, in trying to reconstruct the circumstances under which he wrote we have not engaged in useless sport. The perception that the *Secretum* manuscript may very well not have left Italy again after late 1347 offers a possible alternative to the theory that the *Secretum* text was composed in toto during Petrarch's last months in Provence. How viable that alternative is will ultimately depend on whether when Petrarch referred in his chronological note to 1353 he was thinking of the part of the year spent in Italy. However, this question cannot be answered before another one, namely, whether any additions to the *Secretum* were made in Italy in 1353 — a problem which will be tackled in Chapter 6.

(2) The Dangers of Interpreting in Purely Psychological Terms: Why Petrarch Persevered in His Work on the *Africa* and *De Viris Illustribus*

I

In the preceding chapters we have repeatedly become aware that the most productive way to initiate our analyses is to find homologies between the *Secretum* and other contemporaneous works by Petrarch. One such concordance profoundly influences our interpretation of the last, climactic pages of the third book of the *Secretum:* the scene where Franciscus refuses to accept Augustine's advice to free himself

---

[10] See nn.4 and 5, above.

[11] See Wilkins, *Studies in the Life,* p. 96: "It is possible, but improbable, that Petrarch worked on the *Africa* . . . during his stay in Provence" — the same opinion expressed by him in regard to the *De Vita Solitaria* and *De Otio.*

for a fuller spiritual life by abandoning his work on the *Africa* and *De Viris*.

But let us follow Augustine's demands in detail. "Cast down this great burden of histories," he admonishes Franciscus. "The deeds of the Romans have been celebrated quite enough both through their own fame and through the genius of others. Get out of Africa and leave it to its possessors. You will add nothing to the glory of your Scipio or to your own. He can be raised no higher. . . . Therefore leave all this behind and give yourself back finally to yourself!"[12] These lines might seem to suggest a sense of futility in Petrarch with respect to the soundness of his two major works dealing with Scipio. For since the Augustine of the cited passages personifies some of Petrarch's own thoughts and desires, his insistence that Franciscus abandon the *Africa* and *De Viris* could reflect Petrarch's own disappointment in the two works he had begun with such fervid hopes. This in essence is the reasoning which has repeatedly been pursued in recent years, and it has resulted in the claim that with its help we can obtain a better understanding of the meaning of the third book.

An argument of this sort is proposed in a study with the revealing title "Dall'*Africa* al *Secretum*" by Enrico Fenzi.[13] In the second book of the *Africa*, Fenzi argues, there is a "quasi perfetta corrispondenza" to what we find in the third book of the *Secretum*. For in *Africa* II Petrarch distinguishes three kinds of "deaths," which put an end to the presumed immortality of a name by gradually destroying the memory of a famous person. After the destruction of the body, a second death occurs when the tomb and the inscription carved in honor of the deceased crumble away, and in the course of time a third and final death takes place when even books, the most enduring instruments of fame, no longer survive.[14] Precisely the same tripartite scheme is used in Book III of the *Secretum*, where the argument of the

[12]"Abice ingentes historiarum sarcinas: satis romane res geste et suapte fama et aliorum ingeniis illustrate sunt. Dimitte Africam, eamque possessoribus suis linque; nec Scipioni tuo nec tibi gloriam cumulabis; ille altius nequit extolli, tu post eum obliquo calle niteris. His igitur posthabitis, te tandem tibi restitue . . ." (Carrara, p. 206).

[13]"Dall'*Africa* al *Secretum*," in *Il Petrarca ad Arquà*, Atti del Convegno di Studi nel VI Centenario, ed. Giuseppe Billanovich and Giuseppe Frasso (Padua, 1975), pp. 61–115.

[14]"Iam sua mors libris aderit" (*Africa* II 455).

inevitability of the three deaths helps Augustine shake Petrarch's trust that his name will be perpetuated by the successful completion of the *Africa* and *De Viris*. [15]

In Fenzi's eyes, Augustine's condemnation of Petrarch's continued work on his two major humanistic writings is not motivated by the general concern of the *Secretum* for Petrarch's unhampered spirituality. Rather, it must be explained by the psychological experiences manifested in the *Africa*. As Fenzi puts it, [16] what Augustine echoes in the *Secretum* are "le parole già lette nell' *Africa*," those verses in the second book of the *Africa* on the triple perishability of all fame, where we find "quei profondi motivi di dubbio e di sfiducia" regarding the epic itself, Petrarch's "paralizzante senso d'inutilità" in striving for his own and Scipio's glory — from which Petrarch in the *Secretum* "arriva a fil di logica ad esortare Francesco ad abbandonare il poema," the demand put into the mouth of Augustine. The key to understanding the *Secretum* and its "Augustine" is thus considered to be Petrarch's skepticism about his work, expressed in both writings.

How convincing is this reasoning? Fenzi offers neither internal nor external evidence to prove that the skepticism evinced in the second book of the *Africa* is actually connected with Augustine's warning in the *Secretum* regarding Petrarch's further occupation with the *Africa* and *De Viris*. Moreover, Fenzi himself is aware that we have insufficient knowledge of such a link, for he declares that we would need a clearer picture of Petrarch's whole "esperienza letteraria e umana sino a quel punto" of his life in order to prove the direct relationship between the *Africa* and the *Secretum*. [17] What convinced Fenzi of the correctness of his theory was the supposed proximity in time between the two works: after correcting and enlarging the first version of the *Africa* (at Parma and Selvapiana in 1341) in the wake of his Roman coronation, Petrarch, during the summer–autumn of 1342, at Avignon and in the Vaucluse, "shows himself [in the *Secretum*] to be equipped with sufficient coldness of intellect to contemplate the possibility of giving up the poem." [18] In brief, the pessimism in *Africa*

[15] Carrara, pp. 202, 204.
[16] Fenzi, "Dall'Africa al *Secretum,*" p. 85.
[17] Ibid., p. 109.
[18] "... arriva sino al punto di contemplare, con sufficiente freddezza intellettuale, l'eventualità di abbandonare il poema" (ibid., p. 87).

II and Augustine's advice in *Secretum* III are roughly contemporaneous and therefore able to develop in what Fenzi calls a "dialectical" relationship.

Fenzi's specific argument, then, stands or falls with the old 1342–43 dating of the *Secretum* and clearly loses its validity with the redating of the *Secretum* to 1347. This chronological shift, however, does not preclude some variant of the new psychological approach capable of accommodating to the changed *Secretum* chronology. It was Rico who endeavored to work out such a variant.

Although Fenzi and Rico were unaware of each other's studies,[19] the reasoning they follow is strikingly similar: if Augustine, the representative of Petrarch's own convictions, requires Franciscus to abandon his humanistic works, the psychological explanation must be that when Petrarch formulated Augustine's reaction he was himself doubtful about continuing his *Africa* and *De Viris,* that by then he had grown desperate about the "inutility" (Fenzi's word) of his writings or — as Rico says — about the unlikelihood that they could ever be completed. Rico argues further: if the occasion on which that discouragement occurred could be identified, our understanding of the concluding controversy of the *Secretum* would change. After his discovery that the *Secretum* was begun not in 1342–43 but in 1347, he concluded that the most likely time for Petrarch's disillusionment was his last biennium in Provence, or, more exactly, the year 1352, when he commenced and then abandoned the composition of the pre-Romulean biographies in his attempt to make a fundamental alteration in the plan of the *De Viris* and when his concern for the *Africa* — from February through November 1352 — gave rise to those distressed and disappointed letters indicating the end of consistent, systematic work on the epic.[20]

Rico, indeed, has made use of every possible observation that would support such an interpretation. "In sum," he argues, "Petrarch [in 1352] did exactly what Augustine admonishes Franciscus to do": he abandoned his two works.[21] Moreover, because Petrarch's regular progress on the *Africa* and *De Viris* ceased in 1352, the motivation behind Augustine's words must have been Petrarch's concern over how

---

[19] Fenzi's study came out in 1975, Rico's book in 1974.
[20] See above, p. 119f.
[21] Rico, *Lectura,* p. 419f.; esp. p. 422.

he would appear to readers of the 1353 version of the *Secretum;* one must assume that he wanted to place himself in a favorable light, whatever might happen in the future. If he should succeed in completing his two works in the years ahead, the impression given in the *Secretum,* that he had finished them rapidly because his sights were on higher goals, would lead his readers to accept their defects with forbearance. If he never finished them, Augustine's authoritative advice to abandon them would stand him in good stead. "In either case," Rico concludes, "the *Secretum* hides an apology for the faults and defects in his works. . . . I will even venture to say that . . . the *Secretum,* and not only in a secondary respect, was created to explain and excuse the fact that the epic poem and the 'liber historiarum' [the later *De Viris*] were never published; that the *Secretum* represents symbolically [*mitifica*] Petrarch's dissatisfaction and disillusionment with respect to the *Africa* and *De Viris Illustribus,* a feeling of personal frustration (after so much hope) and a fear of criticism by others (after so many expectations) that kept him from publishing them."[22]

There is a world of difference between this picture of a psychological device intended to cloak or mitigate Petrarch's personal failure in the eyes of his readers and an evaluation of the *Secretum* as a defense of Petrarch's longing to complete his two major humanistic works despite his strong monastic desire for a religious life safe from the distraction of literary pursuits: an inner struggle (the "secretus conflictus curarum mearum" to which the title refers) leading to the hope — so characteristic of the transitional age of the Italian Trecento — that earlier years of humanistic writing would eventually be followed (and paid for) by a spiritually directed old age.

How can we choose between these alternatives? At this point it becomes clear how important, not only for dating but also for understanding the third book, our systematic invalidation of the 1353 thesis is. What in the preceding chapter may at times have looked like nothing more than the refutation of an exaggerated claim for a date now proves to be essential for judging Petrarch's intention. Since (as established in Chapter 4) Book III cannot have been cast or recast as a whole in 1353, but rather belongs in substantial part to 1347 or 1349, the detection of homologies between *Secretum* III and other writings of Petrarch's from the early 1350s must lead to the question

---

[22] Ibid., p. 423.

whether those paragraphs and phrases in which the concordances occur are insertions added to the *Secretum* text in 1353. But again, to be fully aware of what happened, we must turn to the details.

II

In Petrarch's continually informative *Epistola Familiaris* XI 12 of July 19, 1351, the mention of his plan to complete some writings begun in the Vaucluse within the next two years is followed by an expression of hope for his future. As the letter describes it, "after the completion [of those writings], provided that completion is granted to me, another way of life awaits me for which I have long yearned and sighed with great inner turmoil, if only I were not weighed down by my own heaviness."[23] Compare with this Franciscus' final reaction to his conversation with Augustine on the last pages of the *Secretum:* "What should I do, then? Abandon my unfinished works? Would it not be better to hasten them on, to put the finishing touches to them, if God consents, and once rid of these cares, to go with a freer mind to greater things? For I could hardly bear the thought of leaving half completed a work so fine and rich in promise of success." "And I now hurry to my other [literary] concerns so eagerly only in order to return, once they are completed, to these [spiritual concerns]. I am not unaware that . . . it would be much safer for me . . . to relinquish the bypaths and follow the straight path to salvation. But I am unable to suppress my desire."[24]

These passages in the letter and the *Secretum* show the same state of mind, with some of the same key words appearing in both. The comparison is of special interest methodologically, because here we have a correlation in which one of the compared writings (the letter) is dated and consequently all the decisive questions can be posed.

[23]". . . quibus [i.e., libellis meis], si datur, explicitis, alia michi restat vite via, ad quam iampridem, nisi ponderibus meis premerer, anhelo et magna mentis agitatione suspiro" (*Fam.* XI 12 [11]).

[24]"Quid faciam ergo? Labores ne meos interruptos deseram? An accelerare consultius est, atque illis, si Deus annuat, summam manum imponere, quibus curis exutus, espeditior ad maiora proficiscar? Tantum enim ac tam sumptuosum opus vix possum equanimiter medio calle deserere" (Carrara, p. 206). ". . . neque aliam ob causam propero nunc tam studiosus ad reliqua, nisi ut, illis explicitis, ad hec redeam: non ignarus . . . multo michi futurum esse securius . . . , deviis pretermissis, rectum callem salutis apprehendere. Sed desiderium frenare non valeo" (ibid., p. 214).

Of course, as 1351 is not one of the three years in which Petrarch worked on the *Secretum*, the quoted similarities do not denote simultaneity of conception. They must mean either that Petrarch remembered the letter of 1351 when he wrote the conclusion of the 1353 version of the *Secretum* or, vice versa, that he remembered the 1347 or 1349 version of the *Secretum* when he wrote the *epistola* of July 1351. The latter alternative would of course mean that Petrarch's plan to complete his literary works quickly before embarking on a more religious life was already in the original draft of the *Secretum*.

The first of these two possibilities — that the letter of 1351 is older than the concluding part of the surviving *Secretum* text — was proposed by Rico, and his conclusions must be accepted by all those who accede to the theory that the *gloria* section of Book III was totally rewritten in 1353. Yet grave doubts are bound to arise as soon as one considers the circumstances in which Petrarch found himself by 1353. As I have emphasized,[25] during the second half of 1351 and during 1352 he abandoned the original design of the *De Viris Illustribus* of Rome and began working on a basically different kind of book, a combination of biblical and classical biographies — "illustrious men of all ages" — only to leave them in an entirely fragmentary shape. As for the *Africa,* 1352 was the year (according to evidence we have for February through November) in which he first admitted to himself that he did not know how the deep-rooted maladies of this most beloved of his brain children could ever be cured. By the beginning of 1353, in other words, his attempt to bring his labors on the *De Viris* and the *Africa* to a rapid end had decisively failed, proven impossible not merely in the sense that more than a biennium would be needed, but in the deeper and more ominous sense that predictions concerning the fate of his two works could no longer be made.

One must not, of course, confuse the biographical aspects of this moment in Petrarch's life with the literary question of how much of Petrarch's two *magna opera* was actually written during later years (that is, after the disappointments of 1352). Recent research has demonstrated[26] that, almost up to the time of his death, Petrarch never entirely stopped adding to and changing details of his *Africa,* even

[25] See above, pp. 120, 122f.

[26] First Guido Martellotti, in several of his later writings, and more recently Ettore Paratore, "L'elaborazione padovana dell'*Africa*," in *Petrarca, Venezia e il Veneto,* "Civiltà Veneziana," saggi 21 (Florence, 1976), pp. 71–74.

though he had resigned himself to the thought that his epic would be found incomplete among his papers. Similarly, one might legitimately argue[27] that by far the two largest and most important biographies in the *De Viris Illustribus* — the third version of the *Vita Scipionis* and the biography of Caesar — belong to the time after 1353, and consequently that more than half of the pages written for Petrarch's biographies were composed after he left Provence. But it is precisely Petrarch's single-minded concentration on those two book-length biographies that completes the destruction of the original balance and meaning of the *De Viris* in the crisis which befell the work in 1351–52. When we try to clarify for ourselves what Petrarch's reactions after that crisis must have been, the fact that two new biographical designs eventually came to the fore does not make up for the abandonment of the originally planned, comprehensive *De Viris*.

In 1353 it must have been uppermost in Petrarch's mind that his Provençal biennium was drawing to a close and that the task for which he had remained in the Vaucluse was not only unfinished but presented serious and perhaps fatal problems, which destroyed any hope of completing the *Africa* and *De Viris* rapidly. If it were true that the final scene of the *Secretum*, in which Petrarch vows quick completion of these works, was written at the close of his stay in Provence, the whole situation would be incomprehensible. For at the very moment when reality was thwarting his design to speed up his work for the sake of his future life, he would be proposing this plan to Augustine and having him resignedly accept it with the solemn words: "So it must be, if it cannot be otherwise; I pray to God that He will go with you wherever you go."[28] To make it true that the concluding part of Book III breathes the spirit of the early 1350s,[29] the entire conversation between Augustine and Franciscus would have to be the opposite of what it is. Augustine would have to answer: You, Franciscus, have already tried to finish your works quickly, within a period of time you yourself have judged reasonable, and you have found that your plan does not work. It would then have to

[27] As Martellotti did, pp. 1398b–1399a.

[28] "... sic eat, quando aliter esse non potest, supplexque Deum oro ut euntem comitetur, gressusque licet vagos, in tutum iubeat pervenire" (Carrara, p. 214).

[29] As Rico proposed. See esp. *Lectura*, pp. 468, 525.

be the burden of Franciscus' reply to show why it would be sensible to try once more, despite the past failure. Yet we do not find the slightest awareness of Petrarch's problematic situation in Franciscus' confident answer: "What should I do then? Abandon my unfinished works? Would it not be better to hasten them on, to put the finishing touch to them, if God consents, and once rid of these cares, to go on with a freer mind to greater things?" How can we avoid the conclusion, therefore, that what we read in these lines flagrantly contradicts Petrarch's thinking and expectations in 1353 and must have been written in the 1340s?

So long as we cling to the theory that the quoted words originated in 1353, there is only one way to account for them: namely, to fall back on the tired assumption that Petrarch sometimes depicts himself as he was in 1342–43, even though he is writing at a later time. But can we seriously believe that if Petrarch formulated the central problem of the *Secretum* — the gradual reconciliation of his humanistic work with his religious longings — as late as 1353, he would have remained silent about his negative experience with the *Africa* and *De Viris* and made the *Secretum* disputation end with the proposal of an experiment the hopelessness of which a practical attempt had already demonstrated?

The student who shrinks from the artificiality of such a construction is left with the conclusion that the final pages of the *Secretum* show no trace of Petrarch's disillusionment with the *Africa* and *De Viris* in the early 1350s; in other words, that the text we possess must basically be the one written in 1347 or 1349.

III

It remains for us to make certain that nothing in the letter of July 19, 1351, or in the conditions under which it was composed, jeopardizes the assumption that the passages we have examined had, indeed, long been part of the *Secretum* when the letter was written.

Fam. XI 12 is basically an apology by Petrarch for having abruptly altered his plans when he decided to spend two years in the environment of the Vaucluse to complete certain of his works. As recently as the eve of his Alpine crossing — so he says in his letter — he was honestly informing his correspondents that he intended to remain away from Italy only for the summer. "This is what I thought at the time" (*ita tunc opinabar*). Furthermore, since a letter of about June 1351 (*Fam.* XI 6) is preserved, in which Boccaccio is informed that "autumnus me revehet, ut spero," that is, that the autumn would bring him back to Italy, and since Petrarch was in Verona, at the very outset of his long journey across the Alps, when he wrote that letter, we can be sure that when he changed his mind on July 19, he could not yet have been in the Vaucluse for any length of time (at most a few weeks, and perhaps only a few days).

In these circumstances it is difficult to imagine that the beginning of Petrarch's stay in the Vaucluse not only occasioned his sudden decision to take advantage of this inspiring environment in order to complete the *Africa* and *De Viris* but also gave birth to the plan to free himself, after their completion, for a more spiritual existence. A more plausible alternative is clearly that his hope for an intensification of his religious life had long been part of his conception of the future and that the new element in his decision in July 1351 was nothing but the intention to extend his stay in the Vaucluse for two years and to experiment with the *Africa* and *De Viris* while he was there.

That this interpretation of *Fam.* XI 12 is not only possible but probable is further suggested by a particular feature of the letter. Since it essentially concerns Petrarch's plan for the impending biennium, ten of its eleven paragraphs serve to apologize for his inconsistency — the letter is superscribed "Ad Olimpium, de mutabilitate propositi" — while only the eleventh (in fact, only its second half) suggests a connection between Petrarch's intention to complete his two works rapidly and his hopes for beginning a more intense spiritual life afterwards. Clearly, the purpose of the last half paragraph is merely to set the newly made plan within a wider framework.

When he made up his mind in 1351 to stay on in the Vaucluse for a fixed period, Petrarch probably remembered what he had written at the end of the *Secretum* in 1347 or 1349 about two successive periods of his future life. He thus phrased his letter of July 19 in almost identical terms, adding that the completion of his two humanistic works was not to take more than two years in the Vaucluse. To put it differently, the appearance in the letter of the ideas, intentions, and wording of the concluding scene in the *Secretum* is far more convincingly explained by the assumption that Book III, as we know it, had long been in existence by the summer of 1351.

(3) Book III and Petrarch's Attitudes toward Fame before and during the Early 1350s

I

The discussion of Petrarch's "desiderium gloriae" in the third book of the *Secretum* is built on two premises: he is inextricably chained to this passionate desire, and it is the most destructive of his *affectus,* unworthy of a philosopher and a spiritually minded being. To convince Franciscus of this, Augustine explains in various ways what true glory is and how one should aspire to it.

Since there can be no doubt that Petrarch's longing for fame abated in the course of his life and that his idea of true glory also did not remain what it had been, we can chart the successive changes in his way of thinking and see where the concluding pages of the *Secretum* fit in.

There has been some hesitation in recent years to believe that any of Petrarch's convictions changed in a lasting way. Enrico Fenzi has proposed that his thoughts on *gloria* lack a "schema evolutivo."[30] According to him, Petrarch reacted differently on different occasions ("a stimuli diversi risposte diverse"), as seen in his letters, speeches, and canzones, and later made use of these diverse reactions in major works like the *Africa* and the *Secretum* without definitively reorienting his view. Let us see whether this rather tortuous notion does not yield to a more straightforward one when we view Petrarch's sundry reactions within their biographical framework.

One cannot accurately measure the strength of Petrarch's "desiderium gloriae" without paying close attention to the speech ("collatio" in the Latin of Trecento humanists) he gave on the Roman Capitol on the occasion of his coronation as poet in 1341, about six years before the initial draft of the *Secretum*. It was on that unique day in his youth, when he was crowned as the author of the nascent *Africa* — although only King Robert of Anjou, the patron of the Roman event, had yet seen any part of the epic — that Petrarch got his first real taste of the "glory" which Augustine and Franciscus were later to discuss. In the ceremony on the Capitoline Hill, dressed in a purple cloak given to him by King Robert, the poet laureate introduced his speech with a quotation from Virgil's *Georgics:* "But a sweet longing

---

[30] Fenzi, "Dall'*Africa* al *Secretum,*" pp. 81–82.

urges me upward over the lonely slopes of Parnassus" (*Sed me Parnassi deserta per ardua / dulcis raptat amor*). This reference to a poet's impulses was followed by the general comment that "without loving effort, profound joy, and rapture" no work of the spirit will reach its goal.[31]

The subject of the oration that Petrarch then delivered was the power of the poet's thirst for glory. Its argument was based on the fourth book of Cicero's *Tusculanae Disputationes,* one of the most influential sources of the stoic doctrine that calls for the suppression of all *affectus* and passions in the name of reason. In the nineteenth chapter of the fourth book of the *Tusculans,* Cicero rejects the belief that the *affectus* might work as a positive force, as a spur to virtue: anger, he reports, is thought by the Peripatetic school to stimulate fortitude; Themistocles' unique energies are said to have developed because envy of the glory of Miltiades did not allow him rest; and some have argued that without a "burning longing" (*flagrans cupiditas*) philosophy would not have advanced and the earth would not have been explored by eager travelers.

To the author of the *Tusculanae Disputationes* all this was ultimately false teaching, interesting only because it revealed man's innate longing for immortal fame, therewith providing indirect proof of immortality.[32] To Petrarch, in his oration of 1341, the examples in the *Tusculans* were, on the contrary, evidence of the need for great passion and for striving after glory. They show, he said, that even among sages and philosophers hardly anyone will be found who is not spurred on by the thirst for glory. Many great minds have admitted this motivation. Did not Cicero himself say that no man is willing to exert great effort and face danger "unless he may hope for glory as a kind of reward," and did not Ovid express the opinion that "the thought of glory is a powerful spur"? The conclusion, as the speaker on the Capitol is not afraid to admit, is that "the desire for glory is

---

[31] The *Collatio* was first published in *Scritti inediti di Francesco Petrarca,* ed. Attilio Hortis (Trieste, 1874), and is now available in a critical edition by C. Godi, "La *Collatio laureationis* del Petrarca," in *Italia Medioevale e Umanistica* XIII (1970), pp. 13–27. An English translation is found in Wilkins, *Studies in the Life,* pp. 300–313.

[32] The same applies to Cicero's use of related examples in *Tusc.* I 14, 31, as well as in I 15, 33–34, where the remark was made: "quid? nostri philosophi nonne in iis libris ipsis, quos scribunt de contemnenda gloria, sua nomina inscribunt?" (*Tusculanae disputationes,* ed. T. W. Dougan, vol. I [Cambridge, England, 1905]).

innate not only in ordinary men but to the highest degree in those who possess wisdom and excellence."[33]

It is not easy to define the function of this speech in Petrarch's intellectual life. It obviously failed to influence his evaluation of *gloria*. During the generations after him, the examples in the *Tusculans* were often used to justify "desiderium gloriae" and great passion. Yet in judging Petrarch's attitude, it would probably be misleading to say that in 1341 he took the first steps along a road which humanists of the Renaissance were later to follow.[34] What happened was that no sooner had he ventured in the excitement of the Roman event to draw conclusions so adverse to the spirit of the *Tusculans,* than he became persuaded that his oration had echoed his own indomitable passions and had failed to point the way to an acceptable system of values.

That this doubt concerning his judgment developed almost immediately we can surmise from two considerations. One is that although the Capitoline coronation was often recalled by him as an unforgettable event in his life, his *Collatio,* unlike almost all his other writings, is preserved in a single manuscript, which was not published until the late nineteenth century.[35] Second — and still more significantly — very soon after the coronation and speech, one of his early philosophical canzones — "Una donna piú bella" — made the interpretation of *gloria* found in the *Tusculans* its own. As the canzone puts it: although *virtus* and *gloria* are sisters and both are "immortal," *gloria* is nothing but a "shadow" accompanying true *virtus,* not an objective to be striven for in its own right.[36]

---

[33] "*Collatio laureationis,*" ed. Godi, pp. 18–19. For the translation, I have made use of Wilkins, *Studies in the Life,* pp. 305–306. I am applying here what I first pointed out in *Florilegium Historiale: Essays Presented to Wallace K. Ferguson* (Toronto, 1971), p. 30.

[34] What follows is a qualification of my judgment of many years ago, namely, that in his early writings Petrarch "seems often to be travelling straight toward the Quattrocento" (Hans Baron, "Moot Problems of Renaissance Interpretation," *Journal of the History of Ideas* XIX [1958], p. 27).

[35] According to Godi (see "*Collatio laureationis,*" pp. 7, 12), no other manuscript has been found. This copy is from the second half of the fifteenth century, possibly from the beginning of the sixteenth (ibid., p. 9). It is not at all visibly connected with Petrarch and his "scriptorium" but rather is a product of the Florentine tradition concerning Florence's three great poets; it has been handed down together with a copy of Giannozzo Manetti's *Vitae* of Dante, Petrarch, and Boccaccio.

[36] "Ciascuna di noi due nacque immortale"; "i' per me sono un'ombra" ("Una

In the concluding scene of the *Secretum,* this Tusculan postulate reappears exactly: while Petrarch tolerates his longing for fame as a biographical fact (although deeply deploring it), the doctrine to which he consents as a philosopher and which he makes Augustine lay down as a moral precept is the one commended in the *Tusculans* and already accepted in "Una donna piú bella"; it is presented in even greater detail and with a keener awareness of the consequences. This is how Augustine addresses Franciscus in the *Secretum:* "I will never counsel you to live without ambition, but I must warn you with equal insistence not to put the striving for glory before *virtus.*" He then turns to the doctrine that glory is the "shadow" of *virtus:* "Therefore, just as it is impossible that your body should not cast a shadow when the sun shines, so it is impossible that virtue should exist and become visible with God's help but its glory remain unseen. Whoever, then, wishes to take away true glory must of necessity take away virtue as well." Thus our rule should be: "Follow virtue, and let glory take care of itself." According to Cato (as quoted by Augustine): "The less you seek it, the more you will find it," and according to a verse of the *Africa* (also quoted by Augustine): "illa [i.e., *gloria*] vel invitum, fugias licet, illa sequetur."[37]

The other side of the coin, as we find in the quoted *gloria* section of the *Secretum,* is a Petrarch still driven by an irrepressible desire to do the opposite of what Augustine recommends, thus revealing the same tension between life and doctrine that had been characteristic of him in the period of his Capitoline coronation. The very first words of Augustine's stern reproof, which introduces the *gloria* section, leave no doubt about this psychological trait: "More than you ought, you are striving for glory among men and for the immortality of your name." Fr.: "I freely confess it, but I have found nothing to

---

donna piú bella," verses 92, 99). The passage in the *Tusculans* (I 45, 109) runs: "etsi enim nihil habet in se gloria, cur expetatur, tamen uirtutem tamquam umbra sequitur," doubtless understood by Petrarch in the light of Seneca's even more sweeping application (*Ep. Mor.* 79, 13): "Gloria umbra virtutis est: etiam invitam comitabitur." The date of "Una donna piú bella" has long been disputed, ranging from shortly before to shortly after the coronation. Most probably we can be more exact: the final evidence lies in an allusion in the text of the canzone (verses 26–28) to what can hardly be anything but Petrarch's recent coronation: "I' dico che pur dianzi [a short time ago], / qual io non l'avea vista infin allora / mi si scoverse.../" i.e., the nature of the glory. See Fenzi, "Dall'*Africa* al *Secretum,*" pp. 71–73.

[37] Carrara, p. 206.

help me keep my desire within bounds." Aug.: "But I greatly fear that this pursuit of a false immortality through fame may obstruct for you the road to true immortality." Fr.: "I, too, fear this more than anything." Franciscus then urgently requests help, saying that Augustine had already given him effective "remedia" against his worst spiritual maladies; but Augustine replies: You know very well "that no sickness from which you are suffering is worse" than the striving for glory.[38]

This full rendition of Augustine's critique and Petrarch's reply leaves no doubt that, notwithstanding his acceptance of the doctrine that *gloria* is a mere "shadow" of *virtus,* there is no abatement of Petrarch's "cupiditas gloriae" in the *Secretum.* Consequently, the section on *gloria* in Book III must have been written before the time when those reliable indicators of Petrarch's changing sentiments, his vernacular poems and familiar letters, show any diminution of his desire.

Judging from these two sources, Petrarch's state of mind had not yet changed when he wrote his canzone "I'vo pensando" in 1347 or during the first months of 1348.[39] To show this we need only quote Petrarch's lament at the end of the poem about his entanglement in *gloria* as well as *amor:* "Though I see the better, I cling to the worse."[40] Another testimony from the same period is found in the *De Vita Solitaria* of 1346, where he confesses in the preface that he had not as yet curbed his more than average thirst for glory, either emotionally or through reason.[41] But when we come to the *epistola familiaris* that throws so much light on Petrarch at the moment of his return to Provence in July 1351 — *Fam.* XI 12 — we find that his feelings have

[38] Aug.: "Gloriam hominum et immortalitatem nominis plus debito cupis." Fr.: "Fateor plane, neque hunc appetitum ullis remediis frenare queo." Aug.: "At valde metuendum est, ne optata nimium hec inanis immortalitas vere immortalitatis iter obstruxerit." Fr.: "Timeo equidem hoc unum inter cetera...." Aug.: "Nullum profecto maiorem tibi morbum inesse noveris, etsi quidam forte fediores sunt" (ibid., pp. 188, 190).

[39] See above, p. 51f.

[40] "Et veggio 'l meglio, et al peggior m'appiglio" ("I'vo pensando," verse 136). See also another document from this period, *Metr.* II 18 (probably 1344, or possibly 1347–49), where Petrarch answers a friend's questions: "What am I working on? the *Africa* /and why? For empty glory."

[41] "... pro non mediocri glorie cupiditate — si tamen hanc nondum freno animi ac ratione perdomui — providendum est ..." (*De Vita Solitaria,* in *Prose,* p. 288).

changed. To his own astonishment, his longing for fame and glory has greatly diminished, and this has played a role (he decides when questioning himself) in his decision to seek refuge once more in the seclusion of the Vaucluse. "Known in my native land well beyond my satisfaction, and in flight from the ensuing annoyance," he writes, "I am searching for a hidden place where I can stay alone, without glory and unknown. How strange, in view of the desire so many people have, to follow empty glory above all else! Yet this is the fact; this is what I cling and aspire to. Nor do the glamour of that formerly sought or hoped-for fame and the pleasant life of a celebrity divert me from what I have said."[42]

We are not interested here in the question whether these feelings persisted in Petrarch's later life, whether he was indeed a changed man with regard to the allurements of glory.[43] What we must ask, rather, is whether, during the biennium in the Vaucluse introduced

---

[42]"Usque ad satietatem notus in patria fugiensque fastidium quero ubi lateam solus, inglorius et ignotus; mira cupiditas, inter tot presertim inanis glorie sectatores. Sed sic est: hoc sequor, hoc appeto, nec me hinc quesite olim vel sperate fame claritas ac celebrioris vite iocunditas retrahit ..." (*Fam.* XI 12 [4]). It should be pointed out that Petrarch's use of some of the same words in describing Scipio's disenchantment at the height of his fame — *Africa* II 12-15: "Sed revertor ad Scipionem ... , gloriam enim sibi non ad satietatem modo sed pene ad fastidium obtigit"; Rico, *Lectura*, p. 377, n.440, refers to this conformity — does not, of course, diminish the veracity of Petrarch's characterization of himself. On the contrary, if the fact that he applies the same words to himself and to the experiences of his greatest hero tells us anything, it is that Petrarch's epistolary portrait has significance. Even more important is our ability to trace the gradual growth of this sense of satiation with fame. It is already clearly delineated in the *De Vita Solitaria*, although the degree of boredom with and indifference to *gloria* characteristic of *Fam.* XI 12 has not yet been reached. In the preface to the *De Vita*, probably a few years before the letter of 1351, one reads the following analysis of Petrarch's feelings about the consequences of his fame: "I am already known and read and judged, already without hope of escaping the verdict of men and of hiding my talent. Whether I go out into the open or remain sitting at home, it is my part to attract attention to myself" (*Iam noscimur, legimur, iudicamur, iamque hominum voces evadendi celandique ingenium nulla spes, et seu prodeuntibus in publicum seu domi sedentibus apparendum est; Prose,* p. 290. Translation partly according to *The Life of Solitude,* trans. Jacob Zeitlin [Urbana, Ill., 1924]). So there is something very real behind the experience depicted in *Fam.* XI 12.

[43]But this does not mean that it is clear there was no continued effect of the lessening of Petrarch's "cupiditas gloriae." Proof of this is that when around 1358 he judged he had reached a sound "mediocritas" in most aspects of his life, he excepted his relationship to fame; for in that respect, he felt, he surpassed "mediocritas," having more fame than he would choose. See *Fam.* XIX 16, of 1357.

by his searching self-examination of July 1351, Petrarch could reasonably have claimed that an excessive striving for glory was his worst sickness. Of course, it might be argued that Petrarch could have claimed this even between 1347 and 1353, because he was describing a fictive visit of Augustine in 1342–43. But this would be methodological folly, since it would disregard the other available evidence, that is to say, the fact that from the travel page (page 172) to the end of Book III the *Secretum* repeatedly echoes the conditions of 1347 or somewhat later, and not those of the time of the imaginary visit.[44]

In sum, quite apart from the several specific aspects of Book III that prove to be at variance with the period of Petrarch's last sojourn in the Vaucluse, the general mood of the last section of the *Secretum* (the undiminished ardor of Petrarch's striving for fame) bears out the conclusion that the general structure of the ending of *Secretum* III cannot have been conceived at so late a date as 1353.

II

There is, however, another dimension to the debate between Augustine and Franciscus on "desiderium gloriae." Immediately before Augustine's endorsement of the Tusculan view of fame as an inevitable reward for virtue, we encounter two pages of warning against the belief that in this unstable world there can be any value at all in transient fame. Fame is confined to a small island, Franciscus is told, since most of the earth is unfit for human habitation due to burning heat or arctic cold, impenetrable deserts or unnavigable oceans, and since it is impossible to visit the earth's antipodes. There is no hope, therefore, that fame can be widespread, and it is just as much a myth that it can be everlasting. For even if the ancient teachings of the periodic destruction of the earth by deluges and conflagrations sound dubious to Christian ears, all monumental tombs, including their laudatory inscriptions, will crumble on a not too distant day, destroying the remains and the grave of the enshrined and causing him to die a second death; and though his precarious fame may be kept alive a while longer through books, in the end, given the world's

---

[44] I am thinking of pp. 94–97 and 112–113 above. We shall return to these reflections presently (pp. 149–151, below).

instability, all books will be destroyed — a third and final death for those who imagine they can win everlasting fame.[45]

"Habes de gloria iudicium meum," Augustine concludes his speech on the certainty of these "three deaths" — the same Augustine who, only half a page later, will repeat for Franciscus the description of *gloria* in the *Tusculans:* just as the human body is bound to cast a shadow in the sun, so it is impossible for virtue to show itself without glory; "the less you seek glory, the more you will find it," as Cato says.[46]

It would perhaps be too much to claim that the two verdicts on "desiderium gloriae" thus ascribed to Augustine are contradictory.[47] But it would be equally wrong to close our eyes to the fact that the two consecutive paragraphs express very different points of view. What we can say is that the warning concerning the instability of fame exudes a deep pessimism in comparison to the Tusculan conviction that by seeking virtue you will inevitably gain glory. And since this Tusculan doctrine was the one adhered to by Petrarch in his early years (and voiced, as we have seen, in a canzone as early as the time of his Capitoline coronation), there is the possibility that the paragraph which insists on the transitoriness and unimportance of all fame is an insertion that needs to be fully explored.

We should begin by observing that for the time of the first *Secretum* draft (1347), the *Familiares,* our frequent guide, does not yet provide a parallel to Augustine's insistence on the eventual "inevitable" loss of all books and their memories of great men. Quite the contrary, precisely in 1347 or 1348 the opposite idea — the belief in the permanence of the written word—was expressed in *Fam.* VII 15 (10): "Fickle are the memories of men, paintings have nothing to protect

---

[45]To give this important paragraph in extenso, after pointing out that the term "seconda mors" is used in the second book of the *Africa* as well, Augustine continues his condemnation of glory: "En preclara et immortalis gloria, que saxi unius [i.e., of the tomb] nutat impulsu! Adde librorum interitum, quibus vel propriis vel alienis manibus vestrum nomen insertum est. Qui licet eo serior videatur, quo vivacior est librorum quam sepulcrorum memoria, tamen inevitabilis casus est, propter innumerabiles pestes nature fortuneque pariter, quibus, ut cetera, sic et libri subiacent. . . . Quid ergo? adhuc ingerere tibi non desinam versiculos tuos: *libris equidem morientibus ipse / occumbes etiam; sic* mors tibi tertia restat [*Africa* II, 464–465]" (Carrara, p. 204).

[46]For details, see pp. 135–136 above.

[47]Both — one ending and the other beginning — Carrara, p. 204.

them, statues are prone to be overturned; but among the inventions of mortals nothing is more stable than the *litterae*."[48] This dictum, to be sure, cannot be accepted as final proof that the idea of the dreaded "librorum interitus"[49] was still alien to Petrarch when *Fam.* VII 15 was written. Nevertheless, one of the central ideas of the "desiderium gloriae" section — the ultimate fragility of fame due to the inevitable "librorum interitus" — was certainly not yet fully developed in Petrarch's mind in 1347–48.

A few years ago, as already mentioned,[50] Enrico Fenzi drew attention to the fact that there exists an astonishing homology between some of the concluding pages of the *Secretum* — especially Petrarch's laments regarding the transitoriness even of man's literary creations — and a paragraph in the second book of the *Africa*. In itself, the mere fact that there is such a concordance is nothing new, since Petrarch's text in the *Secretum* refers to the kindred verses in *Africa* II in so many words and even quotes from them. What Fenzi added was the important observation that Petrarch's quotations form only the high points of a lengthy discussion which is essentially identical in the two works, the corresponding portions comprehending almost 150 verses of *Africa* II (verses 361 to 500), and pages 200, line 17, to 204, line 17, in Carrara's edition of *Secretum* III.[51] As Fenzi puts it, in this entire section of text the *Africa* and the *Secretum* proceed "in parallelo," in "quasi perfetta corrispondenza." Actually the two works have at this point a "parte comune"; Petrarch has "trasferito" the verses of the *Africa* "nella prosa, sì che i due testi finiscono per sovrapporsi e combinarsi in un tutto unico."[52]

These characterizations may not sufficiently bring out the fact that the two versions differ considerably in detail. However, it can be shown that such variations result primarily from the need to adapt the text to the diverse roles of the two main speakers: Scipio's father, the Roman patrician, in the one case, and Augustine, the church

---

[48]"Fluxa est hominum memoria, picture labiles, caduce statue, interque mortalium inventa nichil literis stabilius." Fenzi (in "Dall'*Africa* al *Secretum*," p. 84, n.1) has drawn attention to this revealing passage.

[49]Carrara, p. 204.

[50]See pp. 124–126, above.

[51]From "Illud equidem ex ore tuo auditum esse doleo" to "nisi forte nunc etiam fabulosa tibi hec omnia videntur" (Carrara, pp. 200–204).

[52]Fenzi, "Dall'*Africa* al *Secretum*," pp. 65f., 86.

father, in the other. This is true even of the two chief variations that can be detected in the parallel accounts. One is that in the philosophical inquiry of the *Secretum* the rapid waning of human fame is partly attributed to psychological causation, to the workings of "invidia," not only on an individual basis but as a result of the natural dynamics in the rise of successive generations. "The ever increasing praise of *novi homines,* which during their time of flowering detracts not a little from venerable fame, always makes people feel that the more they disparage their predecessors the more they themselves will be praised."[53] It is easy to understand why this topic does not appear in the version of the "instability" digression presented in Scipio's dream conversation with his dead father in *Africa* II. Similar contextual reasons account for the second major variation, the failure in the *Secretum* to apply the lament about the instability and diminutiveness of states to the Roman Empire; we will return to this subject presently.

A third example of an obvious difference between the two versions can ultimately be attributed to a mere change in emphasis. When Scipio's father comes to talk about the "interitus librorum" in *Africa* II, he states that the most powerful of the causes that bring about an illustrious person's third and final death are the great floods and fires that blot out the last memory preserved in books: "Books too soon die, / . . . so numerous / are the impediments. Destructive floods, / fierce fires that burn whole cities to the ground, / assaults of tempests from both sea and sky / . . . nay, more: the earth itself / must die and take with it its dying scrolls; / so yet a third death you must undergo."[54] In *Secretum* III, Petrarch's difficulty must have been how to let Augustine, the church father, voice a thought so clearly based on the classical notion of the world's cyclical growth and destruction. Petrarch solved the problem by having Augustine mention this classical idea and its appeal to the mind and then point out its remoteness from Christian thinking: "I certainly am not one to admonish you to go back to those opinions of the ancients which fill Plato's *Timaeus*

[53] "Semper quoque subcrescens novorum laus hominum, que flore suo nonnichil interdum veteribus titulis derogat, quantumque maiores deprimit tantum ipsa sibi videtur assurgere" (Carrara, p. 202).

[54] *Africa* II, 454ff. (Thomas G. Bergin and Alice S. Wilson, transs., *Petrarch's Africa* [New Haven, 1977]).

and the sixth book of Cicero's *Respublica,* where frequent fires and floods on earth are foretold. For such opinions, though they seem credible to many people, are surely alien to the true religion into which you have been initiated."[55]

However interesting such variations between *Africa* II and *Secretum* III may be, the inevitable conclusion is that when Petrarch wrote the two versions of his instability digression he presented the same arguments in the same order, although he adapted them, as suggested, according to the speaker in each work. One must also not overlook the fact that the observations which are made in these digressions are by no means casual borrowings from other authors. The notion of the three deaths of famous people is a carefully reasoned idea of Petrarch's. He did not simply imitate a classical author, although he found a guide in Boethius' *De Consolatione Philosophiae,* which strongly influenced him while he was writing the *Secretum.* Practically everything Petrarch says about the smallness of the inhabitable world and the brevity of human life and fame is derived from Boethius' Book II, Prose 7 and Poem 7. The latter, in fact, ends with a reference to a "secunda mors": "If you hope to live on in the glow of your mortal name, the day will finally come when that, too, will be taken away and the result will be a second death for you."[56] A few lines before this, Boethius has made it clear that he is talking about the preservation of famous names in books; he does not mention monuments or tombs and their inscriptions. So Petrarch initially learned to think of the "librorum interitus" as an inevitable "second death." Eventually, after making himself more independent of his ancient model, he distinguished three phases, and the "librorum interitus" became the "third death." Thus the distinction between three deaths of fame is, indeed, Petrarch's own — a part of his reservations concerning *gloria* — and we must certainly conclude with Fenzi that the appearance of this notion in both digressions is evidence that they were composed "in momenti molto vicini" to each other and must stem from one and

---

[55]"Non ego te ad opiniones illas veterum revoco, qui crebra terris incendia diluviaque denuntiant, quibus et platonicus *Thimeus* et ciceronianus *Reipublice* sextus liber refertus est. Ea enim, quanquam multis probabilia videantur, vere tamen religioni, cui initiatus es, aliena sunt profecto" (Carrara, p. 202).

[56]"Quod si putatis longius vitam trahi / mortalis aura nominis, / cum sera vobis rapiet hoc etiam dies / iam vos secunda mors manet."

the same period of Petrarch's thinking about fame and the instability of life.[57]

This conclusion posed no problem so long as it was believed that Petrarch wrote the first draft of his *Secretum* as early as 1342-43; as Fenzi argued, this was also the time when the first two books of the *Africa* were fundamentally rewritten.[58] But once we accept the theory that the first draft of the *Secretum* was no earlier than 1347, we are confronted with a puzzle. To transcribe into philosophical prose about 150 verses of his epic poem five years after writing them (or even ten years afterwards, if the *Secretum* digression was written in 1353) would be totally out of character for Petrarch. Thus in the final analysis, if we are sure (as we ought to be) that the earliest draft of the *Secretum* did not antedate 1347, the critical question is how the two digressions in *Africa* II and in *Secretum* III could have been written "in momenti molto vicini."

I can imagine only one answer that would serve: if both forms of the instability digression were written more or less contemporaneously either about 1347 or about 1353 (with the form presented in *Secretum* III following closely upon that in *Africa* II), the puzzle would be solved. This conjecture, which would presume an insertion in *Africa* II, is not audacious, for there is evidence that two other insertions were made in the 1338-39 text of *Africa* II after 1343.[59] There is no reason, therefore, to exclude from the outset the possibility that Petrarch might have done the same with verses 361-500 of *Africa* II. With this in mind, we turn to the *Secretum*.

III

Let us begin an anatomy of the *gloria* section in *Secretum* III by recalling some observations made earlier. One is that the pages contain-

[57] Fenzi, "Dall'*Africa* al *Secretum*," p. 67.

[58] Ibid., p. 107.

[59] One of these insertions is verses 510-530, a brief digression dealing with the necessity of distinguishing between two Scipios and two Laelii in Roman history — a discovery not made by Petrarch until 1343 (see Guido Martellotti, "Sulla composizione del *De Viris* e dell'*Africa*," in *Annali della Scuola Normale Superiore di Pisa*, ser. 2, vol. X [1941], pp. 257-258). The other insertion is verses 303-312, which contain an allusion to Cola di Rienzo, if modern critics are correct — an allusion that would reveal an insertion made no earlier than 1347 (first seen by Martellotti in his partial edition of the *Africa*, in Francesco Petrarca, *Rime, trionfi e poesie latine*, ed. Ferdinando Neri et al. [Milan, 1951], p. 626f., and supported by Paratore, "L'elaborazione padovana dell'*Africa*," p. 74).

ing the instability digression have not been culled from the text arbitrarily. They comprise a distinct portion of that section, for these very pages, more or less the same, reappear in the *Africa*. Because of this, there is no doubt what belongs to the digression, where the suspect pages begin and where they end. These are favorable conditions for deciding whether we have an interpolation. The situation is not unlike that in the second book of the *Secretum*, where it was possible to arrive at conclusions on the basis of the concordance of two works, one of them Petrarch's *luxuria* diary. The argument that the digression of the third book is an insertion can be built on similarly firm ground.

As for the date of the digression, we have already seen[60] that *Fam.* VII 15 of 1347–48 makes it at least questionable whether as early as 1347 or 1349 Petrarch could have sounded a warning against the belief in the immortality of fame by insisting on the inevitable "librorum interitus," as he does in both versions of the digression. We must ask, however, if there is any information available that would tie the instability digression through external evidence to the time about 1353.

The awareness that the digression is basically a "parte comune" of both the *Africa* and the *Secretum* can be of help at this point, since it tells us that what we learn about the digression in the *Africa* may also shed light on the digression in the *Secretum*. This brings us back to one of the details encountered only in the *Africa* version, the application of the lament concerning the narrow limits of earthly fame to the great topic of the Roman Empire.[61] The question of the destiny and final memory of Rome is, in fact, one of the major topics of the dream conversation between the two Scipios. What value has the bloodstained glory of Rome, it is asked in the *Africa* digression, if Roman domination is actually nothing but predominance over a small fraction of the earth?[62] Moreover, not only is the Imperium Romanum tiny when considered from geographic and cosmic perspectives, but we see that it has grown old and weak. The *Africa* digression presents what might be called a special introduction (*Africa* II, 344–361) to this aspect of the later empire — the notion of transi-

---

[60] See p. 140f., above.

[61] See p. 142, above.

[62] "Quo sanguine parta / Gloria? quo tanti mundo fugiente labores? / ... Cernis quam parva pudendi / Imperii pateant circum confinia nostri? / ... : totius sola sit Orbis / Roma caput, ... / Quid tamen hic magnum? ... tanto quid nomine dignum / Invenis?" (*Africa* II, 350–360).

toriness applied to the image of Rome. The introduction begins: "*All that is born / must die and after ripeness comes decay* [my emphasis]; / no thing on earth endures, wherefore what man / or race of men can hope for what's denied / even to cherished Rome? In hasty flight / the ages pass; all time is swept away, / and ye who rush towards death, ye are but shades / and only shades, light dust or wisps of smoke / tossed by the wind. This bloodstained glory, then, / what boots it?"[63]

This is unquestionably a variation on a Sallustian theme, because it is virtually impossible that Petrarch could have written the initial phrase, "Omnia nata quidem pereunt et adulta fatiscunt," without having had Sallust's *Iugurtha* II 3 in mind: "Omnia orta occidunt et aucta senescunt." In fact, Petrarch imitated Sallust, trying to rival or surpass him. This Sallustian echo may serve as a clue when we look for homologies in other Petrarchan writings.

There was an occasion, in a letter of 1353, when Petrarch extended the lament over the transitoriness of life in like manner to the rise and fall of Rome and made the thought and the very tone of Sallust his own. In September of that year, a few months after he had settled in Milan, the Republic of Genoa was totally defeated by her maritime adversaries and decided to offer lordship over Genoa to Archbishop Giovanni Visconti of Milan in the hope of gaining a strong patron. During the critical weeks, Petrarch sent his old friend Guido Sette, then archdeacon and soon to be archbishop of Genoa, a letter of sympathy counseling submission to the inevitable. This letter — *Fam.* XVII 3 (especially the concluding paragraphs, 42–48) — is in one respect merely an adaptation of the patristic and medieval doctrine of the consecutive world empires to Genoa's past history: none of those empires lasted forever, so no one should expect Genoa's Mediterranean state to be everlasting. However, this idea is combined in the letter with a more original and personal philosophy of history, based on the theme that all states, however successful, eventually grow old and come to the end of their existence; this is the point, the letter suggests, which the Republic of Genoa may now have reached.

---

[63] "*Omnia nata quidem pereunt et adulta fatiscunt* [my emphasis]; nec manet in rebus quicquam mortalibus; unde vir etenim sperare potest populusve quod alma Roma nequit? . . ." (*Africa* II, 344ff.; Bergin-Wilson translation).

We must read the next few sentences in extenso: "What people's *virtus* can be everlasting, since even the *virtus Romana* has proven to be mortal? Cities, even the entire orb, have their old age, their decline, their death. All things hurry towards their end; the common lot of all created things must be borne with fortitude; 'omnia orta occidunt et aucta senescunt.' Even if Sallust had not said this, we would know it to be true, but we ignore it and try to deceive ourselves."[64] This is almost identical with what we have just quoted from *Africa* II: "Omnia nata quidem pereunt et adulta fatiscunt. No thing on earth endures, wherefore what man or race of men can hope for what's denied even to cherished Rome?" Here we again find the Sallustian idea of the inevitable death of all states as well as the argument that what the Romans could not avoid no other people will be able to avoid. Finally, there is a clear third concordance of ideas in Petrarch's subtle explanation why Rome remains a model of perfection, different from other states. In the letter of September 1353, Rome is characterized as "not annihilated by anyone else, but . . . destroyed by the rusting inherent in old age,"[65] and the same distinction appears in poetic form in *Africa* II: "Though fallen, Rome / shall n'er be vanquished. To her and to her stock, / alone of all the nations of mankind, / this grace is granted. [Old] age will sap her strength; / she will grow weary and in crumbling dust / decay."[66]

This homology satisfies all the criteria required to inspire confidence: a striking similarity in tone, outlook, and expression between two works, which indicates their contemporaneity, as well as the establishment of their date of origin by chronological information provided in an epistolary source.

IV

Acceptance of the year 1353 as the date of the two digressions encourages the conclusion that the version in the third book of the *Secretum*

---

[64]"Cuius enim gentis immortalis erit virtus, cum fuerit romana mortalis? et urbibus et orbi senectus est sua, suum declivium, sua mors; ad finem cuncta festinant, subeunda magno animo creatarum rerum omnium sors comunis; 'omnia orta occidunt et aucta senescunt.' Id si Sallustius non dixisset, scimus tamen, sed dissimulamus et nos ipsos fallimus . . ." (*Fam.* XVII 3 [42]).

[65]". . . non ab alio confractum, sed . . . rubiginosa consumitur senectute" (ibid., [47]).

[66]*Africa* II, 391–396 (Bergin-Wilson translation).

must be an interpolation. We should, however, assume the presence of such a major addition with caution until we have determined how the suspected insertion fits in with the course of the *Secretum* conversation.

When we view the digression in the framework of the *gloria* section, we immediately become aware that it is not a part of the routinely progressing debate; it could be removed without destroying the logic of the advancing argument. It might indeed be described as a delayed and complementary resumption of a point made earlier in the conversation, a paragraph that may or may not have been written later than the rest. To recognize this, one need only turn back from the digression (pages 200–204) to page 194. There Franciscus already touches upon the diminutiveness of man's world in space and time: "Well do I know that old story bandied about by the philosophers, how they declare that all the world is but a tiny point . . . ; yet fame cannot fill even that spot. . . . These are fables with which they seek to divert the minds [of people] from the love of glory." This philosophical wisdom has little impact upon Franciscus, however; his defense is that he does not "think to become as God, or to win immortality, or to embrace heaven and earth. Such glory as belongs to human beings is enough for me." For the next few pages, therefore, the burden of the conversation is whether a way can be found now to live a life on earth and seek worldly fame, leaving the preparation for eternity for later years — a discussion which concludes with Augustine's warning that such an attempt to have one foot on earth and the other in heaven has prevented the salvation of countless souls who "neque hic consistere neque illuc ascendere potuerunt. Itaque miserabiliter lapsi sunt."

This is the gist of the conversation from pages 194 to 200, where the text of the *Secretum* instability digression begins. When the two sections are read together, one cannot help observing the abruptness of the return of the debate on page 200 to Franciscus' complaints about the smallness of the human world, which had appeared on page 194. The transition reads as follows. Fr.: "May the most High in His mercy save me from that much misery!" Aug.: "Though divine mercy may deliver a man from folly, yet it will not excuse it. . . . If God abhors those who lose hope, He also laughs at those who put their trust in false hope. To be sure, it grieves me to have heard fall from your lips [on page 194] that phrase in which you disparaged what you called the old fable of the philosophers concerning this matter."[67] There follows the lengthy advice of the digression, beginning with the ridicule of the smallness of the accessible areas on earth and continuing with the three "deaths" that inevitably bring an end to fame. The digression closes with Franciscus' affirmation that he no longer thinks the opinions of the philosophers about the smallness of the earth are "fables." The remainder of Book III (pages 204–214) continues Augustine's pre-digression warning not to try to have one foot on earth and the other in heaven and climaxes in the final advice that Franciscus abandon further work on the *Africa* and *De Viris,* followed by Franciscus' counterproposal that he should try to complete them as rapidly as possible before embarking upon a more spiritual life.

What can we learn about the *Secretum* digression from this summary of the major turns of the conversation? In itself our synopsis does not prove that the digression is necessarily an insertion. The device of delaying the presentation of certain aspects of a debate so that some other train of thought can first be brought to completion could have been employed by Petrarch hours or days as well as years after his first draft. But although the discovery of a pattern of delayed presentation does not amount to evidence of an interpolation, its occurrence draws attention to the existence of a situation frequently connected with major insertions. In the case of the *Secretum* digression, there are good reasons for thinking that it is an interpolation: we have found no other explanation for the existence of basically identical forms of the digression in two different works, one of them datable (by its Sallustian elements) to 1353; and now we have found all this inside a section of Book III whose origin in 1347 or 1349 has been elsewhere proven in various ways.

(4) The Time of Origin of the "Desiderium gloriae" Section

This chapter will conclude with a statement on the over-all construction of the *gloria* section as it has emerged from our observations.

---

[67] Fr.: "Misereatur Altissimus ne ista contingant." Aug.: "Misericordia divina liberet, quamvis humanam tamen non excusat insaniam. Nolo autem de misericordia nimium speres. Sicut enim desperantes odit Deus, sic inconsulte sperantes irridet.

Apart from the probably interpolated instability digression (pages 200–204), we have encountered nothing in this section that points to 1353.[68] Wherever we probed the surviving text, all signs directed us to 1347 or 1349.

To refresh the reader's mind, those signs include the following. At the very start of the *gloria* section, Augustine characterizes Franciscus' "desiderium gloriae" as his greatest and most perilous desire — a judgment that would no longer have been true after 1350. In the same context, Franciscus declares with Augustine's approval that when the *Africa* is finished it will be a "preclarum rarumque opus et egregium" — a verdict more in accord with Petrarch's mood before 1352 than after his deep disillusionment of that year.[69] Near the beginning of the *gloria* section, Augustine accuses Petrarch of devoting such immense scholarly and poetic efforts to the *Africa* and *De Viris* that he "forgets himself while writing about others" — a remark hardly possible as late as 1353, when Petrarch was no longer working systematically on the *Africa* and *De Viris,* and the *De Vita Solitaria* and *De Otio Religioso* were all but complete. In the next paragraph, there are evident homologies with the original 1349 version of *Fam.* VIII 2–5 — a version that was only partially replaced in the *Secretum* by the approximately 1353 phrasing of the letter.[70] On pages 208 and 210, following Augustine's paraphrase of the Tusculan teaching that *gloria* is necessary but is in any event an inevitable companion to *virtus* (Petrarch's belief during the 1340s) there are again parallels to the original 1349 version of *Fam.* VIII 2–5. Near the end of the section, the Hypanis episode — which may or may not be an interpolation —

Illud equidem ex ore tuo auditum esse doleo philosophorum in hac re veterem, ut ais, fabellam posse contemni" (Carrara, p. 200).

[68] Except perhaps the short aside concerning the Hypanis creatures, which might have been interpolated in the draft of 1347 as late as 1353. See pp. 108–113, above.

[69] That the disillusionment he suffered in 1352 forms a real boundary line and is no fantasy or exaggeration of modern scholars we know for certain from his own remarks in later years concerning his early works. According to his retrospective judgment of the epic, sent to Boccaccio in 1363, the *Africa,* which in Petrarch's youth had been more famous than its author desired, afterwards became "retarded on account of many serious problems and grew senile": "... *Africa* mea, que tunc iuvenis notior iam famosiorque quam vellem, curis postea multis et gravibus pressa consenuit ..." (*Sen.* II, 1, March 1363, to Boccaccio. See *Prose,* p. 1034).

[70] The existence of these homologies was noted above in the Appendix to Chap. 4, p. 113f.

is surrounded by concordances with the original 1349 text of *Fam.* VIII 2–5,[71] by a quotation from an *epistola metrica* of 1337–39, and by the words Augustine addresses to Franciscus, "tu quoque, qui nunc etate florida," which look entirely as if they were directed toward a man younger than Petrarch was in 1353. Finally, Franciscus' idea on the concluding pages of the section, of completing the *Africa* and *De Viris* rapidly and then beginning a more religious life, maintains the very plan that was called in question in 1352, and thus it, too, points to 1347 or 1349.

The ultimate result of this analysis is clear: we have before us in the *gloria* section the same pattern of growth that characterizes Books I and II. In all three books substantial additions and corrections were made in 1349 and 1353, but the discovery of these insertions does not change the fact that the bulk of the work consists of a largely untouched older draft.[72]

---

[71] See p. 112, above.

[72] It has not been due to forgetfulness that I have referred nowhere in this discussion to the at first sight telling evidence (in Book III; Carrara, p. 192) that the *De Viris* is cited with its original title, "a rege Romulo in Titum Cesarem," which Petrarch normally would no longer have used in the 1350s. I have not made use of this fact in defining the chronological layers of Book III because on further consideration there can be no doubt that in Augustine's biographical report the citation of that early form refers to the start of Petrarch's occupation with the *De Viris,* not to the time of Augustine's and Franciscus' conversation. At this point, Augustine is trying to explain how Franciscus' absorption in the *Africa* and *De Viris* had gotten under way in past years. "Not content with your daily work, ... you have been longing for a posterity of fame. And in pursuit of this end, putting your hand to ever greater tasks, you began to write a history from the time of King Romulus to that of the Emperor Titus, an enormous undertaking that would swallow up an immensity of time and labor. Then, without waiting till this was finished, goaded by the pricks of your ambition for glory, you sailed off in your poetical barque towards Africa; and now you are hard at work on those books of your *Africa* without having relinquished the other [enterprise]. In this way you are devoting your whole life to these two absorbing occupations. . . ." In other words, at that past moment when the *De Viris* was first planned, it was indeed intended to be a history from Romulus to Titus, whether or not the title and design of the work were changed by the time of Augustine's talk with Franciscus. There is no need, therefore, for Rico's audacious speculation that Petrarch may have gone back to his original Roman version in his later years and that this might be the reason why he cited the title of the Titus version in the *Secretum* (*Lectura,* pp. 386ff., n.478). Instead, it should be emphasized that the available sources make it certain that Petrarch never returned to the Roman/ Titus plan after 1351–53. This conclusion is supported by three pieces of evidence. In the first place, when Emperor Charles IV asked Petrarch during the mid-1350s whether there would be room for his biography in the *De Viris,* he was told that this would depend on whether he had earned a high place for himself in the course of his

Appendix
The *Amor* Section of Book III

In this chapter, I have analyzed the *gloria* section of Book III but disregarded the *amor* section. It has seemed preferable not to retell the chronological story of the latter, because the present chapter is already a crowded one. Besides, in Chapter 4 it was established in detail that the "travel page" in the *amor* section (Carrara, page 172) is attributable to 1349 rather than 1347 or 1353 (see above, Chapter 4, pages 86–103). The only question that should still be raised is the extent of the 1349 interpolation. I believe there is no doubt about its boundaries. However, I must correct a mistake I made in *From Petrarch to Leonardo Bruni* (pages 92–93), where I assumed that everything said by Augustine and Franciscus about the need for "peregrinationes" outside Provence refers to 1349. Actually, the insertion of 1349 does not begin until the travel page, the preceding part of the text (Carrara, pages 164–172) being void of any sign that Petrarch's reference to a "peregrinatio" abroad means a sojourn in Italy. Rather, in the preceding part of the *peregrinatio* paragraph, his flight from Provence is compared with his earlier travels northward to the Atlantic Ocean, and his planned "peregrinatio" is called an "exilium" from Provence. With the travel page, Augustine's advice for Franciscus to travel to his "patria," Italy, becomes the heart of the *peregrinatio* idea; this means that we are no longer in Provence in 1347 but in Italy in 1349. This is confirmed by two references to *Metrica* III 25, which dates from as late as autumn 1349, and to the *Psalmi Penitentiales* of about 1348. In brief, an interpolation of rather modest length (Carrara, page 172, perhaps pages 172–174) was added to a vast, surviving text of 1347. This is a

---

life — an answer which makes sense only if Petrarch maintained the "universal" design that could include an emperor of the fourteenth century (*Fam.* XIX 3). Second, the one revival of the Roman plan during Petrarch's final years, as a result of the wish of Francesco da Carrara of Padua to realize the concept of the *De Viris Illustribus* by erecting an actual hall of fame decorated with portraits and brief comments written by Petrarch, was insisted upon by the Carrara prince, not by Petrarch, as the latter tells us in his letters (see Ernest H. Wilkins, *Petrarch's Later Years* [Cambridge, Mass., 1959], p. 286). The third piece of evidence is found among the additions made in the *Africa* during the last decade of Petrarch's life: Ennius, who is talking about himself "as if he were a Petrarch *ante litteram,* alludes to a work that includes 'gli uomini illustri di tutte le età,' that is, precisely to the *De viris illustribus* as it took form after 1352" (Paratore, "L'elaborazione padovana dell'*Africa,*" pp. 82–83). For the reader of the *Secretum,* it is impossible under these circumstances to determine reliably how and when the Titus reference was put into the *Secretum* text, and our only safeguard against committing a blunder lies in the total exclusion of the reference to the Titus version from critical discussion.

counterpart to what occurred in the *gloria* section, the only difference being that the insertion in the *amor* section was made in 1349, whereas the additions to the *gloria* section were made in 1353.

One problem remains — or seems to remain — in the *amor* section, to which Rico has drawn attention (pages 284–285). What is the meaning of Augustine's warning to Franciscus (Carrara, page 138) that Laura might die before him, as she indeed did in April 1348? After her death, Augustine says, Franciscus will have to look upon her disfigured body and will feel ashamed ever to have thought of her immortal soul as intimately connected with that frail shell: "Atqui cum oculos illos, usque tibi in perniciem placentes, suprema clauserit dies; cum effigiem morte variatam et pallentia membra conspexeris, pudebit animum immortalem caduco applicuisse corpusculo, et que nunc tam pertinaciter astruis, cum rubore recordaberis." Is this not prophecy *ex eventu*, Rico asks; that is, was it not written after life had proved that Laura, though younger than Petrarch, was to die first? Is this not a warning that the entire text of the *amor* section, even where there are no signs of interpolation, may have been written or rewritten in 1349 or 1353? This seems to me a misinterpretation caused by a disregard for Petrarch's absence from Provence at the time of Laura's death during the plague of 1348. He never saw the cruel spectacle that Augustine prophesies Franciscus will some day see. Moreover, we know from Petrarch's famous entry in his copy of Virgil that his reaction when he received the news of Laura's death was the very opposite of terror at the thought of Laura's lifeless body, which Augustine insisted he would feel. "Her chaste and lovely form," Petrarch noted in his Virgil, "was laid to rest . . . on the same day on which she died. . . . I am persuaded that her soul returned to the heaven from which it came." Far from arousing the suspicion of a late insertion of a reference to Laura's death in the *Secretum,* therefore, the evidence makes it hard to believe that Petrarch needed the experience of her death in order to write Augustine's words. What he did add to Book III in Italy in 1349 was the travel page and, perhaps, little else.

CHAPTER SIX

The Last Repercussions in the *Secretum*
of Events in Petrarch's Life

(1) Paragraphs Written after Petrarch's
Final Return to Italy

I

The question whether the *Secretum* was worked on after Petrarch settled in Milan has arisen repeatedly in this discussion, as it frequently
has in the history of *Secretum* research. Readers of the *Secretum* have
usually concluded that certain passages take up problems known
from the *De Remediis Utriusque Fortunae*. In other words, they have
pointed to homologies between the *Secretum* and a work composed
after Petrarch moved to Milan.[1] Taken together with the long-
prevailing assumption that the final autograph may be as late as
1358, this has been interpreted by many a reader as meaning that the
Secretum text received some final touches between 1353 and 1358.
Such was the conclusion drawn by Enrico Carrara in his edition of
1955,[2] and through his influence it became the belief of most Petrarch
students, even though the scrupulous among them did not forget
that no specific *Secretum* passages had actually been detected "that are
definitely assignable to the period of Petrarch's residence in Milan"
(as stated by Ernest H. Wilkins in 1958).[3]

It was against this relatively vague and uncertain background that
Rico thought it defensible to conclude that nothing of significance
was added to the *Secretum* after Petrarch moved to Italy in June 1353.
"A good sign of the inattention paid to many problems in the *Secretum*," he observed, "is that E. Carrara's 'ritoccato tra il 1353 e il 1358'
has been repeated despite the fact that not a single date points to this

[1] The dates of the *De Remediis* will be referred to in n.38, below.

[2] The *Secretum* was "ritoccato tra il 1353 et il '58" (Carrara, in *Prose,* p. 1162).

[3] Ernest H. Wilkins, *Petrarch's Eight Years in Milan* (Cambridge, Mass., 1958), p.
234.

. . . period."[4] What Rico puts in its place, however, is not based on any newly established facts but on a number of unacceptable inferences. Why, after all, should we assume that the absence in Tedaldo's copy of any notes on changes indicates that the *Secretum* was not touched in Milan? Why should not their lack rather mean that the final autograph was written relatively late, when all the changes occasioned by Petrarch's move to Italy had already been made in the original text?[5]

Now, it is true that Rico's hypothesis that the manuscript used by Tedaldo was written in Provence is accompanied by several minor arguments intended to reach the same conclusion in their own right. But the dominance of a purely speculative procedure is even more pronounced in these supports than in the major thesis. The most explicit of Rico's auxiliary arguments is the following. Whereas it was appropriate for Petrarch to rewrite the earlier versions of the *Secretum* during the weeks of "haste" before his departure from Provence because a period of his life was closing, after his arrival in Milan "a [new] period opens: there are no reasons to hurry; rather, everything invited him to engage in long-term projects such as the *De Remediis*. Thus clues and proofs converge: the remaking of the *Secretum* . . . took place in Provence, during the winter and in the days just before the beginning of spring 1353."[6]

In reality the situation was just the opposite. In the case of his *Invective Contra Medicum* Petrarch did what we are told he could not have done with the *Secretum:* he reorganized and revised the four invectives which had occupied him during his Provençal years, "certainly soon after his establishment in Milan."[7] And he must have

---

[4] Rico, *Lectura,* p. 16, n.23.

[5] I have suggested above, pp. 76–77, that both explanations are conceivable but that the one allowing for changes in Milan (and therefore for the making of the final autograph copy there) is more probable.

[6] "Las pistas y las pruebas convergen: la refundición del *Secretum,* intensa y decisiva, del *incipit* al *explicit,* se efectuó en Provenza, en el invierno y en días próximos al principio de la primavera, en 1353" (Rico, *Lectura,* p. 468).

[7] According to Ernest H. Wilkins, *Studies in the Life and Works of Petrarch* (Cambridge, Mass., 1955), p. 174. To be precise, the first invective was written in the form of a long letter in March 1352 and the other three in early 1353. According to the editor of the *Invective,* P. G. Ricci (who is reporting on the results of Umberto Bosco's research on the genesis of the *Invective*), Petrarch "riassettò in un'opera sola gli scritti di risposta all'avversario, facendo della lettera il primo libro, e dell'opusculo il secondo, terzo e quarto libro delle *Invective . . .*" (*Prose,* p. 1172).

done something similar in the case of the *De Vita Solitaria* of 1346, for his accurate description of Milan in Book II of the *De Vita* cannot be earlier than his move to that city in mid-1353.[8]

Another assumption proffered to exclude the possibility that Petrarch worked on the *Secretum* in Milan seems equally dubious. "If Petrarch inserted any new material into his work during his stay in Milan . . . it is inconceivable that he would have passed over the opportunity to make the changes indispensable for explaining or excusing his stay in Lombardy."[9]

I have cited these arguments in order to make even clearer how purely deductive and abstract is the reasoning behind the thesis that the *Secretum* was not touched after Petrarch's departure from Provence. What we must try to find is more facts.

II

So far in our discussion, less has been said about Book II than about the other books of the *Secretum*, although it has supplied perhaps our clearest information on the obvious changes that occurred in Petrarch's conduct between 1347 and 1349 with respect to *luxuria*. Since Book II reports on Petrarch's behavior regarding all the Seven Deadly Sins, it may provide evidence of similar changes where sins other than *luxuria* are concerned.

Our relative neglect of Book II does not mean that the same methods that proved themselves in the analysis of the other two books will not work for this one. In Book I we distinguished with relative ease between Petrarch's original Augustinianism and his stoicizing bent of mind in the early 1350s. In Book II a similar contrast is apparent in Petrarch's treatment of the sin of *superbia*. There the heart of the confessional scrutiny is Augustine's disparagement of Petrarch's talents, pride in which brings Petrarch near to *superbia*. Just as his gift of eloquence is not as magnificent in Augustine's eyes as Francis-

---

[8] As B. L. Ullman demonstrated in "The Composition of Petrarch's *De Vita Solitaria*," *Miscellanea Giovanni Mercati*, vol. IV, Studi e Testi 124 (Vatican City, 1946), p. 123.

[9] ". . . de haber insertado en la obra algún nuevo material entre 1353 y 1358, durante la estancia en Milán . . . , es inimaginable que Petrarca renunciara a efectuar las modificaciones imprescindibles para explicar o excusar el asentamiento en Lombardía" (Rico, *Lectura*, pp. 470–471).

cus is inclined to think, so his propensity toward learned conceit is a danger to him. How often has his knowledge deserted him, how often has he found that the acumen of lowly people excels his own! But in the midst of these warnings against committing a sin, we hear the voice of the more philosophical Petrarch of the early 1350s, who inveighs not only against learned conceit but also against a kind of learning that ignores the exploration of one's own nature and spiritual destiny.

There are three crucial passages in Augustine's critique of Franciscus' *superbia:*

(1) Of what relevance is it to know a multitude of things? What if you learn all the circuits of the heavens and the earth, the reaches of the sea, the courses of the stars, the virtues of herbs and stones, the secrets of nature, and remain ignorant of yourself? What will it profit you?

(2) If with the help of books you discover the straight, ascending path, what use will it be if passion makes you turn aside onto a crooked, downward path?

(3) Suppose you remember the deeds of illustrious men of all ages, what value will it have if you do not care what you do with your life?[10]

Of the first of these three passages it may be said that it would not be surprising to encounter this idea in the *Invective Contra Medicum* of the early 1350s, where self-knowledge is confronted in entirely the same fashion with the allegedly sterile facts of Aristotelian natural science; and this passage would be just as congenial in the context of the *De Sui Ipsius et Multorum Ignorantia,* written a decade later. But it would definitely be out of place in a text written before the early 1350s. As for the third of the quoted passages, the phrase "cum omnis evi clarorum hominum gesta memineritis" points to or beyond the time when Petrarch composed the pre-Romulean *vitae* for his *De Viris* and was planning to replace the original Rome-oriented text with the expanded design "ex omnibus terris ac seculis illustres viros in unum contrahendi." Again we are in the early 1350s.[11]

---

[10](1) "Quanquam vel multa nosse quid relevat si, cum celi terreque ambitum, si, cum maris spatium et astrorum cursus herbarumque virtutes ac lapidum et nature secreta didiceritis, vobis estis incogniti?" (2) "Si, cum rectam virtutis ardue semitam scripturis ducibus agnoveritis, obliquo calle transversos agit furor?" (3) "Si, cum omnis evi clarorum hominum gesta memineritis, quid vos quotidie agitis non curatis?" (Carrara, p. 72).

[11] As has been mentioned above, pp. 70f. and 129. This implies, of course, that at

This conclusion may be tested by asking whether the general context of the *superbia* section remains intact when the passages under review are removed. Before them, Augustine has just accused Franciscus of false pride in overrating the capacity of his erudition and literary talents: "I nunc, et ingenio gloriare!" After them, the debate again turns to the scrutiny of his *superbia* and his vaunted eloquence: "Will you not readily confess how often your confidence in this power has proved vain?" When the two or three suspected passages are omitted, not only does the general context remain unimpaired, but the structure of the entire section seems more coherent. Just as he did repeatedly in Book I, Petrarch in the *superbia* section of Book II reveals the more philosophically minded moralist he became in his later years. These observations are admittedly based upon a single page, but there may well be other, less evident insertions in Book II. It would be strange, for instance, if the learned discourse on the respective richness of the Latin and Greek languages, which appears on another page of the *superbia* section,[12] belonged to the first draft of the *Secretum* rather than having been added in 1349 or 1353.

Moreover, what is striking in the second book is the inclusion of information on Petrarch's real or imagined sinful behavior. In this lies the opportunity to learn about changes in his way of life, not just in his thinking. Petrarch's changing relationship to *luxuria* has already yielded new information, as we have seen. But it has also been known for nearly twenty years that the unusually long sections on *accidia* and *avaritia* in Book II hide major changes in Petrarch's life between the late 1340s and his final emendations in 1353.[13] More remains to be said — and more systematically — about the vital information that can be extracted from those two crucial sections.

III

When we read the long section on *accidia,* we quickly come to realize that we are confronted by a text of the late 1340s, considerably en-

---

the time of his occupation with the *Invective Contra Medicum,* Petrarch must have been thinking of the *De Viris* as "ex omnibus seculis illustres," comparable to what we read in the *superbia* section of the *Secretum.* This is indeed so, since the latter title is the form in which the *De Viris* is cited in the second of the *Invective.* See Baron, *From Petrarch to Leonardo Bruni,* p. 26.

[12] Carrara, pp. 74–76.
[13] See p. 2f., above.

larged during the early 1350s — which can only mean when the *Secretum* received its last revisions in 1353.

There is no reason to suspect that the first pages of the section, which give a psychological analysis of Petrarch's *accidia* — pages 106–110 in Carrara's edition — were not part of the text from the very start. After all, it must always have included an analysis of this kind on *accidia,* and there is no trace of later changes anywhere in this fundamental part of the section. Portions of the next few pages, where later experiences required interpolations, look quite different.[14] The changes begin at the point where Petrarch singles out Fortuna's often malevolent treatment of him as a major cause of his *accidia.* Augustine, who considers this complaint an indication of latent avarice, charges that the root of the evil is Franciscus' ambition for a "primus locus" in life when he should be seeking "mediocritas." "If men were aware of the misery of high status, they would tremble at the thought of it, instead of desiring it." No one should know this better than Franciscus, "whom experience has long persuaded that the gift of very high status is nothing but toil, trouble, and misery." Franciscus roundly denies the charge. "That I have never aspired to first place, Lady Truth here . . . is my witness." She knows he has always been convinced that "the tranquility and serenity of mind" for which he longs is alien to the "supremum fortune culmen"; therefore, he has "abhorred a life of anxiety and care and prudently preferred a mediocre state." As proof he refers to criticism that he has received for "indolence and lack of energy" (*secordiam atque segnitiem vocant*) because he has not striven for more.[15]

If there was no truth to Augustine's accusation, why such a dispute in a book in which he serves as the voice of Petrarch's conscience and the unveiler of his hidden thoughts? Presumably, the presence of these charges in the *Secretum* means that Petrarch had, at least at times, entertained hopes for a higher position in life than was compatible with the "mediocritas" he professed. We must also consider it probable that his normal reluctance to aspire to the higher curial offices open to a man with his connections and gifts had been criticized as "secordia atque segnities."

Petrarch's experience during his last stay in Provence in 1351–53

[14] Carrara, pp. 111–120.
[15] Ibid., pp. 112–114.

accurately fits the account given in the *Secretum*. The sins with which he was charged at the time by friend and foe alike did include suspected aspirations for a high curial office, even though nothing came of them; afterwards Petrarch defended himself with precisely those arguments in favor of an unburdened lower station which he puts into the mouth of Augustine.[16]

One office offered to him by the pope was that of papal secretary — an offer made and declined for the first time in 1347. But in 1351–52 Petrarch's reaction was no longer entirely negative, for he did work out and present a draft of a chancery document, which, however, merely proved to everyone that he was not suited for bureaucratic work.[17] And why, on learning in 1351 that he was wanted at the papal court, did he move back to Avignon at all, against the advice of several Italian friends who tried to dissuade him?[18] If his reaction to the offer of a position as papal secretary was half-hearted, were even higher aspirations perhaps one of his reasons for crossing the Alps? His letters are ambiguous on this point, but it has been suspected that he may have been dreaming of as much as a cardinalate. Ernest H. Wilkins, in the latest reexamination of this possibility, has concluded that the conflicting evidence reflects a real struggle in Petrarch's mind, and that if he ever wrestled with such desires, he must have done so between 1350 and 1352.[19] In any event, rumors were circulating, and Petrarch was painfully aware of them. At the same time, some of his friends were reproaching him for his lack of interest in a papal secretaryship — a burdensome but esteemed and richly paid office — with the same arguments against which Franciscus defends himself before Augustine in the *Secretum*. "You and all my friends, to whom I appear too indolent [*quibus segnior appareo*], should know," he wrote to Nelli in March 1353, "that I have vowed to keep my aspirations within the bounds of moderation."[20]

Thus, the complex situation presupposed in the *accidia* section — Petrarch aspiring for a "primus locus" in spite of all his denials, and at the same time reproached for not aspiring enough — actually existed in 1351–53, but not before.

[16] Baron, *From Petrarch to Leonardo Bruni*, p. 74, n.60.
[17] Ibid., n.61.
[18] See Wilkins, *Studies in the Life*, p. 76.
[19] Ibid., pp. 75ff., esp. p. 80.
[20] *Fam.* XVI 3 (3).

Having detected events of the early 1350s behind the reproof of Petrarch's aspiration for a "primus locus," we may wonder whether the passages professing "mediocritas" of fortune as his ideal do not equally well suit the conditions of those later years. In the sentences immediately following the discussion of a "primus locus" we find two extensive quotations from Horace's *Odes* (the *Carmina*), which are cited as illustrations of Horatian *aurea mediocritas*.[21] Although arguments based solely on the dates of Petrarch's first familiarity with certain ancient authors are sometimes dangerous, it is a fact that Horace's *Carmina* was not well known during the Middle Ages, and that Petrarch did not read it thoroughly and use it widely until 1350–51.[22]

The portion of the *accidia* section with which we are dealing[23] does not, however, exclusively reflect experiences of the 1350s. It is clear that an older layer of thought is also present in this stretch of text. After the references to Horatian *mediocritas,* Franciscus explains to Augustine why he is unable to live by the ideals he so firmly proclaims. He is not free to lead a life in accordance with his avowed values, he says, because until now "I have been living for others, which is the most miserable of all states."[24] On the next page he returns twice to his lament regarding his "aliis vivere," making Augustine remark that Franciscus' complaints are due not to poverty but to servitude — "servitus," an expression clearly equated with submission to a master. Franciscus, he says, is right to believe that this is a miserable state, and Franciscus himself takes this additional cause of *accidia* so seriously that when he finally vows to change in the future, he includes both servitude and poverty among the things about which he will no longer complain.[25] In other words, Petrarch must be alluding to a significant situation in his life, one, moreover, which had not yet come to an end when he placed Franciscus' lament about his submission to a master in the *Secretum.*

[21] Carrara, p. 114.

[22] Baron, *From Petrarch to Leonardo Bruni,* p. 76, n.66. Moreover, Rico has now added another piece of evidence by pointing out that Petrarch's classical literary model, Horace's *Carmina,* was acquired for his library in Genoa in November 1347, that is, later than the first form of the *Secretum.* (See n.36, below).

[23] Carrara, pp. 111–120.

[24] "... hactenus aliis vivo, quod miserrimum ex omnibus est" (ibid., p. 116).

[25] Fr.: "Movisti animum fateor, ut iam nec servum me nec inopem indigner" (ibid., p. 118).

Did such a situation occur more than once in Petrarch's life during the 1340s and early 1350s? To ask this question is to answer it. Petrarch can only have been thinking of his relationship to Cardinal Giovanni Colonna, in whose "familia" he served as a household chaplain from 1330 to 1347. The cardinal had been like a father to him, but this bond was now to be broken. When the 1347 version of the *Secretum* was being written, Petrarch was still under the strain of that unresolved dependence, of which much evidence has survived. In 1349 and 1353, on the other hand, there was no longer any "servitus" in his life from which the lament in the *accidia* section can have sprung. However unsure we may be of the details, it is most unlikely that the allusion to an onerous submission to a master would have been put into the *accidia* section after the relationship had come to an end: that is, after July 1347 when the cardinal died. This is a second bit of evidence — the first being the introductory analysis of *accidia* — that the basis of the *accidia* section dates back to 1347.

However, in 1353 the obsolete complaint about submission to a master, whose retention among the causes of Petrarch's *accidia* is easily understood, was not left untouched by the work of adaptation to new ideas. For before the 1350s Augustine could not have been made to exhort Franciscus to be patient because even men who are highly placed, like Caesar, must live for others. In a sense, Augustine explains, Julius Caesar lived for those who murdered him, that is "for D. Brutus, T. Cimber, and the other participants in a perfidious conspiracy, whose covetousness could not be satisfied by the munificence of such a liberal giver."[26] This is a strong condemnation of the motives of those who claimed to liberate Rome from its tyrant. In his youthful work on the *Africa*, Petrarch had taken a passionate stand against Caesar. In 1341, in one of his canzones, he had called Cato "quel si grande amico di libertá, che piú di lei non visse," and in a letter of about 1342 he had described Marcus Junius Brutus as a "vir acer [i.e., ardent] et strenuus." But by the time he grew old, he was to ask whether Cato's suicide was not due to envy of Caesar's glory, whether it was really necessary to fear Caesar so much, the "most clement and benevolent, not only of all tyrants but of all princes." In 1366 (in part somewhat later) he composed the *De Gestis*

---

[26] "... vivebat ... D. Bruto, T. Cimbro ceterisque perfide coniurationis auctoribus, quorum cupiditates explere non valuit tanti munificentia largitoris" (ibid.).

Caesaris, the first modern picture of Caesar as a great statesman and personality.[27]

Can we date the transition from one point of view to the other? The first sign in Petrarch's correspondence is found in a letter defending Cola di Rienzo which Petrarch sent to the people of Rome in October or November 1352. In it he raises the question whether one should not talk rather of "Caesar's monarchy" than of his "tyranny."[28] A year later, in a letter to Emperor Charles IV, Caesar — "to whom I often refer" — is presented as the paragon Charles ought to emulate in ruling the Roman monarchy.[29] Perhaps the earliest preparation for the change is in the first draft of the *triumphus Fame,* where Caesar outshines Scipio. Most probably, the first draft of this triumph was written soon after Laura's death, in the second half of 1348 or perhaps a year or two later.[30] Thus, we find traces of the reversal of Petrarch's estimation of Caesar's adversaries and of Caesar himself only *after* the 1347 draft of the *Secretum.* In other words, if the outspoken designation of the assassins as participants in a "perfida coniuratio," whose "cupiditas" could not be satisfied by Caesar's munificence, was written in 1347, it would stand alone in its time. There is no difficulty in ascribing it to either 1349 or 1353, but in view of the fact that it occurs in a portion of text where every other sentence points to 1353, we can be reasonably sure that the change in Petrarch's judgment is attributable to the latter year.

Franciscus' reference to the banishment of his family from Florence is another indication that this section dates from the early 1350s. "Have you never heard," he asks, "how cruelly Fortuna used me, this stepmother who in a single day laid low with her ruthless hand all my hopes, my resources, my family, and my home?" And Augustine answers, "I see tears in your eyes and I pass on."[31] This emotional outburst almost two generations after the event comes as a surprise; there are none comparable in other works of Petrarch's. Why does he contend that this was one of the experiences which caused his *accidia*? The answer must be that during his Provençal biennium old memories suddenly came back to him with great force. In 1351 the Floren-

---

[27] Baron, *From Petrarch to Leonardo Bruni,* pp. 15, 38, 98.
[28] Ibid., p. 36.
[29] *Fam.* XVIII 1, November 1353; see Baron, *From Petrarch to Leonardo Bruni,* p. 37.
[30] See Baron, *From Petrarch to Leonardo Bruni,* pp. 27, 35f.
[31] Carrara, p. 118.

tine *signoria* offered him restitution for his paternal fortune together with a chair at the University of Florence. In April 1351 he sent an answer to the *signoria* (*Fam.* XI 5), in which he expressed deep appreciation for their readiness to return the property that had been his father's; Florence, he said, was restoring his childhood home to him.[32] When it became clear in 1352–53, during his stay in Provence, that he would not accept the chair or come to Florence, the offer of restitution was withdrawn. It was then, we may assume, that Petrarch with deep feeling wrote his lament about the final loss of his family fortune and his house in Florence.

Another major cause of Petrarch's *accidia,* discussed on the same page, is the suffering inflicted on him by the hated city life of Avignon. "Who could express sufficiently the daily disgust of my life, this most dejected and disorderly of cities, narrow dark sink of the earth, where all the filth of the world is collected? Who could find adequate words for the nauseating spectacle: streets full of disease and infection, dirty pigs and snarling dogs," the noise of vehicles, the pandemonium of so many races of men, the great poverty and wealth, everything inimical to the work of the poet.[33]

The tone of these phrases attacking Avignon deserves attention. They are followed by a citation of the verse "Silva placet Musis, urbs est inimica poetis" from Petrarch's *Metr.* II 3, a poem probably written in the summer of 1342. There we find a similar bitter reproof of life in Avignon, but with a basic difference. The noise of Avignon, we are told, kills every contemplative and creative mood; people from all nations converge at the papal seat and make Avignon the loudest and most unpleasant of cities. The often farcical street scenes forced upon the onlooker's attention are described with despair.[34] The same complaint occurs in other poems and letters of the late 1330s and early 1340s. However, there is no counterpart in this poem, or in any of Petrarch's contemporaneous letters, to the disgusted description — the very heart of the *Secretum* passage — of Avignon as the stinking

[32] See Ernest H. Wilkins, "Petrarch's Last Return to Provence," *Speculum* XXXIX (1964), p. 79.

[33] "Quis vite mee tedia et quotidianum fastidium sufficienter exprimat, mestissimam turbulentissimamque urbem terrarum omnium, angustissimam atque ultimam sentinam et totius orbis sordibus exundantem? Quis verbis equet que passim nauseam concitant: graveolentes semitas, permixtas rabidis canibus obscenas sues . . ." (Carrara, p. 120).

[34] *Metr.* II 3, verses 11–51.

dregs of the world ("angustissimam atque ultimam sentinam et totius orbis sordibus exundantem") and its streets as foul with the confusion of savage dogs and revolting pigs ("graveolentes semitas, permixtas rabidis canibus obscenas sues"). In fact, it is not until the early 1350s, when Petrarch composed his *Epistolae Sine Nomine* and others of his most bitter attacks against the Curia, that he uses the motif of impure Avignon, a place of moral contagion and pestilence, reeking with evil smells.[35]

Rico has succeeded in giving this observation, which I originally made in 1963, a still more factual basis. The changed tone of Petrarch's criticism of Avignon was not solely the fruit of his increasing disagreement with the Curia but also of his expanded reading in classical literature. Certain charges against ancient Rome in Horace's *Carmina* introduced him to the more violent form that he, in turn, was to use against Avignon. We still have the manuscript copy of Horace which Petrarch bought for his library in Genoa on November 28, 1347, and which proves his active interest in the new acquisition by its numerous marginal notations.[36] When this purchase was made, the original draft of the *Secretum* had already been in existence for months, and the wording of the attack on Avignon in the *accidia* section cannot therefore have been entered in the *Secretum* manuscript before 1349 or 1353. In view of our observation that similarly phrased criticisms of Avignon do not occur before the early 1350s and that all the chronologically verifiable allusions in this paragraph point to 1353, we have every reason to believe that this invective against Avignon, and with it the entire paragraph as we have it, is in fact no earlier than 1353.

IV

But we have not yet tackled the central problem. Although there can be no doubt that most of the surviving text of the *accidia* section (following the introductory analysis of the nature of *accidia* written in 1347) stems from 1353, we have not yet ascertained whether from the first or the second half of the year, from the end of Petrarch's sojourn in Provence or the beginning of his Milanese years.

---

[35] Baron, *From Petrarch to Leonardo Bruni,* p. 99, n.120.
[36] See Rico, *Lectura,* pp. 228–231.

The last few pages of the *accidia* section lead to this vital question.[37] There we find two groups of references that seem to point to the time when Petrarch was already in Milan. One group includes two clearly identifiable allusions to Petrarch's *De Remediis Utriusque Fortunae*. This is a work which was composed for the most part between late 1356 and mid-1357 and was presumably not started before 1354, even though the idea for it had begun to take shape in Petrarch's mind about 1347.[38] At least two pages of the *accidia* section are clearly imbued with the spirit of the *De Remediis*.[39] On the first of these, Augustine advises Franciscus to store in his memory suitable passages from writings on human conduct, so that "no matter when or where some urgent case of illness occurs you will, like an experienced physician, already have the remedy, so to speak, written in your head. For among the maladies of the soul, just as among those of the body, there are some for which delay is fatal; if you defer the remedy you take away all hope of recovery; . . . a tardy remedy is a useless one." In his edition of the *Secretum*, Carrara notes that this is *in nuce* the objective of the *De Remediis*.[40] That this work was indeed what Petrarch had in mind becomes even more evident on the second of the two pages, where he questions whether Fortuna exists and promises "ego autem quid sentiam, aliud forte tempus ac locus alter fuerit dicendi" — which is, of course, the *De Remediis,* where the theme of the existence of Fortuna is treated in considerable detail. The allusions in the *Secretum* are clear enough to suggest that, given the probability that Petrarch did not do his major work on the *De Remediis* before 1354, he must have interpolated them when he was in Milan, that is, during the second half of 1353, if not later.

The second group of references touches the crucial evidence: reminders of Petrarch's scorn for city life in general and his unbounded

[37] Carrara, pp. 120–128.

[38] See Klaus Heitmann, "La genesi del *De remediis utriusque fortune* del Petrarca," *Convivium,* XXV (1957), pp. 9–30, and Wilkins, *Petrarch's Eight Years in Milan,* pp. 69–71, 235f. The emphasis on 1356–57 is the result of research done by both these scholars, and Wilkins has shown it to be probable that Petrarch began writing in 1354. He resumed work, in order to make substantial additions (15 percent of the length, in Heitmann's estimation), as late as 1366. See above, p. 85, n.27, and Baron, *From Petrarch to Leonardo Bruni,* p. 97.

[39] Carrara, pp. 122, 128.

[40] Ibid., p. 122.

hatred of Avignon in particular.[41] His complaints contain a curious element: a protest against his life in the city which is in clear conflict with his relationship to Avignon. As Augustine says, the ultimate cause of Franciscus' complaints appears to be that he is in an unsuitable place for his studies ("Doles quod importunum studiis tuis locum nactus es"), and if he could but find peace of mind, the environment would affect only his senses, "sed animum non moveret."[42] This advice for a philosopher living in a city was found by Petrarch in Seneca's writings,[43] so one might argue that it need not reflect a specific situation. But did Petrarch think in 1351–53 that he would have to remain in Avignon for an indefinite length of time? Of course, during the autumn–winter of 1351–52 he had to stay there for a few months under depressing conditions; our sources make us familiar with the details of his despair in that period.[44] But beyond those few months he was not bound to live in Avignon. In these circumstances he thought continuously of getting away from the hated city just as soon as his various transactions at the Curia could be terminated.

Yet what we read in the *accidia* section of the *Secretum* has a totally different ring to it: Franciscus feels tied to the city in which he is residing. This is the tacit premise of what Augustine says and Franciscus replies. As Augustine puts it when he tries to encourage Franciscus: when you complain about a life surrounded by the "tumultus urbium," you forget that "since you have come to this pass through your own doing, you can also escape of your own free will, if only you wish it."[45] This seems to imply that Petrarch has settled in the city for an indefinite length of time — he never did this in Avignon — but would consider leaving it again if only it were possible. That we have correctly understood his situation is clear from Franciscus' answer to Augustine: the strangest thing you have said is that "to leave the world of cities [*urbes relinquere*] would be easy for me and

---

[41] The name, Avignon, does not appear in the *Secretum,* of course, but in the paragraph under discussion the allusion is phrased in such a way that it is definite that Franciscus is talking about that city.

[42] Carrara, p. 120.

[43] Seneca, *Ep. ad Lucilium,* 56, 15. Quoted by Petrarch in *De Vita Solitaria,* Lib. I, in *Prose,* pp. 338–340. See also below, Chap. 8, n.47.

[44] See p. 169f., below.

[45] "... quod tua sponte in hos incideris anfractus tuaque sponte, si omnino velle ceperis, possis emergere, ..." (Carrara, p. 126).

purely a matter of my own will."[46] Is it believable that Petrarch would have reacted with such despair merely because he was forced to spend a few months of his biennium in Avignon, that he would have incorporated this false picture in the *Secretum* in a moment of discouragement when his original plans for settling in Italy had failed and he had to bide his time for a while in Provence?[47]

We know exactly what caused Petrarch's despair in Avignon from early autumn 1351 until early April of the next year, and we can determine whether it had anything to do with a feeling that he might be imprisoned in urban surroundings for the indefinite future. A mere look at his sojourn in Avignon reveals it to have been one of the most crowded and preoccupied periods of his life. The most urgent business he had to deal with there was the recent request of the pope to come and see him, one of the major reasons for Petrarch's traveling to Provence. The pope's intention in asking for him was to renew earlier offers of a papal secretaryship or a bishopric. Both were unacceptable to Petrarch, but their rejection required time-consuming and difficult diplomacy on his part. As if this were not enough, he had to settle two affairs in which he had allowed himself to become deeply involved as a father and as a friend — the procuring of a canonry for his son and of an abbacy near Vallombrosa for a friend of Florentine friends — strenuous efforts which to his despair consumed months of his time, as we know from his letters from Avignon. When both benefices had at last been procured, he described ruefully how he had waited in antechambers as he would never have waited on his own account, and how if anyone had seen him, a lover of freedom and solitude, haunting the papal palace among the courtiers, he would have been moved to laughter and pity. Ernest H. Wilkins, in his *Life of Petrarch,* has collected a number of Petrarch's testimonies to his state of mind during those months in Avignon: "This tempest of affairs hardly leaves me time to breathe." "So many things press upon me . . . that there is not time enough to take care of them all: there is

---

[46]". . . multa me vellicent, atque illud in primis quod urbes relinquere quasi rem facilem mei censes arbitrii, . . ." (ibid.).

[47]This is the interpretation proposed in Rico, *Lectura,* passim, and esp. p. 349, n.342, where Rico refers to sources which actually say that Petrarch did not intend to remain in Provence.

no end of them." "I am worn out, I am tormented, I am distressed, I am indignant, and I am wasting my time."[48]

During the same months, Petrarch was drawn by other problems into an ever-increasing state of irritation and restlessness. His position in Parma, until then the seat of his ecclesiastical benefices, was being undermined by the hostile attitude of Ugolino de' Rossi, Bishop of Parma, with the result that Petrarch had to try, unsuccessfully as it turned out, to conciliate him. At the same time, rumors were circulating in Avignon, even among the cardinals, that Petrarch was reading Virgil so avidly because he was involved in necromancy; for according to medieval legends, Virgil was himself a necromancer. Petrarch had to visit certain cardinals to justify himself and lost still more time. Besides all this, after his move to Avignon he frequently wrote scathing attacks (found in his *Epistolae Sine Nomine*) against the "Babylon" of the Avignonese Curia, becoming engaged during the early months of 1352 in a feud with one of the pope's physicians that culminated in a polemical pamphlet on the respective values of medicine and poetry: the later introductory book of his *Invective Contra Medicum*. As Wilkins summarizes this period from mid-September 1351 to March 1352: "During these crowded months in Avignon Petrarch can hardly have done much writing other than the writing of letters. He did . . . write a few brief *epistolae metricae,* and may have done a little more work on the *De viris illustribus.* "[49] Last, but not least, he was again cut off during these six months from his library in the Vaucluse.

This lengthy description of the reasons for Petrarch's despair in Avignon during 1351–52 shows that it has nothing in common with his lament in Book II of the *Secretum* against imprisonment in the city. Clearly, the *accidia* section must be interpreted in an altogether different light. We must ask whether there is a time and place other than Petrarch's brief confinement in Avignon in 1351–52 with which the words "urbes relinquere" can be associated. During the second half of 1353, after his return to Italy, Petrarch was living "in urbibus" with the intention of remaining there for the indefinite future. If this was the occasion which inspired the *accidia* section, Franciscus and Augustine could well have had different opinions as to whether there

[48] Ernest H. Wilkins, *Life of Petrarch* (Chicago, 1961), p. 112f.
[49] Ibid., p. 114.

was a chance to leave the city in which Franciscus was residing. Petrarch could easily have conceived the picture of his incarceration "in urbibus" by fusing what he had so recently lived through in the papal city with elements of his present life in Milan.

Of course, the hypothesis that parts of the *Secretum* text were written in 1353 in a city other than Avignon must be proven beyond a doubt. Although the *accidia* section is alone insufficient to do this, the shortly preceding section dedicated to *avaritia* (which is related to the *accidia* section, where *avaritia* also plays an important role) provides the information needed to understand what Petrarch meant when he used the words "urbes relinquere." We must turn our attention, then, to the *avaritia* section.

V

The central theme of Petrarch's discussion of *avaritia* is how he can make the golden mean his standard rather than great wealth or spartan poverty. Franciscus and Augustine agree that he should do so; but what is true "mediocritas"? Are Petrarch's present possessions, which he is anxious to increase, not already far beyond the golden mean? As Augustine says, "why do you continue to torment yourself? If you measure yourself according to your nature, you have already long been rich enough, but if you follow the standard of the world you will never be rich; you will always find something wanting, and in rushing after it you will be swept away by your passion."[50]

At this point, Augustine abruptly interrupts the discussion and reproaches Franciscus for his recent change of heart and style of living, which has corrupted his discernment of true values. The page on which this reproach appears comprises three passages: (a) With no transition from the previous subject, Augustine asks Franciscus whether he does not recall what a different person he was when he roamed his valley and hills, forever occupied with great thoughts, and came home at evening feeling himself the richest and happiest of men. Whereupon Franciscus replies that he "now recalls." (b) Augustine then asserts that it was only when Franciscus began to scorn the simple clothing and food of country people that "in medios urbium tumultus, urgente cupiditate, relapsus es," and that his words and

---

[50] Carrara, p. 86.

looks testify to his present unhappiness. (c) Augustine's concluding words are menacing: God's punishment may be that Franciscus, who was forced to live his youth at another's discretion, will now waste his miserable old age of his own free will."I was present," he adds, "when, still young and unstained by avarice and ambition, you gave promise of becoming a great man; now that you have alas changed your moral conduct [*nunc mutatis moribus*], the nearer you come to the end of your journey the more you trouble yourself about provisions for the way." On the day you die "you will be found, I say, still hungering for gold, poring half-dead over the calendar of your revenues." With this, the *avaritia* section returns to its major theme, what "mediocritas" really means to Petrarch.

This looks to me like the very model of an insertion and a perfectly clear allusion to Petrarch's change of heart and style of living upon leaving the rural solitude of the Vaucluse for city life in Milan.[51] What other meaning could this page have? However, the dating of these additions and a better understanding of their character require a more precise reading of all of them.

VI

(a) Aug.: "Do you remember with what delight you used to wander in the country? At one time . . . you would listen to and drink the water murmuring over the stones; at another, seated on some open hill, you would let your eyes wander freely over the plain stretched at your feet. Then again you would enjoy sweet slumber under the shady trees of the sunny valley, relishing the silence. Never idle, you would always ponder some great thing, with only the Muses for your friends — you were never less alone than in their company. Like the old man in Virgil who reckoned himself

> 'As rich as Kings, when, at the close of day,
>   Home to his cot he took his happy way,
>   And on his table spread his simple fare,
>   Fresh from the meadow without cost or care,'

you would come back to your humble house at sunset. Content with what you had, did you not feel yourself the richest and happiest of mortals?"

---

[51] "Rus" is Petrarch's code word for Vaucluse and "in urbibus" that for Milan in his letters as well. Cf. *Fam.* XXI 13 (11), Milan 1359: "prope alius rure michi videor, alius in urbibus. . . ."

Fr.: "Woe is me! I recall it all now, and the remembrance of that time makes me sigh with grief."[52]

A convincing reality seems to lurk behind this confrontation between Petrarch's memories of his past life and his present longing for it, now that his situation has so greatly changed. There can be no doubt that this idyllic picture depicts his life in the Vaucluse and not an episode of his distant youth before he settled on the Sorgue in 1327, even though the name Vallis Clausa does not appear in the *Secretum* paragraph.[53] For the features of his beloved refuge are apparent throughout: the quiet valley surrounded by hills from which he could look down upon a wide plain (the land around the Rhone) and from which he returned at nightfall to his "angustam domum." (He had never possessed another modest home in such a setting.) There are very similar descriptions in his letters of his actual life in the Vaucluse, above all in a letter (*Fam.* VI 3) probably written in May 1342, in which he describes precisely the same sort of idyllic country existence in order to entice a Roman friend to visit him. His friend will find a man without want and not intent on great gifts of Fortuna, "a solitary country dweller from early morning to evening"; a lover of meadows and hills, "disliking intensely the chores of the Curia, fleeing the tumult of the cities, . . . at leisure all day and night, full of happiness in the company of the Muses, the songs of birds, and the murmur of brooks; with few servants but accompanied by many books; now at home, now walking, now . . . stretching out weary limbs and relaxed head in the grass; and what is not the least part of this solace, no one comes near except very rarely."[54]

---

[52] "Meministi quanta cum voluptate reposto quondam rure vagabaris, et nunc herbosis pratorum thoris accubans murmur aque luctantis hauriebas, nunc apertis collibus residens subiectam planitiem libero metiebaris intuitu; nunc in aprice vallis umbraculo dulci sopore correptus optato silentio fruebaris; nunquam otiosus, mente aliquid altum semper agitans, et, solis Musis comitantibus, nusquam solus? Denique virgiliani senis exemplo qui

    regum equabat opes animo, seraque revertens
    nocte domum, dapibus mensas onerabat inemptis

sub occasum solis angustam domum repetens et tuis contentus bonis, nunquid non tibi omnium mortalium longe ditissimus et plane felicissimus videbaris? Fr.: "Hei michi! nunc recolo, atque illius temporis commemoratione suspiro" (Carrara, p. 86). The translation of the Virgilian verses is that by William H. Draper in his *Petrarch's Secret* (London, 1911), p. 64.

[53] Petrarch's youth before 1327 has been proposed by Rico. We will discuss the consequences presently. See n.56, below.

[54] *Fam.* VI 3 (66–70).

When can the crucial first passage of the *avaritia* page, full of longing for a past existence, have been written? Certainly not in 1347, when Petrarch had finished composing the *De Vita Solitaria* and *De Otio Religioso* and was at the high point of his life in the Vaucluse; and certainly not in the first half of 1353, near the end of the biennium during which he was again living this kind of life and would not have "recalled it with a sigh." The passage must, rather, have been written either in 1349, when Petrarch was living in Parma and often visiting other cities in northern Italy, or in the second half of 1353, when he was in Milan and knew that his life in the Vaucluse would never return.

The choice between these two times should not be difficult. In 1349, as we have seen,[55] Petrarch was leading an agreeable life in the middle-sized cities of Emilia and Romagna and along the Po; he was so happy there that he did not return to the Vaucluse for several years, although nothing prevented him from doing so. He could not possibly have grieved at that time for his past life in the Vaucluse. Only the second half of 1353 remains; which means that the passage reminiscing about the loss of the Vaucluse must have been written in Milan.[56]

---

[55] See pp. 95–97, above, and pp. 223–224, below.

[56] Some comment is needed about why Rico missed this point though it was already clearly made in 1963 (in the first version of my "Petrarch's *Secretum:* Was It Revised — and Why? The Draft of 1342–43 and the Later Changes," *Bibliothèque d'Humanisme et Renaissance* XXV [1963], pp. 489–530). He started from the daring assumption that the rural life depicted on the *avaritia* page reflects not Petrarch's early life in the Vaucluse but an episode of his childhood, presumably during the quadrennium spent in Carpentras, 1312–16. Rico felt entitled to this hypothesis because Augustine, on the same page of the *avaritia* section (Carrara, p. 86), also speaks of a time when Franciscus had been "adhuc adolescentulus." However, there is no indication that the designation "adolescentulus" (applied by Augustine to a period in which Franciscus had not yet developed *cupiditas* or *ambitio*) has any relationship to the time when Franciscus is portrayed as coming home in the evening to his own house, like Virgil's old man in the *Georgics*. The two passages are separated by nearly the length of a page and have nothing in common. Besides, in classical usage "adolescentulus" can be applied to someone over thirty, often even to someone near forty (see Hans Baron, "The Year of Leonardo Bruni's Birth and Methods for Determining the Ages of Humanists Born in the Trecento," *Speculum* LII [1977], p. 606). Sallust (*Catil.* 49) calls Caesar an "adulescentulus" at thirty-three or perhaps thirty-five, an example which must have been known to Petrarch. So even if the term "adolescentulus" on page 86 is connected in some way with the passage we have discussed, Petrarch might have been called an "adolescentulus" ca. 1342, and there is no reason to go back to his school days in Carpentras. Rico is well aware of a

VII

(b) Since you first began to scorn the fruits of your own trees and to find despicable the plain clothing and food of country people, you have again plunged into the tumult of city life, urged on by cupidity, and how happily and tranquilly you pass your time there one reads in your face and speech.[57]

It is impossible to date this sentence to any time before Petrarch had permanently left behind the rustic life of the Vaucluse and his manner of living and dressing had again become citified. As in the case of (a), this nostalgic passage could not have been written in 1351–52 during the six months Petrarch spent in Avignon, nor in

---

parallel problem: the characterization of Petrarch as "nunquam otiosus, mente aliquid altum semper agitans, et, solis Musis comitantibus, nusquam solus" (Carrara, p. 86) clearly would not fit his boyhood days in Carpentras, whereas it does fit the life of the mature Petrarch of ca. 1340. But he argues: since the picture of Petrarch's aspirations (identified with Petrarch's world before 1327) does not agree with what was possible in his boyhood days, we should reason rather that in real life he never had "the idyllic experience" presented in our passage. As a consequence, the assumed move "from the countryside to the cities" is judged as Petrarch's clinging to a medieval conceit without connection to the conditions of his early life. In his actual development, "we cannot find the transition between an habitual peasant life and a sin-ridden return to the city" (*no cabe establecer el tránsito de un vivir campestre habitual a una vuelta empecatada a la ciudad en las circunstancias y a la altura cronológica en que se atribuye a Francesco*). "Everything in Franciscus," says Rico, "is allied to theoretical paradigms and literary designs" such as had dominated literature for centuries. (See Rico, *Lectura,* pp. 160–163 and 519–520.) With all this, Rico is only the most impressive representative of a broader trend in recent criticism. Its first incentive may have come from Francesco Tateo, who maintained in his essay *Dialogo interiore e polemica ideologica nel "Secretum" del Petrarca* (Florence, 1965), p. 37, that the Franciscus of the *Secretum* is not "una figura autobiografica, ma una finzione letteraria, un termine polemico, creato secondo il costume letterario medievale, che oggettivizza umilmente nel personaggio autobiografico la miseria e l'errore." For the recent spread of this school of thought, see also David Marsh, *The Quattrocento Dialogue* (Cambridge, Mass., 1980), p. 35: "The *Secretum* is closely bound to medieval tradition and portrays a symbolic debate in which, as Petrarch observes in the prohemium (p. 26), the figure of Franciscus represents all mankind." Should we begin, under the impact of this school of thought, to believe in a more medieval Petrarch than the one with whom generations of scholars thought they were dealing? The answer depends on our capacity to perceive the realities of Petrarch's inner life, which prove to have much greater significance than his dependence on medieval literary conventions.

[57] "Ex quo primum cepisti ramorum tuorum bachas fastidire amictusque simplicior et agrestium hominum sorduit convictus, in medios urbium tumultus, urgente cupiditate, relapsus es, ubi quam lete quamque tranquille degas frontis tue habitus et verba testantur" (Carrara, p. 86).

1347 when he was still in the Vaucluse, nor in 1349 when he was contentedly living in northern Italy. It must have been written in the second half of 1353.

It has been claimed that in this passage Petrarch wrote fiction in the style of medieval symbolism, largely without regard for the actual conditions of his life.[58] However, there is ample epistolary evidence that he depicted reality. In his earlier correspondence he shows no interest in country dress and food. The first indication of it seems to appear in the ever-informative letter of July 19, 1351, *Fam.* XI 12, where the assertion that his once overpowering thirst for fame has lost its urgency is followed by the remark that "here [in the Vaucluse] everything is the opposite [of his previous life in northern Italy] and, moreover, the coarseness of the rustic food frightens one off" (*et pretecrea ruralis victus deterret austeritas*). In *Fam.* XIII 8, we are given a detailed picture of Petrarch's sojourn in the Vaucluse the summer of the following year. One of its highlights is the description of the stern but kindly demeanor of the old peasant couple who took care of Petrarch's personal needs and small estate. He lives with them, the letter reports, dressing almost like a peasant himself and sharing their coarse bread. "What shall I say about my clothes and shoes? All that is changed. . . . You would take me now for a peasant or shepherd." "I have finally trained my palate and stomach to be satisfied and often even delighted with my herdsman's bread. . . . My overseer, who is devoted to me and is himself a man of iron, quarrels with me only on this score, saying that the food I eat is too coarse for me to tolerate for any length of time. But I am convinced that I can put up with it longer than I could with a delicate diet."[59] His relish in imparting this piece of news suggests that these were fresh experiences and not mere reiterations of something he had already known during his previous stays in the Vaucluse in the 1330s and 1340s.

When Petrarch moved to Milan a year later he began an essentially new way of life in a refined urban milieu, henceforth living in a comfortable house well staffed with servants. We learn from his correspondence that during his early years in Milan he began to pay greater attention to clothes and that this was a change from his former style in the Vaucluse — a change which made him question his

---

[58] This claim is commented upon in n.56, above.
[59] See Baron, *From Petrarch to Leonardo Bruni,* p. 78, n.74.

earlier proclivities. He remarks in a *familiaris* of 1359, in which he recalls his letter of 1352, that what he had reported about his love of plain country dress in the Vaucluse should not be understood as a reflection of innate modesty; it was, rather, the effect of his rural environment. After he moved to Milan, he said, his tastes changed — "prope alius rure michi videor, alius in urbibus" — and only recently had he begun to practice greater simplicity as a principle.[60]

These are vivid images, about whose autobiographical character there should be no doubt. Nor can there be any doubt about the period to which Augustine's criticism — quoted in (b) above — must be ascribed. It is clear that at some point after he had left the Vaucluse behind, Petrarch felt that he had made the wrong choice and that a secret discontent with the simple life of the Vaucluse had driven him from his paradise, sinner that he was, back to the tumult of the cities. This may have been no more than a brief moment of disappointment in his acclimatization to Milanese and north Italian conditions; but however long it lasted, whether months or only weeks, it was then that the *accidia* and *avaritia* sections were extended to include the despairing idea that "avarice" had caused him to "fall back," probably irrevocably, into the noise and restlessness of city life.

Can we be sure that Petrarch experienced such a mood of despair at having robbed himself of the chance to retreat again to the Vaucluse?[61] Such feelings understandably did not come to the fore during the first few weeks and months of his new life. An *epistola metrica* composed during the summer of 1353 (*Metr.* III 18) presents a Petrarch wholly content with his new environment. But by September he was telling Francesco Nelli that many unwanted tasks had replaced the "leisure and sweetness of my beloved solitude." "I had been happy too long and too completely!" Either God or fate or the wantonness of his own nature, he now brooded, had caused him to be untrue to his former intentions — perhaps because, contrary to what he had believed, he had not been free enough of "passion" to live in solitude forever.[62] On the first day of the new year he again wrote, "I do not know whether my own fault or Fortuna has be-

---

[60] *Fam.* XXI 13. See ibid., n.75.
[61] I basically made this claim already in 1963.
[62] *Fam.* XVI 14 (14–15), Missive version.

grudged me my sweet hiding place." Petrarch was now truly looking back with longing to his lost *solitudo* in the Vaucluse. "Since my
youth," he said, "I have been such a great lover of solitude and woods,
and now that I am older I must labor in the city among the crowd,
and I feel ill at ease." Nothing was left to him, he added, but "to
think, in chains, of liberty; in the city, of the country; in labor, of
quietude; and, reversing a dictum of my beloved Scipio Africanus
[i.e., *in otio de negotiis cogitare*], to think of leisure while at work [*in negotiis de otio cogitare*]."[63]

Why have students of the *Secretum* ignored such clear and simple
facts and thereby cast a veil of uncertainty over the vicissitudes of the
text after Petrarch moved to Milan? The cause is undoubtedly a misinterpretation of the third and last of the passages which we have
singled out in the *avaritia* section.

VIII

(c) What miseries have you not endured since then? . . . And still you
hesitate, perhaps because you are held by the bonds of sin and because
God wills that there where you spent your *pueritia* under an alien whip
[*sub aliena ferula*], you will also spend your pitiable *senectus* now that you
are legally your own master.[64]

When and where did Petrarch spend his "pueritia" under "an alien
whip"? Carrara suggests, in the short commentary accompanying
his edition, that Petrarch was "alluding" to Avignon. But he does not
indicate who forced Petrarch to spend his *pueritia* there, or take into
account that almost immediately on their arrival Petrarch's father
had moved his wife and two sons to rural Carpentras, where Petrarch
began his regular schooling. Rico, too, fails to show whose "ferula"
was compelling Petrarch, although he makes Carrara's conjecture
the basis of his thesis that nothing in the *Secretum* text stems from a
time later than Petrarch's biennium in Provence, and that the passage
in question was prompted by Petrarch's fear in February and April
1353 that he would be forced to remain in Avignon permanently.[65]

---

[63] *Fam.* XVII 10 (26–28). See Baron, *From Petrarch to Leonardo Bruni*, p. 80, n.78.

[64] "Quid enim ibi miseriarum non vidisti, . . . et adhuc hesitas, peccatorum forsitan illigatus nexibus, ac favente Deo ut, ubi sub aliena ferula pueritiam exegisti,
ibidem, tui iuris effectus, miserabilem conteras senectutem" (Carrara, p. 86).

[65] Rico, *Lectura,* passim, esp. pp. 345–346, 468–469. ". . . Agustín atemorizaba a
Francesco con la amenaza de que tal vez ('forsitan') fuera voluntad divina dejarle

This question is, of course, a crucial one. If any of the closely connected passages we have quoted could be shown to belong to the time
before Petrarch's departure from Provence in June 1353, it would
inevitably introduce an element of doubt into the thesis that this section of text originated in Milan. But the circumstances in which
alone Petrarch's words make sense are clear and incontestable. Only
once in his life was Petrarch sent to a place against his will, "sub
aliena ferula," namely, when his father sent him to Bologna in 1320
to study law — a career he abandoned immediately on becoming his
own master after his father's death in 1326. Indeed, everything falls
into place when we recall the following facts: although Bologna was
not Milan, it was part of the Milanese state between 1350 and 1360,
that is, at the time when the final version of the *Secretum* was taking
shape. By then Petrarch had chosen to return to the north Italian region to which his father had sent him against his will and from which
he was now beginning to look back longingly to his voluntarily abandoned Vaucluse.

Presumably, scholars would have found this solution to the *sub
aliena ferula* enigma long ago were it not for Petrarch's use of the term
"pueritia." Could he really have used this word to refer to the time of
his university studies in Bologna? He not only could, but does so in
another literary document of the early 1350s, *Fam.* IV 1 on the ascent
of Mont Ventoux. Among his alleged thoughts on the mountaintop
we find him reminiscing about his return to Provence after his father's death: "Hodie decimus annus completur, ex quo, *puerilibus
studiis dismissis* [my emphasis], Bononia excessisti."[66] In other words,
Petrarch thought of his years in Bologna as a preliminary to his real
studies and development and therefore included them in the period
of his "pueritia" instead of the more normal "adolescentia," which is
the term he uses in the original text of *Fam.* VIII 2-5 of 1349 in reference to Bologna: "in qua, ut meministi, primum adolescentie tempus
exegimus."[67] In the *Secretum*, he is contrasting childhood and old age
in a form which he also uses in another work of the period, the *Invective Contra Medicum*. There, speaking of someone else, he says: "ibi

---

apurar una vejez miserable en la misma Avignon donde transcurrió su infancia" (p.
345). To be exact, Petrarch said in his letters at that time only that he might have to
remain in the Vaucluse until conditions changed in Italy.

[66] *Fam.* IV 1 (19).

[67] *Fam.* VIII 2-5 (γ), Rossi's ed., vol. II, p. 201.

senectutem agis, ubi pueritiam exegisti."[68] His use of the word "pueritia" is thus no obstacle to our conclusions.

IX

We have repeatedly become aware of how much depends on the certainty that Petrarch made at least one addition to the *Secretum* after
his return to Italy. In both the present and preceding chapters, we
encountered situations in which all signs pointed to Petrarch's stay
in Milan but in which there was no ultimate certainty as long as not
a single passage could be shown whose composition in Milan was
more than "possible."

A case of such semi-certainty was found in the *accidia* section. The
passages in question made no real sense without the assumption that
Petrarch had moved to the Italian cities but gave no clear proof of
this before the evidence offered by the *avaritia* page was also considered. A similar initial uncertainty prevails in the *Secretum* digression
on human instability and the "deaths" of fame, as well as in the various allusions to the *De Remediis*. All these apparent references to the
Milanese period change from "possible" to "highly probable" once we
are assured in one specific case — the *avaritia* page — that Petrarch
was indeed working on the *Secretum* in Milan. Even the conjecture
that the original draft of the *Secretum* was not taken out of Italy in the
summer of 1351 becomes more acceptable in the light of what we
have learned about the circumstances in which the *avaritia* page was
rewritten. In short, it is difficult to believe that if a page was added
in Milan, others which look as if they were composed there, particularly the part of the *accidia* discussion that is so similar to the *avaritia*
page, were not also inserted in Milan under identical conditions.[69]

[68] *Invective Contra Medicum*, ed. P. G. Ricci (Rome, 1950), p. 75.

[69] The correctness of the general direction of my conclusions is confirmed by some
observations made in the Appendix to Chap. 4 on "Analogies between the *Secretum*
and *Epistolae Familiares* VIII 2–5" (pp. 115–116, above). One is that the final version
of *Fam.* VIII 5, which is related to the 1353 version of the *Secretum,* presupposes a
thorough knowledge of the Lake of Como, which Petrarch did not have prior to the
last months of 1353. Another is that the rewritten text of *Fam.* VIII 5 in all probability did not yet exist when Petrarch left Provence but was composed between
mid-1353 and mid-1356. There seems to be no conceivable way in which these two
situations could have come to pass unless the 1353 form of the *Secretum* — like the last
version of *Fam.* VIII 5 — was composed after Petrarch returned to Italy in mid-1353.
I have refrained from making these observations in the text of the present chapter
because the analysis of the *avaritia* and *accidia* sections seems self-sufficient and ought

(2) A Summary: The Growth of the *Secretum* from 1347 to 1353

With this we have come to the end of our attempt to identify the changes made in the text of the *Secretum* during the years listed in Petrarch's dating note. Let us review these changes one last time before considering the meaning of the *Secretum* and Petrarch's truthfulness in regard to it.

1347

Although it cannot be proven statistically, because minor corrections and polishing are bound to escape our attention, there is no reason to believe that the bulk of the *Secretum* text was ever systematically amended after 1347. We can rely on its early origin, partly because throughout the *Secretum* Franciscus clearly shows himself to be under the impact of *cupiditas gloriae*, whereas this passion no longer dominated Petrarch in 1353, and partly because after 1352 Petrarch had lost the hope of completing the *Africa* and *De Viris* rapidly and consequently cannot have conceived the dialogue's concluding scene as late as 1353.

Moreover, the central subject of the *Secretum* debates remains unchanged throughout the work. By the end of Book I, the pervasive problem has already been tackled, namely, Petrarch's apparent unfitness for spiritual concentration despite his living in an ideal climate of solitude; and at the end of Book III, the proposition to defer a more intense religious life until after the completion of his most important humanistic labors proves to be the logical outcome of the conversation that spans the three books. There are signs pointing to 1347 in each of them. We need not wonder, therefore, whether the gradual process of completing the *Secretum* included major changes in its over-all structure and central theme: as far as these two basic elements are concerned, the *Secretum* is undoubtedly a creation of the year 1347.

1349

But this does not mean that the identification of corrections and additions from later years is relatively unimportant. As Petrarch's

---

to be kept clear of other arguments. But having come to the end of this discussion, the reader should compare the information set forth in the Appendix to Chap. 4.

life changed, its reflection in this book of personal confessions had to change too. Even during the brief two years between 1347 and 1349, Petrarch's existence altered profoundly. One sudden and unexpected change concerned the role of the Seven Deadly Sins in his life. His original point of view had been that he was not a serious sinner; *amor* and *gloria* were the chief causes of his moral lability, but these were not deadly sins. Then, however, a relapse occurred in his sexual behavior, resulting in 1349 in the need to rewrite the *luxuria* paragraph. The original balance of Book II was thereby upset, Petrarch no longer being depicted as almost free of the Seven Deadly Sins. Book II cannot be fully understood unless this reversal is recognized.

By 1349, moreover, Petrarch was no longer living in solitude in the Vaucluse. Although he was still only a visitor to the northern cities of Italy, he had been living in them uninterruptedly since late 1347 and was now guilty of social ambition and tainted by urban life. Thus, in 1349 not only a new *luxuria* paragraph but a section dealing with *ambitio* was added to Book II, and his solitary life in the Vaucluse became a memory of the past. It was then that the "travel page," which exudes a spirit the very opposite of Petrarch's sedentary, reclusive feelings in the Vaucluse, was added to Book III. The resulting contradiction can only be understood when we realize that the *Secretum* reflects successive stages in Petrarch's life.

1353

The new trends that affected the *Secretum* in 1349 continued in 1353, but by that time there was an additional reason for changes: Petrarch was now showing a tendency to conceptualize his inner experience — originally expressed in Augustinian terms — according to the tenets of stoic philosophy. His *De Remediis Utriusque Fortunae,* a piece of genuine stoic philosophy, was probably written between 1354 and 1357. In 1353 this tendency had already begun to influence the final version of the *Secretum;* and since he followed his custom of grouping his insertions in order to interfere as little as possible with the rest of the text, the result was the emergence of a number of recognizable stoic "pockets," dispersed throughout the three books. We have isolated two such areas of stoic thought in Book I, some veiled references to the *De Remediis* in the *accidia* section and an attack against useless knowledge in the *superbia* section of Book II, and a digression dealing with the "three deaths" of fame in Book III — all testifying to the displacement of the Augustinian disciple of 1347 by the philosopher and future author of the *De Remediis.*

It is important to separate this layer of Petrarch's later philosophy from the original core of the *Secretum.* Yet we should not imagine that these intrusions from the *De Remediis* years are as significant for the growth of the *Secretum* as the changes provoked by alterations in Petrarch's environment and conduct. In all three versions of his book, his values and way of life played the foremost role. At the time of the original draft of 1347, Petrarch was — and seemed to himself always to have been — a lover of solitude, and his basic problem was his inability to grow enough spiritually, even as a hermit in the Vaucluse. On the travel page of 1349, on the other hand, Augustine himself sends Petrarch from the Vaucluse to Italy, from sedentary solitude to city life and travels, because solitude and a lack of change in scene are dangerous to a captive of love; and Petrarch now clearly perceives that he had been shunning city life only "dum licuit." In the *avaritia* and *accidia* sections of 1353, Petrarch finds it difficult, if not impossible, to escape from the city life in which he has become ensnared because, in his own judgment, he had been guilty of secret avarice while in the Vaucluse.

In short, it should be amply clear by now that all these interpolations and changes in the *Secretum* text must be read in the light of the specific surroundings in which they were conceived. Otherwise they become sources of the most serious confusion.

CHAPTER SEVEN

The Question of Petrarch's Truthfulness and His Sincerity in Claiming That the *Secretum* Was for His Eyes Alone

(1) The Evidence That Petrarch Did Not Show the *Secretum* to Friends and His Intent in Writing for Himself

I

At several points in our discussion we have touched upon the fact that Petrarch's claim that he would keep his *Secretum* "secret" and not try to gain literary fame with it has been rejected as untrustworthy in recent times. As Rico puts it, the truth is that the *Secretum* was meant "to circulate a predetermined image of Petrarch."[1] Proof that Petrarch never had such an idea in mind is, of course, difficult to produce, but at least one vitally important fact — that he avoided talking about this work — can be established.

We have already seen that Petrarch did not refer to the *Secretum* in any of the works in which such references have been suspected;[2] conversely, there is one case where we would expect him to name the *Secretum*, and yet he is silent. In *Fam.* VIII 2–5 (the report of his endeavor to settle down with three friends in a shared household and of its unfortunate outcome) he offers a list of those of his writings which were inspired by the solitude of the Vaucluse; and since we have the original, May 1349, version of this letter as well as the text in the book edition of the *Familiares* of about 1354–55, we know what Petrarch told others at two different times in his life about the inspiration of the Vaucluse on his writings. In 1349 he mentioned the *Africa*, the *Bucolicum Carmen*, and his *Vulgaria Cantica* (the *Rime*) as having been conceived largely in the Vaucluse. In 1354–55 he added a

---

[1] "... mientras buen número de otros factores únicamente tiene sentido en la medida en que pretende divulgar una determinada imagen de Petrarca" (Rico, *Lectura*, pp. 32–33).

[2] See Chap. 1 (3) and the Appendix to Chap. 1, above.

longer list of items to these three, which is so exhaustive that it is obvious he intended it to be reasonably complete. In addition to his letters (the *Familiares* and *Metricae*), he named three other books: the expanded version of the *De Viris,* the *De Vita Solitaria,* and the *De Otio Religioso.*[3] The one work missing in both versions of *Fam.* VIII 2–5 is the *Secretum.* Is this omission what one would expect for a work that Petrarch longed to bring to the attention of his contemporaries? Is it not, rather, what one would expect for a work he intended to keep "secret"?

Now, it is only fair to state that the belief in frequent references and allusions to the *Secretum* would hardly have arisen in the first place if it were not obvious that three of Petrarch's closest friends — Boccaccio, Nelli, and Barbato da Sulmona — did know that Petrarch had composed a work identifiable as the *Secretum.* "To be sure," said Rico when he drew attention to this information, "the *Secretum* does not seem to have circulated during the lifetime of its author, but everyone knows that 'he constantly refused to release the master copies of his writings.'"[4] On the other hand, "he did announce [*anunció*] the *Secretum* on repeated occasions [refuted in our first chapter], and in fact Boccaccio knew of the book [*sabia del libro*] between 1347 and 1350, when it was still in first or second draft."[5]

A more realistic assessment of Boccaccio's information would be something like the following. We can establish with near certainty that his original knowledge of the *Secretum* was not due to any written "anuncios" of Petrarch's to him or any oral communication beween them. For Boccaccio's earliest allusion to the *Secretum* in the first draft of his *De Vita et Moribus Domini Francisci Petrarchi de Florentia* — the so-called "Notamentum" in his miscellany volume Ms. Laur. lat. XXIX, 8 — was made in 1347, only weeks or months after the first drafting of the *Secretum,* whereas Petrarch and Boccaccio did not have any personal contact until the summer of 1350. The puzzle of how Petrarch's literary efforts in the Vaucluse could, in these circumstances, have become known to Boccaccio in Florence in 1347 was solved by Wilkins not many years ago. An intimate friend of Petrarch's — "Lelius," with whom he was in close contact in Provence during the

---

[3] *Fam.* VIII 2–5, Rossi's ed., vol. II, pp. 160, 198.
[4] Rico, *Lectura,* p. 33.
[5] Rico, *Lectura,* p. 33.

spring of 1347 — traveled to Naples that summer, and it is reasonable to think that he stopped in Florence and brought the latest news to Petrarch's Florentine circle of friends. Much of the information in Boccaccio's *vita* of Petrarch, Wilkins tells us, "points to someone who had known Petrarch's life at Vaucluse; and as far as we know the only person who had such knowledge and could have passed it on to Boccaccio was Laelius."[6] Now, what we read in Boccaccio's "Notamentum" touching upon the *Secretum* is that "Petrarch has composed the following works: An *Africa* in verse, a dialogue in prose, and others."[7] No one has ever doubted that this "dialogue" can only be the *Secretum*.

For our purposes, of course, we must try to determine whether Boccaccio had any concrete knowledge of the *Secretum* which could not have come to him through such channels as the talk of an occasional traveler. For the maximum extent of his information we may consult the final text of his *vita* of Petrarch, finished a year or two after the "Notamentum": "In addition, he [Petrarch] produced a dialogue in prose embellished by such marvelous and artistic beauty of speech that it appears beyond any doubt that nothing which Cicero could have had in his mental armory has escaped him."[8] This is all we need to be certain that Petrarch had not given away the least bit of solid information on the nature of his work. When he found it necessary to respond to his friend Lelius' questions about what he was writing (or had just written), he evidently said only that he was working on a dialogue in Cicero's style and trying to apply whatever he could learn from the Ciceronian model. If he gave a demonstration of this style, it was not extended to the content.

Boccaccio's *vita* is also valuable in that it gives us a distinct answer to Rico's query whether there is, after all, any real difference in intention between Petrarch's general habit of not permitting copies of his major works to be made for many years (or even during his lifetime) and the words he addressed to his *Secretum:* "so I bid you, little

---

[6] Ernest H. Wilkins, "Boccaccio's Early Tributes to Petrarch," *Speculum* XXXVIII (1963), pp. 84–85.

[7] "Composuit quidem usque in hodiernum diem libros, videlicet *Affricam* metrice, dyalagum [*sic*] quendam prosaice et alios" (Giovanni Boccaccio, *Opere latine minori,* ed. A. F. Massèra, Scrittori d'Italia 3 [Bari, 1928], p. 366).

[8] Petrarch "insuper edidit dialogum quendam prosayce tam mira ac artificiosa sermonum pulcritudine decoratum, ut appareat liquido, nil eum quod Tullius arpinas noverit latuisse" (ibid., p. 244).

book, to flee the company of people and be content to stay with me, true to your name; for, my 'secret' you are and will be called, and when I am occupied with higher things, everything spoken in seclusion, which you remember, you will in seclusion recall to me."[9] The difference becomes clear when we compare Boccaccio's vague and formal remarks on the "dialogue" in his *vita* with his detailed and reliable description of the *Africa*, a work which Petrarch likewise did not release for copying during his lifetime: "He wrote that outstanding work in which — in heroic poetry and diction, with admirable artistic richness — he dealt with the deeds of Scipio the elder against the Carthaginians, especially Hannibal their leader, and with the wondrous virtue of Scipio's thoughts and actions; a work which he named the *Africa*, because [Scipio] Africanus' deeds in Africa are mainly discussed, and which he dedicated to King Robert [of Naples]. . . ." To this precise characterization of the *Africa* Boccaccio added: "And although no copy of the aforesaid work has yet been conceded by him [Petrarch] to anyone, nevertheless it is considered by many to make a Homer-like impression."[10] Surely, we cannot disregard the inevitable disparity between the author's way of dealing with a work not yet released but freely discussed with his friends (so much so that in 1341 Petrarch was crowned as the poet of the unfinished and unpublished *Africa*) and a work about whose nature and intention his first biographer (in 1347) was unable to learn anything but that it was modeled on Ciceronian dialogues.

Do the other two references to the *Secretum* made by friends during Petrarch's lifetime — those of Francesco Nelli and Barbato da Sulmona — belie the conclusion that Petrarch kept all detailed information about the work to himself? "Nelli," says Rico, "hoped to see it [the *Secretum*] in 1354."[11] This is correct. We would be much mis-

---

[9]"Tuque ... libelle, conventus hominum fugiens, mecum mansisse contentus eris ... ut unumquodque in abdito dictum meministi, in abdito memorabis" (Carrara, p. 26).

[10]"Nam primo et principaliter opus illud egregium compilavit, in quo heroyco carmine ac oratione arte multiplici admiranda, Scipionis primi gesta in cartaginenses potissime et Annibalem eorum ducem penosque reliquos mira virtute tam animi quam corporis operando tractavit, cui eo nomen imposuit *Affrica*, quia de Affricani et in Affrica rebus gestis loquatur ut plurimum, intitulavitque illud Roberto regi ... et quamvis predicti libri adhuc ab eo [Petrarch] nemini copia concedatur, tamen a multis visus homericus reputatur" (Boccaccio, *Opere latine minori*, p. 243f.).

[11]"Nelli esperaba verlo en 1354 ..." (Rico, *Lectura*, p. 33).

taken, however, if we took the statement to imply that Nelli knew anything about the nature of the work he wanted to see. What he asked Petrarch was only, as he put it, to "tell me, when can I read you in your *Africa?* when in all the parts of the *Bucolicum Carmen?* when in comedies? and in the dialogue?"[12] To be sure, Nelli was aware of the existence of the work which we know as the *Secretum,* but this does not allow us to assume that Petrarch was his source of information or that any knowledge of the *Secretum* was the common property of Petrarch's circle of friends.

Since the Florentines Nelli and Boccaccio were close neighbors and friends, we can venture the theory that Nelli was merely repeating what Boccaccio had written in his *vita* about six years before. To ascertain whether Nelli was influenced by this source is not beyond our reach, especially in view of his inclusion of such a rare item as Petrarch's early "comedy," a lost work presumably already discarded by its author in 1354. If we consult the short annotated bibliography of Petrarch's writings at the end of Boccaccio's *vita,* we find that this comedy (erroneously called "Philostratus" instead of "Philologia") is given special merit; it is a "pulcerrima comedia," which Boccaccio hesitates to call a work "in the manner of Terence," because this would blur the fact that Petrarch was "merito preponendus."[13]

Boccaccio's high appraisal, then, explains why Nelli was so eager to read Petrarch even "in comediis." Thus encouraged to assume that Nelli depended on Boccaccio, we proceed to a closer comparison of Boccaccio's bibliography and Nelli's short list of desiderata. Both enumerate the same three major works, that is, the *Africa,* the *Dialogus,* and Petrarch's "comedia," the only difference being that Boccaccio adds the second *Eclogue* (one of the pieces which were to form the later *Bucolicum Carmen*) and alludes to a few of Petrarch's *epistolae metricae,* while Nelli's list includes the collection of the *Bucolicum Carmen* in book form[14] and omits any reference to *epistolae metricae.* This

[12] "Dic michi quando te in Affrica tua legam? quando in buccolicis omnibus? quando in comediis? et dyalogo?" (*Un ami de Pétrarque,* ed. Henry Cochin [Paris, 1892], p. 217).

[13] A parallel to this influence of Boccaccio's note concerning Petrarch's comedy is the request of Lapo da Castiglionchio, another member of Petrarch's Florentine circle, for a copy of the comedy in 1351, two or three years after the composition of Boccaccio's *De Vita.* See Ernest H. Wilkins, *Life of Petrarch* (Chicago, 1961), p. 102.

[14] "Buccolicis omnibus." The volume was put together between 1347 and 1354.

omission is easily understandable, for Nelli's name does not appear among the receivers mentioned in the three books of the *Metricae*. He consequently could not entertain any illusion that after they were collected Petrarch might choose to dedicate or send a special copy of the *Metricae* to him.

Except for these minor differences, Nelli simply copied Boccaccio's list of three major works, asking Petrarch soon after the latter had settled in Milan whether any of the three were now accessible and could be sent to Florence. Thus, the inclusion of the *Secretum* in Nelli's list of desiderata does not provide evidence that he had seen the work or heard anything about it from Petrarch. Relying as Nelli's letter does on Boccaccio's bibliographical information, it is no more than a footnote to the history of the circulation of Boccaccio's *vita*. In other words, since we have already ascertained that in Boccaccio's case Petrarch cannot have divulged anything concerning the nature of his unpublished work, the short record of known situations in which he might have talked about his "secret" to friends has shrunk to one: that connected with the name of Barbato of Sulmona. His would thus be a unique case in which Petrarch reneged on his promise in the *Secretum* proem — unless a careful analysis of Barbato's words should reveal that he, too, was ignorant of the vital features of Petrarch's work.

In Rico's eyes, Barbato is "el unico amigo que in vida de Petrarca *muestra un conocimiento exacto* [my emphasis]" of the *Secretum*.[15] Yet it seems to me highly questionable whether one can ascribe to him even a superficial knowledge of the work, if knowledge means more than hearsay. Early in 1361 Barbato pointed an accusing finger at Petrarch, claiming he had received a promise in Petrarch's own hand that copies of the "magnum opus" of the *Africa* and of the collected *Epistolae Metricae* (which had been dedicated to Barbato) would be sent to him. In the end, however, Barbato lost courage: "But if my own unworthiness gets in the way of my wish to receive such magna opera," he wrote, he would ask Petrarch to be good enough to send him at least "libellum illum trialogum *de conflictu curarum*," which would have been welcome to him at any time, but was especially so now that he had himself entered old age.[16]

---

[15] Rico, *Lectura*, p. 508.

[16] "... sed si tam magnis habendis operibus mea repugnat indignitas, saltem li-

On the surface it appears reasonable to argue that this passage shows a deeper knowledge of the *Secretum* than Boccaccio's and Nelli's, who used the generic term "dialogus" as a title and quite possibly had never heard of the heading "De conflictu curarum" or the division of Petrarch's "libellus" into three parts.[17] But knowledge of the phrasing used in a title and the number of subdivisions of a literary work is not the same as "un conocimiento exacto de la obra." When Boccaccio had written about a "dialogus" nearly fifteen years before, he had intended to convey that Petrarch was resurrecting the art form of the Ciceronian dialogue. Even though the experiences and ideas dealt with in the *Secretum* have little to do with this, the novelty of restoring the ancient dialogue as a literary form and as a humane exchange of personal opinions was, after all, one of its significant aspects.[18]

If Barbato had been familiar with Boccaccio's *vita* and his appreciation of the role of the dialogue form in Petrarch's work, it seems to me quite improbable that he would have replaced the key word "dialogus" by the word "trialogus," with its reference to the number of books. The use of "trialogus" implies that Barbato's notion did not rest on deeper knowledge of the *Secretum* than Boccaccio's did. Of course, someone — conceivably Petrarch in a letter — must have told Barbato that the work was tripartite and that the title included the words "de conflictu curarum." But not even the latter information would have revealed anything about its real nature. Barbato's designation of a "libellum illum trialogum *de conflictu curarum*" does not

---

bellum illum trialogum *de conflictu curarum,* semper mihi gratissimum, sed nunc senescenti perutilem, ut mictere digneris exoro" (in Marco Vattasso, *Del Petrarca e di alcuni suoi amici,* Studi e Testi 14 [Rome, 1904], p. 14).

[17] That "trialogus" means a three-unit work and cannot be a reference to the circumstance that Veritas is a third, silent partner in the *Secretum* seems to me self-evident, even though Du Cange defines the term as conversation between three persons. Rico is of the same opinion, dismissing Du Cange in this case. Perhaps one should add, in order to illustrate fourteenth-century usage, that when Wyclif was occupied with a systematic presentation of his theology in three parts, toward the end of the century, he gave this work the title "trialogus."

[18] Cf. the appropriate estimate of Petrarch's transitional position in David Marsh, *The Quattrocento Dialogue* (Cambridge, Mass., 1980), p. 44: "In several respects, then, Petrarch's *Secretum* anticipates the relativity and freedom of discussions in quattrocento humanist dialogues. Yet the structure of the work still adheres to the pattern of instructive exchange represented in Christian dialogues from Augustine onwards. ... Because the *Secretum* deals with the introspective problems of Petrarch's spiritual crisis, it also lacks the social dimension which shaped the ... quattrocento dialogue."

give cause to assert that he "da el titulo correctamente,"[19] since the true title of Petrarch's work is "De conflictu curarum suarum" (or "mearum"). Unaware of the possessive pronoun, Barbato was also unaware that the *Secretum* is an autobiographical work. As Rico notes correctly, Barbato's phrasing shows that he presumed he was asking Petrarch for some didactic guide or preparation for old age which would prove to be especially helpful now that Barbato was himself becoming old ("semper mihi gratissimum, sed nunc senescenti per-utilem").[20] We have no reason to believe, therefore, that Barbato was given any clearer idea of the personal and confessional nature of Petrarch's work than were Boccaccio and Nelli. Far from "announc-ing" his work to friends in violation of his promise in the proem of the *Secretum*, Petrarch managed to keep his secret so well that everyone was left to make his own guesses, and no one, we must conclude, was able to penetrate his taciturnity.

II

One might ask, of course, why Petrarch alluded to his work at all if he was unwilling to talk about it. However, it is not difficult to imag-ine how, hard-pressed by Lelius (or whoever informed Boccaccio and Barbato), he cautiously said a word or two about the work on which he was engaged, choosing to satisfy his interrogator's curiosity by disclosing something about its literary (that is, Ciceronian) quali-ties, as echoed in Boccaccio's *vita*. When we recall that Petrarch spent some time working on the *Secretum* during three separate periods be-tween 1347 and 1353, that he often had friends staying in his home and spent evenings with them discussing literary concerns, and that his enormous correspondence often gave an account of how his time was spent, it is obvious that at least some remarks about a work on which he was engaged for weeks at a time must have been un-avoidable.

Our information is rich enough to let us recognize how generously on such occasions Petrarch allowed his closest friends to look into the work he was doing and discuss problems of publication with him. By 1361, when Barbato made his remarks on the *Secretum*, Boccaccio had already copied some of Petrarch's writings from the originals in his

[19] Rico, *Lectura,* p. 508, n.189.
[20] Ibid., p. 508.

study and talked with him about the possibility or infeasibility of re-
leasing others. Boccaccio visited Petrarch in his house in Milan in
the spring of 1359, and among the works he transcribed there was the
Bucolicum Carmen, for which Nelli had been waiting since 1354. In the
late 1350s, exchanges between Petrarch and his friends figured constantly in his decisions whether his nearly finished works should ultimately be released or judged incurable. The book edition of the *Epistolae Metricae,* which Petrarch had planned to dedicate to Barbato,
was abandoned, and thus another item was added to the list of writings never to be released in Petrarch's lifetime.[21] The most painful
decision of all concerned the *Africa.* Boccaccio himself tells us that he
"did everything he could" during his visit to Milan in 1359 to convince Petrarch that "Scipio . . . should be released from his [long]
confinement and brought forth to public view. But it was all in vain,
since Petrarch adduced many arguments to the contrary."[22]

Boccaccio and Barbato were the most active of Petrarch's friends
in exerting pressure with regard to the *Africa.* In 1361, a group of influential Neapolitan friends planned to change Petrarch's mind with
a communal letter "de publicanda *Africa*"; it was to be sent to Boccaccio with the request that he inform Petrarch about their point of
view. The letter stated that if Petrarch really contemplated leaving
his epic poem unpublished, he should also consider that he had
already robbed his many deceased friends of it and that some unexpected mishap might destroy his plans to have his unfinished
works published posthumously.[23]

These known examples of influence exerted by Petrarch's friends
during the years in which the fate of several of his major works was
being decided give us considerable insight into the circumstances
surrounding their completion and thus the means to make comparisons with the particular situation of the *Secretum.* One might say, no
doubt, that the histories of the *Secretum* and of works like the *Africa*
are similar in so far as their existence was known to Petrarch's friends

[21] See Francesco Petrarca, *Rime, trionfi e poesie latine,* ed. Ferdinando Neri et al.
(Milan, 1951), pp. 865–866.
[22] Ernest H. Wilkins, *Petrarch's Eight Years in Milan* (Cambridge, Mass., 1958), p.
182. Barbato learned all this from a letter written by Boccaccio a few years later. See
Boccaccio's *Epistola* XI of 1362 to Barbato in Boccaccio, *Opere latine minori,* pp. 144–
146.
[23] Ernest H. Wilkins, *Studies in the Life and Works of Petrarch* (Cambridge, Mass.,
1955), pp. 248–250.

during his lifetime and their publication was left to later editors; but the active involvement of his friends in the vicissitudes of the *Africa* illustrates especially well that the *Secretum*, both during its incubation and after its completion, was indeed in a class by itself. Whereas his friends were kept informed about the nature of the *Africa* both orally and in letters, and were even given samples to read, their confusion in the case of the "dialogus," or "trialogus," was such that Petrarch cannot have been a cooperative informant. In a word, his avoidance of relevant details can only be interpreted as proof that he was doing his best to live up to the promise implied in the proem of the *Secretum*, even when he was strongly pressed to divulge more.

III

Why has this vital difference been overlooked by scholars in recent years? The answer is that Petrarch's honesty is now widely distrusted, and a contribution to one of the festschriften of the Petrarch year, 1974, has drawn attention to some major reasons for this. "One quite justly distrusts Petrarch's contention that he did not want the *Secretum* to be counted among his usual writings," says Erich Loos; "he wished to keep it 'secret' because he had greater plans for it. It is self-evident [*selbstverständlich*] that the purely technical references in the proem to the niceties of composition along with the artistry of the *Secretum* dialogues presuppose that the author expected this work to be read."[24] About the same time, Rico expressed a like opinion. "The whole artful literary elaboration of the work," he said, "cannot be explained otherwise than that it was intended for the enjoyment of readers." And as we know, he concluded that we have to assume the very opposite of what Petrarch asks us to believe: that the key to the *Secretum* is an intention on the author's part to "divulgar una determinada imagen de Petrarca."[25]

Do we have any reliable way of judging between the opposing claims of Petrarch and his recent critics? When in the prohemium he asks his "secret" not to strive for glory like his other works but to remain with him "in seclusion" (*in abdito*) — "conventus hominum fu-

---

[24]"Die Hauptsünde der *acedia* in Dantes *Commedia* und Petrarcas *Secretum*," in *Petrarca 1304–1374: Beiträge zu Werk und Wirkung*, ed. Fritz Schalk (Frankfurt am Main, 1975), p. 172.

[25]"... valga solo insinuar que toda la artificiosa elaboración literaria de la obra no se explica sino dirigida al paladeo del lector ..." (Rico, *Lectura*, p. 32). See also n.1, above.

giens" — he is admitting in so many words that he expects a different reward: that the great delight its composition has given him will return whenever he rereads the book. As he puts it, he is writing his work "in order to recapture when I read it the sweetness I once felt when I composed it."[26] One may wonder how Petrarch could have derived such "sweetness" from the composition of a work which largely delves into the weaknesses and sins that could prevent his salvation. Undoubtedly, the sweetness must have lain in his relationship with Augustine — who is presented more as a paternal friend than a saint and austere father of the church — a relationship that Petrarch humanized by recreating the form and spirit of equality characteristic of Ciceronian conversations. Its tenor is perhaps best expressed in a letter from the *Secretum* years, in which Petrarch justifies his boldness in viewing his bond with Augustine as a connection based on mutual "love." When Augustine was still on earth, Petrarch tells us, he wrote in his *De Vera Religione* that he was certain every angel who loved God also loved him. "And I, who am human," Petrarch adds, "also dare to hope for the human love of that most holy soul, which now enjoys heaven."[27]

But can we be sure that Petrarch's alleged intention to write for himself — in order to recapture the sweetness he once felt — is more than a rhetorical artifice? In the very period in which the *Secretum* was being written, Petrarch gave several demonstrations of his awareness that literary success and "glory" were far from being the only, or even the strongest drives in his personal experience. Thus in the 1340s[28] he explained what inspired him in his work: "I write a great deal not to be of any particular use to my times . . . but to unburden myself of ideas and console my mind with writing."[29] And in Italy, during the autumn of 1353, looking back over his years of passionate longing for the "ruralis vita," he wrote in *Fam.* XVII 5 — which contains perhaps the closest parallel to the statement made in the proem

[26]"Non quem annumerari aliis operibus meis velim, aut unde gloriam petam . . . sed ut dulcedinem, quam semel ex collocutione percepi, quotiens libuerit ex lectione percipiam" (Carrara, p. 26).

[27]". . . audebo et ego, qui homo sum, amorem humanum anime illius sacratissime, que nunc celo fruitur, sperare" (*Fam.* II 9 [15], ca. 1352).

[28]In *Fam.* VI 4. See next note.

[29]"Multa . . . scribo, non tam ut seculo meo prosim, cuius iam desperata miseria est, quam ut me ipsum conceptis exhonerem et animum scriptis soler" (*Fam.* VI 4 [10]; trans. Aldo S. Bernardo, in Francesco Petrarca, *Rerum familiarium libri I–VIII* [Albany, N.Y., 1975], p. 314).

of the *Secretum* — that much of his work on the *De Vita Solitaria* and *De Otio Religioso* was due to fear that if he did not record it, he might in the future lose the most deep-seated of his emotions, his longing for *solitudo* and *otium,* "on each of which I composed a separate treatise in the past, not so much for others as for myself, lest the forgetfulness that comes from continued silence should permit my mind to become entangled in new passions."[30] This is certainly a relevant response to the suspicion that Petrarch would not have written such an elaborate work as the *Secretum* had he not been planning to publish it.

We must still consider what might have happened to Petrarch's promised "secrecy" if he had succeeded in carrying out his plan to add to the *Secretum* three books about his "secret inner peace." Could this be the key to the introductory contention that the *Secretum* was to remain with him? Was it to be kept secret because he did not want it to circulate until he could add the books that would proclaim his inner victory? The answer to these questions is that we have not a shred of evidence that the plan to compose a second series of books already existed in Petrarch's mind when the *Secretum* proem was being written. Our evidence of this plan — the title of the *Secretum* autograph, "facturus totidem libros de secreta pace animi," and the marginal note of 1358 — does not predate the 1350s. On the other hand, nothing in the proem makes it improbable that the lines dealing with the secrecy of Petrarch's work derive from 1347 or 1349. Petrarch most probably had not yet conceived his plan to add three books when he stated his intention not to circulate the *Secretum*, and we have no reason to think that his statement was insincere.

(2) Why the Report of the Ascent of Mont Ventoux Is Not Pure Fiction: A Further Criticism of the View That Petrarch Lied about His Life

I

To refute the belief that Petrarch disguised an intent to make the *Secretum* public is not to deny that the work contains ambiguities which were neglected in *Secretum* studies before Rico's research appeared.

---

[30] "Is est autem otii ac solitudinis appetitus, de quibus hactenus singulos tractatus edidi non tam aliis quam michi, ne forte silentium oblivio consecuta novis animum implicaret affectibus . . ." (*Fam.* XVII 5 [3], October 1353).

Quite the contrary, it would be a disservice to scholarship not to agree emphatically that we are today in a position to ask more subtle questions than in the past. Attention can now be turned to the fact that everything concerning the date of the conversation between Petrarch and his unearthly partner, Augustine, is a product of Petrarch's imagination; we are aware, too, that the chronology of his spiritual life — not only in his fictitious letters but also in the autobiographical sections of his other works — has been modeled on Augustine's development.

That this knowledge can help us avoid anachronistic interpretations of the *Secretum* there is no doubt, but the question must still be posed to what extent the changes in Petrarch's thinking are bound to affect our long-standing image of him as it is derived from the *Secretum*. If Petrarch were to reveal himself to be as insincere as Rico and some others before him assume, we might have reason to think that he was unscrupulously falsifying his image. But since the supposition that he frequently talked about his "secret" to friends has proved false, one of the major reasons for distrusting him has disappeared. In the circumstances, the thesis that Petrarch tended to mislead his readers becomes nothing more than an intriguing hypothesis, whose correctness or incorrectness must be determined case by case.

II

Rico never tires of emphasizing that Petrarch's letter on his ascent of Mont Ventoux and the final version of the *Secretum* were written during the same period, in 1352–53; they are inextricably tied together, we are told.[31] This implies that *Fam.* IV 1 can serve as a key to the study of the *Secretum*, and Rico makes use of the parallel to gain evidence for Petrarch's insincerity. He cites Giuseppe Billanovich, who admitted, when discussing the fictitiousness of Petrarch's report of the ascent, that "the neat precision of some particulars" in Petrarch's account "seems to confirm that he really carried out the excursion."[32]

---

[31] Rico, *Lectura,* pp. 73f., 76, 193, 473.

[32] Giuseppe Billanovich, "Petrarca e il Ventoso," *Italia Medioevale e Umanistica* IX (1966), p. 401. Previously, Billanovich had minimized the weight of Petrarch's report: "... anche se durante i molti anni in cui dimorò in Provenza egli possa avere compiuto, del tutto o in parte, l'ascensione al monte famoso nella regione" (*Petrarca letterato,* vol. I, *Lo scrittoio del Petrarca,* Edizioni di "Storia e Letteratura" 16 [Rome, 1947], p. 195).

But Billanovich remains unconvinced of Petrarch's truthfulness: despite its alleged date of 1336, the letter can be regarded for all practical purposes as a composition of the period 1352–53; the companionship of Gherardo on the ascent is questionable, and "it is vain to try to discern when and with whom he could have carried out his enterprise." Moreover, the role played by Augustine's *Confessions* in the scene on the mountaintop is merely rhetorical. Petrarch's alleged consultation of a pocket edition of the *Confessions,* Billanovich suggests, is nothing but a literary device that carries on a long medieval tradition: testing by "sortes biblicae," with the one change that the random opening of the Pauline letters to find a sign of divine will is now replaced by "sortes Augustinianae." "And naturally," Billanovich adds with some mockery, "he used the ritual protestation as an introduction — which may scandalize those who are no experts in rhetoric! — : 'Deum testor . . . that where I first turned my eyes it was written. . . .'"[33]

So far as I can judge, the observation that Petrarch's use of "sortes Augustinianae" basically carries on a medieval custom by no means confirms the fictitiousness of the narrated happenings on Mont Ventoux. Since Petrarch knew that pious readers put the Bible, and especially the Pauline letters, to this use, why should he not have done the same with his own favorite book, the *Confessions,* on the day of the ascent? He knew the *Confessions* well enough to be aware of what he could expect in the tenth book, and he may easily have given a helping hand to chance and thus have found the passage that so perfectly suited his situation.

If we want to find out whether we can trust Petrarch's contention that what he tells us really happened, we must search for personal and truly Petrarchan features in his report. There are, indeed, a few such traits. For instance, in the context of the letter, Petrarch's appeal to "witnesses" who know he is speaking the truth does not look like a mere rhetorical formula; besides God, Petrarch names his own brother, Gherardo, as an observer of his action. As Petrarch describes his "sortes Augustinianae": "My brother stood by attentively to hear me read something from Augustine. May God and my own

---

[33]"Naturalmente premise lo scongiuro rituale — se ne scandalizzino gli inesperti di retorica! — : 'Deum testor . . . , quod ubi primum defixi oculos, scriptum erat . . .'" (Billanovich, "Petrarca e il Ventoso," *passim,* esp. pp. 393, 401).

brother be my witnesses that where I first turned my eyes it was written: 'And people go to admire the summits of mountains and the vast billows of the sea and the broadest rivers . . . and they overlook themselves.' I confess that I was stupefied, and hearing my eager brother ask for more, I begged him not to annoy me and closed the book."[34]

By the early 1350s, Gherardo had long been leading an exemplary life as a Carthusian monk; in a letter of about 1352, for example, Petrarch describes Gherardo's selfless courage during a plague. The two brothers were in epistolary and personal contact during those years. Petrarch visited Gherardo in his Carthusian monastery at Montrieux in 1347, and in 1352 he tried again to see him but was forced to turn back because the roads were unsafe. He did see Gherardo, however, in February 1353 and talked with him about Augustine's *Confessions,* among other things. We know this because Gherardo asked Petrarch to send him a copy as a gift. How should we imagine that conversation? Did Petrarch tell Gherardo that he was currently writing, or planning to write, a fictitious letter in which he called him and God as witnesses to a scene on a mountaintop? Did he inform his saintly brother that he was presenting him falsely as his companion on a mountain climb in 1336 and deceiving his readers by writing "Deum testor ipsumque qui aderat"? Or did he perhaps hide what he was doing from his brother, preferring to run the risk that some monastic reader of *Fam.* IV 1 might later learn from Gherardo that he had not been Petrarch's companion at all?[35] Would it not be more reasonable to conclude that the known contacts between Petrarch and Gherardo at the time *Fam.* IV 1 was being composed and our knowledge that they talked about Augustine's *Confessions* make it improbable that Petrarch would have referred to his brother had he not actually been his companion and "witness" on that ascent?

Among other observations which add to the force of this reasoning, the following comes especially to mind. However lightly the

---

[34] Gherardo, "expectans per os meum ab Augustino aliquid audire, intentis auribus stabat. Deum testor ipsumque qui aderat, quod ubi primum defixi oculos, scriptum erat: 'Et eunt homines admirari alta montium . . . et relinquunt se ipsos.' Obstupui, fateor; audiendique avidum fratrem rogans ne michi molestus esset, librum clausi . . ." (*Fam.* IV 1 [27]; trans. Bernardo, in Petrarca, *Rerum familiarium,* p. 178, with some changes).

[35] Billanovich himself observed that by addressing his fictive letters to people who were already dead when the letters were actually written Petrarch carefully avoided the danger of being exposed as a teller of tales.

words "Deum testor" may occasionally have been taken by others, one would not expect a frivolous use of the formula by an author who on other occasions took such affirmations very seriously, for instance, when he wrote to Boccaccio in 1366: "Christ, my liberator, knows that I speak the truth; he who, when tearfully implored, often gave me his hand while I wept in misery, and himself held me up."[36] We even have Petrarch's account of the source of his religious seriousness on such occasions. About 1348 he advised in a letter that an admirer of classical literature should choose one of the great ancient writers or statesmen and think of him as always present in his life and a witness of his every thought and action, though, he added, Christians may not need this device, since to them Christ himself is always present.[37] Later, he inserted a more detailed version of his advice into the then still unreleased text of the *De Vita Solitaria,* in which he remarked that Christians, although they would do well to follow the ethical prescriptions of the ancients, are after all not bound to choose a human being for such a role, because they have ever-present witnesses in God and Christ: "Since we have the Father who judges us as witness, we are in no need of any imaginary [ancient] witness." "Christ himself is present in all places and at all times, as a true witness of all our thoughts and actions. . . . I would direct attention to this point and ponder it. . . . Every Christian is certain that Christ in person is always present in the innermost recesses of the soul. . . . It is a delusion if, because we do not see with our eyes the presence which we acknowledge in our hearts, we slip back into the error for which Cicero, who surely did not know Christ, rebuked the ancients when he said that they saw nothing with their minds but referred everything to their eyes." What a shame, "if Christ looks on, to live and die badly, or to commit any base or dishonorable deed in so awful a presence."[38]

[36]"Scit me Christus liberator meus verum loqui, qui sepe mihi cum lachrymis exoratus, flenti ac misero dextram dedit secumque me sustulit ..." (*Sen.* VIII 1, *Opera omnia* [Basel, 1554], p. 915). This was confessed to Boccaccio concerning the late date of Petrarch's achieving chastity. See p. 212, below.

[37]*Fam.* X 3, to Gherardo. See the passages in *Prose,* pp. 934–936.

[38]"Habentes ergo testem Patrem iudicem, teste [humano] illo imaginario non egemus...." "... Cristus ipse locis omnibus atque temporibus est presens, non actuum sed et cogitatuum omnium verus testis.... Figere hic animum libet et cogitare.... Atqui Cristum ipsum in abditis etiam anime penetralibus semper assistere ... nemo usquam cristianus est qui dubitet.... Quid hic prestigii est, nisi quia

Is it believable that a writer with such a spiritual sensibility would so readily toy with the truth and lightly invoke "Patrem iudicem" as his witness? How much of the "rhetorical" interpretation of Petrarch's "Deum testor" can stand up when we recall the fact that this part of his invocation on the mountain is so closely woven with one addressed to a beloved and admired human being?[39]

It is my contention that the skeptical approach to the *Secretum* proposed by Rico cannot be fully appraised unless it is viewed against the recent tendency to interpret the letter on Mont Ventoux skeptically. Interpretations of the letter and the *Secretum* show the same disposition to unmask the "true" Petrarch, the same presumption that he lied frequently in the interest of mere rhetoric or in order to spread a false image of himself, and the same ensuing feeling of satisfaction that modern scholarship has at last seen through the poet's tricks, which have deceived generation after generation. "Becoming aware of the huge difference between the fictitious date and the real date of the *Secretum*," says Rico, "forces us to admire Petrarch, who plays like a virtuoso with pasts, presents, and futures; a prestidigitator who dexterously shuffles biography and imagination, without losing track of the cards."[40] There is also a want of readiness to deal in complex ways with the complexity of past situations and to avoid the attitude of a prosecutor. We have already seen some of the dangers of this

---

quem presentem corde credimus oculis non videmus, eoque relabimur in quo veteres Cicero, qui Cristum certe non noverat, arguebat ubi ait: 'Nichil animo videre poterant, ad oculos omnia referebant'?" "... pudebit Cristo spectante male vivere, male mori, aut omnino facinorosum ac turpe aliquid tanto sub teste committere" (*De Vita Solitaria*, in *Prose*, pp. 348–352; trans. partly according to Jacob Zeitlin, *The Life of Solitude* [Urbana, Ill., 1924]). That the passage in the *De Vita Solitaria* from "Habentes ergo testem Patrem iudicem" (p. 348) to "ad propositum sermo redeat" (p. 352) is an insertion is clear from the fact that Petrarch alludes to *Fam.* X 3 of 1348 or 1349, as Martellotti indicates in n.4, p. 348 of his edition.

[39] The same applies to the perspective from which the arbitrariness of Petrarch's spiritual chronology must be viewed. It will never again be doubted that Petrarch derived the date of late April 1336 by remembering the significance of the thirty-second year of Augustine's life, when his conversion occurred, and drawing a parallel with the end of the ten-year period which had passed since he, Petrarch, had abandoned his study of law in Bologna. And here, too, our verdict regarding the fictitiousness of the Ventoux incident may be mitigated once Petrarch's ascent of the Ventoux, including the famous scene on the mountaintop, is understood to have easily been possible and even probable.

[40] Rico, *Lectura*, p. 349.

attitude in the case of Petrarch's presumed "lying" about the purpose
of the *Secretum*, but the danger is the same wherever his autobiographical reports are found to deviate from exact, though often
unimportant, facts and his mendacity is consequently taken for
granted.

(3) Did Petrarch in Book I Try to Mislead
Readers regarding His Acquaintance with
Augustine's *De Vera Religione*?

I

A particularly intriguing incident is encountered in Franciscus' report to Augustine of how he became familiar with and profoundly
impressed by the latter's *De Vera Religione*. Although the story is a
complicated one, the facts can be verified.

Toward the end of Book I of the *Secretum*, Franciscus describes the
moment when the *De Vera Religione* first made its effect on him: "It
was not so long ago [*nuper*] that I came across that work of yours in
one of my digressions from the study of philosophy and poetry, and it
was with very great eagerness that I perused it in its entirety [*perlegi*].
Indeed, I was like someone who, setting out from his country to see
the world and coming to the gate of some famous city quite new to
him, is charmed by the novelty of everything around him and stops
now here, now there, to look intently at all that meets his gaze."[41]
This introduces a description in the *Secretum* of how touched Augustine was in the *De Vera Religione* by an expression of true spirituality
in Cicero's *Tusculans*, which Franciscus immediately remembers as
having helped form his own relationship as a Christian to Cicero and
classical philosophy. And indeed, Petrarch had transcribed that
passage from the *Tusculans* in his copy of the *De Vera Religione*, presumably around 1337 as we shall discover.[42]

Concerning the discussion in the *Secretum*, Rico makes the follow-

---

[41] Carrara, p. 66. I have already referred (p. 31f., above) to this important judgment concerning the impression the *De Vera Religione* made on Petrarch. See p. 32,
n.24, for the Latin text.

[42] The Ciceronian passage is found in the margin of Petrarch's copy of the *De Vera
Religione*, Ms. Paris lat. 2201. See n.51, below.

ing observations:[43] Petrarch dates the dialogue with Augustine between November 1342 and April 1343 and attributes his first reading of the *De Vera Religione* "to a slightly earlier period" (*a un período poco anteriore* [*nuper*]) — to a time when, as he says, he was immersed in ancient literature, and a book like Augustine's meant the crossing of an "ignotum . . . limen" and made him feel "nova captus . . . dulcedine." "However, we can be certain," says Rico, "that this first reading occurred quite a number of years earlier than Francesco claims, and therefore that the *De Vera Religione* could not have been unknown [*desconocida*] to him about 1342." "Undoubtedly, the Francesco of the *Secretum* wants to make us believe that the Augustinian treatise came into his hands under the fictitious circumstances in which the action of the dialogue takes place." Thus we are faced with yet another chronological deception in the service of "the ideal intellectual autobiography that Petrarch was creating for himself." At the same time, "this obvious falsehood is one more piece of evidence that we cannot take seriously the declaration that the *Secretum* was not destined for the public. This leads us, moreover, to distrust the precision of the other chronological details given in the dialogue."[44]

If these claims were fully correct, they would make a significant contribution to the question of Petrarch's credibility. However, some problems lurk beneath the seemingly smooth surface of the thesis. The most obvious is that the final judgment depends greatly on Petrarch's understanding of the term "nuper." As Rico interprets its usage in this case, it means about the winter of 1342–43 ("hacia 1342"), a time when in reality Petrarch had been thoroughly acquainted with the *De Vera Religione* for years. But why should we interpret "nuper" to mean such a short span of time when the same word in the proem to the *Secretum*, where it concerns the amount of time elapsed since Augustine's appearance, is taken to mean five years ago?

At this point we need to be certain that when Petrarch used the term "nuper" he was reckoning from 1342–43 rather than 1347, 1349,

---

[43] Rico, *Lectura,* pp. 113–114, and Francisco Rico, "Petrarca y el *De vera religione,*" *Italia Medioevale e Umanistica* XVII (1974), pp. 350–352; the arguments have been combined here.

[44] "La falsedad, palmaria, es un nuevo testimonio de que no cabe tomar en serio la declaración de ser el *Secretum* escrito no destinado al público; y, por otra parte, invita a desconfiar de las restantes precisiones cronológicas del coloquio" (Rico, *Lectura,* pp. 113–114).

or 1353. It is true that calculations based on an assumption that everything Franciscus says belongs to the period 1342–43 are suspicious; there are pages in which he is clearly speaking like the Petrarch of a later date. One can argue, however, that if there is any point in the *Secretum* at which one would expect a chronology calculated from the perspective of 1342–43, it is where we find *Franciscus* measuring time with the word "nuper," not where the author is speaking in his proem or through the mouth of Augustine. Thus we have to assume that Franciscus is using "nuper" from the vantage point of 1342–43 when he reconstructs the history of Petrarch's acquaintance with the *De Vera Religione,* and "nuper" might take us back from 1342–43 as many as five years. These reflections give a different look to the history of Petrarch's relationship to the *De Vera Religione.* For if it is possible that Franciscus is thinking of a time as long ago as the winter of 1337–38, then there is no reliable foundation to the accusation that Petrarch was deliberately falsifying the date. Scholars who are suspicious of Petrarch's veracity will no doubt observe that he may have become acquainted with the *De Vera Religione* even a few years earlier, possibly as early as 1333,[45] but this does not provide a basis for charging Petrarch with intentional falsehood.

The most persuasive answer to accusations against Petrarch is that he did not become familiar with the *De Vera Religione* all at once. When he first read the manuscript that included the *De Vera* about 1335 (the approximate date of the second list of his "libri mei peculiares," where the *De Vera* manuscript is mentioned)[46] he was not yet aware that he had an Augustinian work in his hands, because the titles of the two parts forming the manuscript — Cassiodorus' *De Anima* and Augustine's *De Vera Religione* — were designated as Liber I and II of some unnamed saint's *De Beata Vita.* Only gradually did Petrarch discover the true authors, and no one has given us a more careful picture of this delayed identification of the *De Vera Religione*

---

[45] Rico has shown that some elements of the text of the *De Vera Religione* were already used in Petrarch's "Oratio quotidiana," written on the endpapers of his copy of the *De Vera* and dated June 1335. Petrarch may even have read the *De Vera* a few years earlier. More about this below. See also n.46.

[46] The date of the lists of the "libri mei peculiares" in Ms. Paris lat. 2201 has not been exactly determined, but the general estimate is 1335, give or take two or three years. See Arnaldo Foresti, *Aneddoti della vita di Francesco Petrarca* (Brescia, 1928), pp. 46, 50–52; B. L. Ullman, "Petrarch's Favorite Books," in *Studies in the Italian Renaissance* (Rome, 1955), esp. pp. 131f., 134; Rico, *Lectura,* p. 487.

than Rico. For a while Petrarch believed that the work consisted of two books entitled *De Beata Vita et Vera Religione*. Thus several years may have passed between his first annotation of the text and his recognition that part of it was by Augustine.

We can make an educated guess concerning the time when this recognition occurred. The endpapers of the manuscript with the *De Vera Religione* contain not only Petrarch's *Oratio quotidiana* of June 1335 but also a long and a short list of books generally thought today to represent a more comprehensive and a shortened list of Petrarch's ideal library: the just mentioned "libri mei peculiares" ("the books appropriate for me"). The one point where the second list is not merely a condensation of the first but adds a new item is an "Iste" entry at the beginning, clearly a reference to the Cassiodorus-Augustine manuscript in which the lists are found — a fact already explained many years ago by B. L. Ullman as an indication that "Petrarch had become thoroughly fond" of this volume of spiritual writings by the time the second list was drawn up.[47]

A further comment can be made on this addition to the "libri mei peculiares"; it concerns the surprising form of the entry. The two lists otherwise present the titles of individual works, not a description of manuscripts in Petrarch's possession, which sometimes include a number of items. A catalogue of manuscripts would have been something quite different from the bibliography of preferred writings Petrarch offers. What, after all, did he intend to add to his bibliography when he wrote the "Iste" reference? Was he including not only the *De Vera* but also Cassiodorus' *De Anima* among the books "appropriate" for him? As Rico's study of the marginalia revealed, the Cassiodorus part of the manuscript is also annotated extensively, but as a rule only by a sort of scholarly commentary, "a little pedantic, basically an erudite exercise," not at all revealing the spiritual absorption apparent in many of the notes accompanying the subsequent Augustinian work.[48] Thus Petrarch's "Iste" entry not only is inconsistent

[47] As Ullman suggests, "the first list was written soon after the acquisition of the book [Ms. Paris lat. 2201], before Petrarch had become thoroughly fond of it" (Ullman, "Petrarch's Favorite Books," p. 131). See also n.46, above.

[48] See Rico's observations in "Petrarca y el *De vera religione*," p. 335. See also de Nolhac's remark that "Cassiodore est représenté deux fois dans nos manuscrits, mais Pétrarque ne le nomme, je crois, jamais dans ses oeuvres" (Pierre de Nolhac, *Pétrarque et l'humanisme,* vol. II [Paris, 1907], p. 106). In fact, Cassiodorus does not appear in

with the true function of his list of writings but seems to include among his favorite authors one — Cassiodorus — who did not play an essential role in the formation of his mind. The only possible explanation for the entry is that Petrarch already loved this manuscript when the entry was made but did not yet know who had written its most spiritually consoling part. The "Iste" entry may have been made two or three years after 1335, and till then Petrarch easily might not have known that the *De Vera Religione* was in his possession.[49]

Are there any other clues to help us determine the time when Petrarch became aware that this manuscript included an Augustinian work previously unknown to him? Some guidance is given by a paleographic finding and a biographical interpretation of it, both originally made by Billanovich.[50] He observed that the small clear script used in the notes with which Petrarch covered the margins of the heavily used manuscripts in his library changed considerably during the second half of the 1330s; essentially from a *scriptura minuscula cancelleresca* to the *minuscula rotunda* which Petrarch was to use as his *scriptura notularis* for the rest of his life. In Ms. Paris lat. 2201, the entire annotation accompanying Cassiodorus' *De Anima* and much of the *De Vera Religione* (from fol. 23v, where the *De Vera* begins, to about fol. 32v/35v) is in the older script, whereas from fol. 32v/35v onward, in notes that can be attributed to the late 1340s and afterwards, the new script begins to dominate.

This fact alone is insufficient to set exact chronological boundaries, but Billanovich's biographical interpretation rounds out the picture. During the early half of 1337, Petrarch visited Rome for the first time and there bought some manuscripts from the estate of the late canon Landolfo of Chartres. After his return to Provence in the second half of 1337, when he had settled down on his newly acquired property in the Vaucluse, he adopted from these manuscripts the *scriptura notularis* which Landolfo had developed for marginal annotations. Wherever the new script appears in Petrarch's notations, we can therefore be sure that the respective note was written no earlier

the index of Rossi's edition of the *Familiares* (whereas Boethius does), nor in the index of G. Billanovich's edition of the *Rerum Memorandarum Libri* (Florence, 1945).

[49] See n.46, above.

[50] See the survey of Billanovich's results by Armando Petrucci, *La scrittura di Francesco Petrarca* (Vatican City, 1967), pp. 37–39.

than the second half of 1337. Now, in this connection Rico added a suggestion of great potential value for the history of Petrarch's acquaintance with the *De Vera Religione.* The characteristics of the new *scriptura notularis* appear not only in the notes from fol. 32v/35v onward but also in a note on fol. 23v, on the very title page of the *De Vera Religione:* "In taking up the subject of this book, it will probably be of the greatest usefulness to keep in mind a passage which Cicero, no Christian but otherwise great and without equal, wrote in the first book of the *Tusculans,* castigating the errors of his time as follows: 'Unable to see anything through their inner light, they referred everything to their eyes. But it is the mark of a great mind to recall the intellect from the senses and to pull our thoughts away from what is habitual for us.'"[51] As Rico concludes his analysis of the changed paleographic character of this note: "It is certain in any case, I believe, that this interesting note is later than all the insertions made in 1335 and that it could not have been written long after the summer of 1337."[52] We will not be far from the mark if we correlate this new phase of Petrarch's annotation of the *De Vera Religione* with his discovery of the true identity of the second half of the "Iste" manuscript.

II

The various bits of information that we can glean on the history of Petrarch's acquaintance with Augustine's *De Vera Religione* thus form a coherent picture. In 1347 Petrarch set the scene of the fictitious apparition of Augustine, and when he declared in the proem of the *Secretum* that the event had occurred "not so long ago" (*nuper*), he meant 1342–43. Within the context of the dialogue, Franciscus tells us that not so long ago ("nuper") his reading of the *De Vera Religione* had added a new world to his studies of the ancient poets and philosophers. Thus Petrarch may have been in the process of becoming acquainted with what he now knew to be Augustine's *De Vera* about five years before 1342.

[51] "Ingredienti libri huius materiam prodesse poterit plurimum sententiam illam habere pre oculis, quam etsi non cristianus, in ceteris tamen magnus et singularis vir, Cicero scripsit in *Tusculano,* libro I, errores temporum suorum perosus, his verbis: 'Nichil enim animo videre poterant, ad oculos omnia referebant. Magni autem est ingenii revocare mentem a sensibus et cogitationem a consuetudine abducere'" (Rico, "Petrarca y el *De vera religione,*" facsimile of fol. 23v facing the text on p. 328).

[52] Ibid., p. 342.

What, then, is seriously wrong with Petrarch's account of when and how he became acquainted with the *De Vera Religione*? One might argue that the two uses of "nuper" are not quite the same, in view of the fact that Petrarch must have read and annotated a part of Augustine's text by about 1335, seven years before 1342. But it is also true that he probably did not yet know the real author at that time and did not come under his profound influence till somewhat later — about five years before 1342–43. Add to this that the *De Vera* did not have its fullest impact on Petrarch until the time of the composition of the *De Vita Solitaria* and *De Otio Religioso,* that is, on the very eve of the first draft of the *Secretum,* as Rico has so convincingly shown.[53] Whatever the details of Petrarch's growing sense of having discovered a new world of spirituality in the *De Vera Religione,* there is no basis for charging him with an attempt to lead others astray, as if he had been, in the usual sense, familiar with the *De Vera* since his early years. Not unless one is already convinced that Petrarch deceived his readers elsewhere would one find deceit in this story.

(4) How True Is Petrarch's Own Version of His Sexual History?

I

Perhaps we should withhold final judgment of Petrarch's truthfulness until we feel sure that his account of his sexual life — the sin of *luxuria* in the *Secretum* — does no more damage to his veracity than his reports of the ascent of Mont Ventoux and his acquaintance with the *De Vera Religione.*

Now that the date of the *Secretum*'s origin has been shifted to 1347, it is in any case germane to inquire into Petrarch's reasons for ascribing the conversation with Augustine to 1342–43; nothing in that year appears to account for his choice of date. Rico was again the first to attempt an explanation. He recalled Billanovich's discovery[54] that Petrarch gave a sort of chronology of his spiritual development in the rewritten or fictitious *familiares,* suggesting the ideal age by which his

[53] See above, p. 5f.
[54] This problem has been mentioned earlier in our discussion. See above, pp. 24, 25.

spiritual progress as a Christian ought to have been completed. As Billanovich argued, when Petrarch surveyed his life in those letters, he rearranged past events to accord with the Augustinian model. To this, Rico added the observation that other works of Petrarch's besides the *Familiares* play a part in the history of this spiritual auto-biography.[55] Thus his fragmentary letter to posterity shows a mysti-fying deviation from the true course of his conquest of *luxuria*. In the *Familiares* and *Seniles* we learn that it was not until after 1350, when Petrarch was forty-six, that he finally overcame his desire for carnal intercourse, whereas the letter *Posteritati*, drafted late in life and found among his papers after his death, tells us that he became chaste before he turned forty. There he writes that, whereas he was not "expers libidinum" in his youth, "soon afterwards, as I was near-ing the age of forty, and while I still possessed sufficient vitality and strength, I so totally abandoned not only that obscene act but any re-membrance of it that it was as if I had never looked upon a woman. I count this among the greatest felicities of my life, giving thanks to God, who liberated me from a vile and hated slavery at a time when I was still in the fullness of my strength."[56]

What Rico suggests is that Petrarch's insistence on having won his freedom before the age of forty must have had a place in his thoughts as early as about 1350. In *Fam.* IV 1 — the letter on the ascent of Mont Ventoux, which is so closely connected with the final version of the *Secretum* of 1353 — Petrarch asks himself the following: if his progress toward "virtus" ("ad virtutem accedere") should be as good in the next ten years as it was during the decade that has slipped by since he gave up his legal studies in Bologna, could he not die at forty with the satisfaction of having reached his spiritual goal and without lamenting the loss of his declining years?[57] In other words, Petrarch already viewed forty as the critical age by which a Christian ought to find fulfillment and overcome the Seven Deadly Sins; this is the stan-dard he would have wished to follow.

[55] Billanovich, in *Petrarca letterato,* passim; Rico, in *Lectura,* passim, esp. pp. 193f., 507.

[56] "Mox vero ad quadragesimum etatis annum appropinquans, dum adhuc et caloris satis esset et virium, non solum factum illud obscenum, sed eius memoriam omnem sic abieci, quasi nunquam feminam aspexissem. Quod inter primas felici-tates meas numero, Deo gratias agens, qui me adhuc integrum et vigentem tam vili et michi semper odioso servitio liberavit" (*Posteritati*, in *Prose*, p. 4).

[57] For the full text, see n.60, below.

Within the *Secretum*, nothing in the *luxuria* paragraph or elsewhere expresses in any way that the age of forty had this spiritual significance for Petrarch. Nevertheless, as Rico suggests, the idea must already have been in his mind when he was composing the *Secretum*. For when we remember, he says, that Petrarch completed his fortieth year on July 20, 1344, it no longer seems strange that he should have dated the *Secretum* conversations as early as 1342–43, even though he drafted them in 1347. Augustine had to make his appearance when Petrarch could still hope to find the right path in good time.

So we have to admit that Petrarch adhered to the fortieth-year mystique many years before he wrote the letter *Posteritati*. But what matters here is the consequence of this fact for Petrarch's veracity. Rico concludes that the two works of the early 1350s (the *Secretum* and *Fam.* IV 1) and the later letter to posterity all reveal a clear, systematic pattern of deceit. It is helpful, he says, "to realize that Petrarch often wanted to give a picture of himself which was embellished out of shame, painted in dark tones in search of the exemplary, retouched with artistic eagerness. . . . There are many reasons why the humanist subjected his own biography to these distortions. And unless one becomes aware, if not of the cause, at least of the existence of a willful distortion, neither the *Secretum* nor a substantial number of Petrarch's other works can be understood."[58]

II

It remains to Rico's credit to have recognized that when, during the last lustrum of his life, Petrarch claimed in the letter *Posteritati* that he had become chaste before the completion of his fortieth year, he was motivated by a mystique of numbers which had indeed impressed him at least as early as the beginning of the 1350s, as the testimony in *Fam.* IV 1 suggests. There is no reason to believe, however, that in the early 1350s Petrarch distorted the actual facts of his life in order to give himself undue credit. In the *Secretum,* as we have seen, the

---

[58]". . . que Petrarca quiso a menudo dar un retrato de sí mismo deliberadamente en desacuerdo con la realidad, embellecido por mor de la vergüenza, pintado con tonos oscuros en busca de la ejemplaridad, retocado por prurito artístico . . . Muchas razones pueden explicar las distorsiones a que el humanista somete su biografía: y si no se advierte, cuando no la causa, por lo menos la existencia de una distorsión voluntaria, tampoco se comprenderán ni el *Secretum* ni bastantes otros textos petrarquescos" (Rico, *Lectura,* p. 194).

element of fiction involves only the time of discussion with the messenger from the beyond — that is, of an imaginary conversation — and not a false autobiographical claim. What we read in *Fam*. IV 1 is that his first thought on the mountaintop in 1336 was of the ten years that lay before him and of the past decade of his life, that is, the twenty years that followed the end of his studies in Bologna. Seven of the past ten years, he muses, had been spent by him as a worldling. Then a new spiritual determination had awoken in him, struggling against the frivolities of his post-Bolognese life. "However, a great deal still remains that is uncertain and troublesome. What I used to love I no longer love. I am lying: I do love it, but less. Again I am clearly lying: I love it, but with more shame and sadness. At last I have spoken the truth. For that is the way it is: I love, but something I would rather not love and would prefer to hate. Nevertheless I love it, but unwillingly, under coercion, with sorrow, and mournfully."[59] He then asks himself whether he might not be able to achieve the maturity of a truly Christian life if another decade should be granted him: "If it should chance that this transitory life of yours were extended another ten years and your progress toward virtue were as considerable as during the last two. . . , would you not then be able to face death in your fortieth year, if not with certainty at least with hope, and calmly forsake the remainder of a life vanishing into senility?"[60]

Would not this expression of hope and good intentions be a strange way of intimating to presumed readers that he had indeed achieved purity before the completion of his fortieth year? To agree with Rico that the *Secretum* and *Fam*. IV 1 "presuppose each other" with respect to Petrarch's alleged liberation from his carnal drive before the age of forty and that the two writings "are tied together"[61] is to go far

[59]"Michi quidem multum adhuc ambigui molestique negotii superest. Quod amare solebam, iam non amo; mentior: amo, sed parcius; iterum ecce mentitus sum: amo, sed . . . quod non amare amem, quod odisse cupiam; amo tamen, sed invitus, sed coactus, sed mestus et lugens" (Carrara, p. 838. Trans. Bernardo, in Petrarca, *Rerum familiarium,* but altered at some points.)

[60]"Si tibi forte contingeret per alia duo lustra volatilem hanc vitam producere, tantumque pro rata temporis ad virtutem accedere quantum hoc biennio, . . . nonne tunc posses, etsi non certus at saltem sperans, quadragesimo etatis anno mortem oppetere et illud residuum vite in senium abeuntis equa mente negligere?" (*Prose,* pp. 838, 840).

[61]The two works "se suponen entre sí" and "enlazan al par" (Rico, *Lectura,* p. 193).

beyond what is written in them. They do, of course, attest to Petrarch's participation in the fortieth-year mystique. But this is only one aspect of the problem, the other being whether and when Petrarch, in violation of the truth, told his readers that he had conquered his sexual urge before he turned forty. And the answer is clear: this claim was not made by Petrarch during the time he was working on the *Secretum* and *Fam.* IV 1 but only toward the end of his life (probably after 1368, to be exact) in the letter *Posteritati.* [62]

One must concede, of course, that it is disquieting to discover any insincerity in Petrarch, even if only in his letter to posterity. But this discovery loses much of its alarming implication when the particulars concerning the letter are considered carefully. Petrarch was by that time so advanced in age that his memory could easily have failed him. This seems especially possible when we bear in mind that he had by then already revealed the true chronology of his struggle to become chaste in both the *Epistolae Familiares* and the *Epistolae Seniles* — letters that were circulating among his friends and were sure to become known to posthumous readers. One of these (*Fam.* X 5 of June 1352) is addressed to his brother and reports joyfully that he has finally succeeded in following the advice Gherardo had given him five years before, to shun the "consortium femine."[63] In June 1352 Petrarch was forty-seven, and almost two years had passed since the Roman jubilee which, later on, he solemnly maintained was the boundary beyond which he finally remained chaste. In *Sen.* VIII 1 of 1366, he gave Boccaccio a final assurance that since the jubilee of 1350 he had been free of desire for sexual pleasure. "Christ, my liberator, knows that I speak the truth," he added, "he who, when tearfully implored, often gave me his hand . . . and himself held me up."[64]

---

[62] The "progettata autobiografia" in *Posteritati* "se anche fu cominciata da tempo," "fu ripresa e stesa *ex novo* molto tardi, . . . cioè tra il 1370 e il 1372" (Enrico Carrara, "L'epistola *Posteritati* e la leggenda petrarchesca," reprinted in the posthumous collection of his essays, *Studi petrarcheschi ed altri scritti* [Turin, 1959], pp. 55–56). "The self-portrait that now opens the letter [*Posteritati*] was written after 1368: it probably contains some elements of the self-portrait that Petrarch had drafted, at least in part, in 1350" (Ernest H. Wilkins, "On the Evolution of Petrarch's Letter to Posterity," *Speculum* XXXIX [1964], pp. 307–308).

[63] *Fam.* X 5. Giuseppe Fracassetti suggested the date 1352 for this letter. Subsequently, in 1932, Salvatore Maugeri proposed 1347 or somewhat later. But Wilkins accepted 1352 (in several of his works) and Rico follows him (*Lectura,* p. 194, n.230).

[64] See p. 200, above. Another bit of information, in *Fam.* XIX 16 (3), Milan 1357 — "Siquidem post compressos adolescentie turbines et flammam illam beneficio

Would Petrarch have had the impudence to make the claim he does in his letter to posterity had he remembered how unequivocally he had revealed the true course of events in those other two letters? Apparently, forgetfulness had combined with a passionate desire to report that he had learned to lead a pure life before completing that critical fortieth year. Moreover, that he was prone to wishful thinking when sketching his self-portrait for posterity we see from what he tells us there about the vicissitudes of his *Africa*. After the original impetus received in the Vaucluse had faltered, he says, he resumed his work on the *Africa* in Selvapiana, in the mountains above Parma, in 1341–42, and there and in Parma "I brought that work to its conclusion [*ad exitum deduxi*] in a short time with such ardent zeal that I am now amazed."[65] When Petrarch wrote these words he knew painfully well that his epic had never been completed; that it remained so fragmentary that his friends decided it could only be readied for publication by another hand after his death; and that his future readers, too, would know it had never been brought "ad exitum." It must have been sweet to him to tell this dramatic tale about his major work — just as he did about his deplored carnal passion — in terms which would have been appropriate had his life been less complicated and more perfect.

Is it so inconceivable that Petrarch neglected at one time to think of the confusing consequences of his claims? How do we know that he would not have reconsidered them had he prepared the letter *Posteritati* for publication? We must not forget that all we have of it is a few sheets with Petrarch's entries from the early 1350s to the late 1360s, in such disarray that even the general order of the items long remained controversial and may well become so again. The very worst thing we can do in the circumstances is to consider this fragment as Petrarch's most mature legacy and to read the autobiographical reports he made throughout his life in its light, or even to interject its half truths into our interpretation of his earlier works. This applies particularly to the *Secretum*. In short, the letter *Posteritati*, dramatic and psychologically informative though it may be, must

---

maturioris etatis extinctam ... prope unus semper vite mee tenor fuit...." — does not add anything new to the chronology disclosed in the two cited letters but is consistent with the information contained in them.

[65]"... tanto ardore opus illud non magno in tempore ad exitum deduxi, ut ipse quoque nunc stupeam" (*Prose*, p. 16).

not become a back door through which an assumption of Petrarch's deceitfulness is slipped into the interpretation of the *Secretum*. The proper measure of the latter's veracity is not an isolated entry in a never-published work of Petrarch's old age but his readiness in 1349 to admit to the *Secretum* the bitter news of a moral fall, even though it destroyed his dream of the spiritual role of his fortieth year.

CHAPTER EIGHT

Reflections on the Role of the *Secretum* in Petrarch's Life and Work

(1) Interpretations of the *Secretum*

I

In their attempts at interpretation, past students of the *Secretum* have emphasized quite different aspects and portions of the work. One approach, which offered what was perhaps the first modern historical perspective on the *Secretum,* focused on Petrarch's confession to Augustine with regard to his inclination toward *accidia*. As one of the Seven Deadly Sins, *accidia* (or *acedia*) had had a strongly monastic hue in patristic and medieval times, whereas Petrarch's characterization is voiced in strikingly individual and psychological terms. He states dejectedly that, unlike the other sins into which he frequently and suddenly fell but from which he was also free again after a short while, *accidia* prevailed for entire days and nights. "And what may be called the high point of my miseries," he adds, "is that I indulge in tears and suffering with such an unhappy pleasure that I can barely tear myself away from it."[1]

Beginning in the latter half of the nineteenth century, scholars began to engage in comparisons of Petrarch's psychological analysis with the romantic discontent and weariness of modern life (Weltschmerz) that typified the mood of the fin de siècle; and thus — as Hugo Friedrich put it in 1942 — the *Secretum* became a forerunner of "the modern cult of melancholy."[2] This approach has often resulted in accusations against Petrarch of eudaemonistic egoism, lability, and a lack of religious earnestness — the result of overemphasizing what is obviously a limited role played in the second book by a single sin. Everything considered, its inherent weakness is the joining of an exceptionally narrow base to exceptionally far-reaching conclusions.

---

[1] "Et (qui supremus miseriarum cumulus dici potest) sic lacrimis et doloribus pascor, atra quadam cum voluptate, ut invitus avellar" (Carrara, p. 106).

[2] Hugo Friedrich, *Die Rechtsmetaphysik der Göttlichen Komödie: Francesca da Rimini* (Frankfurt am Main, 1942), p. 174.

The issue has been most welcomely brought into the open by a recent comparative study of the conception of this sin in the *Divina Commedia* and the *Secretum*.[3] Erich Loos has systematically posed the question whether Petrarch's single-paragraph discussion of *accidia* could serve as a basis for the interpretation of the *Secretum* as a whole. The conclusion he draws is that Petrarch's description of *accidia* has a central position in the *Secretum* and casts its shadow far beyond this single sin. In the prohemium, he maintains, "Petrarch's state of mind is described by concepts and images which are amazingly similar" to those in the *accidia* section. But does our evidence support this contention? In the prohemium, *Veritas* turns toward Augustine and asks him to help free Petrarch from his errors. "You are not unaware how dangerous and long is the illness with which he has been stricken, and that he is much nearer to death than to awareness of the gravity of his disease!"[4] According to Loos, "it is to *acedia,* later discussed in detail, that this passage clearly points. *Acedia,* therefore, turns out to be much more in the *Secretum* than one among several deadly sins; it expresses Petrarch's relationship to the world in general." When seen in the context of the *Secretum*, Loos concludes, it is clear that *accidia* "does not merely occupy a specific place in the catalogue of individually discussed 'diseases' but also serves, in the broader sense of a negative attitude toward the world, as a kind of running theme throughout the work."[5]

That the classical psychology of the passions and the condemnation of sins ("Affektenlehre und Sündenvorstellung," in Loos' words) are brought together in the *Secretum* in a new fusion has long been known, but the suggestion that the prohemium references to diseases of the soul allude to the *accidia* section — presumably because both use the idea of disease as often as that of sin — is peculiar to Loos' approach.

[3] Erich Loos, "Die Hauptsünde der *acedia* in Dantes *Commedia* und in Petrarcas *Secretum,*" in *Petrarca 1304–1374: Beiträge zu Werk und Wirking,* ed. Fritz Schalk (Frankfurt am Main, 1975).

[4] "... nec te latet quam periculosa et longa egritudine tentus sit, que ec propinquior morti est quo eger ipse a proprii morbi cognitione remotior!" (Carrara, p. 24).

[5] "... nicht nur einen bestimmten Platz im Katalog der einzeln behandelten 'Krankheiten' innehat, sondern sich in der breiten Bedeutung einer negativen Haltung zur Welt als eine Art Leitfaden durch das ganze Werk zieht" (Loos, "Die Hauptsünde der *acedia,*" p. 177; see also p. 174f.).

There is, to answer Loos' assertions, another correlation in the *Secretum* which is far more evident. The *amor* section of Book III almost duplicates Augustine's words in the *accidia* analysis in Book II: under the impact of your love, Augustine says to Franciscus, your misery rose to "such a pitch of wretchedness that it gave you morbid pleasure to feed on tears and sighs, passing sleepless nights . . . scorning everything . . . with a melancholy love for solitude, avoiding your fellow men."[6] It is quite clear that Petrarch's "morbid pleasure" (*funesta cum voluptate*) has nothing to do with "a negative attitude toward the world" but is an ingrained part of his sensibility, experienced and dreaded by him not only in *amor* but in other human relations as well. He seemed mysteriously attracted to sadness — as when death destroyed his plan of living with close friends and he again had the curious experience of being in despair and yet enjoying his suffering; "for there is a certain sweetness in one's mourning, in which, unhappy as I am, I often indulge too much."[7]

Considering these facts, is it not obvious that *accidia* did not play the major role in Petrarch's thinking that Loos attributes to it? Indeed, it played so minor a role that when he had to characterize it in the second book of the *Secretum* he offered little more than a parallel to the analysis of scenes from his amorous life. Ernest H. Wilkins, in one of his last essays, has drawn attention to the fact that *accidia* is seldom mentioned in Petrarch's works, except for a few places in the *Secretum* and *De Remediis* where the structure calls for it. "It is not clear that Petrarch regarded it as sinful in the same sense in which pride, envy, avarice, gluttony, wrath, and incontinence are sinful. Augustinus treats it with pity rather than with condemnation, as a healer rather than as an accuser. It would seem that when Petrarch had all but completed his self-examination he still had left one experience that he could not omit, and just one of the Seven Deadly Sins — one that

---

[6] "Cogita nunc ex quo mentem tuam pestis illa corripuit; quam repente, totus in gemitum versus, eo miseriarum pervenisti ut funesta cum voluptate lacrimis ac suspiriis pascereris . . . cum rerum omnium contemptus viteque odium et desiderium mortis; tristis et amor solitudinis atque hominum fuga . . ." (Carrara, p. 156).

[7] "Mestam nimis et miseram historiam aggressus sum; sed est quedam et lugendi dulcedo, qua sepe nimium pascor infelix." So already in the original draft of *Fam.* VIII 9 of 1349 (see Rossi's ed., vol. II, p. 204) and unchanged, though with insertions, in the book edition (ibid., p. 182).

was less definite in scope than the other six — and that he classed this experience, accordingly, as a manifestation of *accidia*."[8] This voice of common sense comes near to the truth. That modern readers of the *Secretum* became so strongly impressed by this specific sin was ultimately due to quite anachronistic comparisons of Petrarch's description with the very different *romantischen Erlebnissen* characteristic of the nineteenth century.[9]

For historically more substantive approaches to the meaning of the *Secretum* we must look elsewhere.

II

During the last fifty years, the *accidia* theory has been largely replaced by what might be called a "conversion" theory: the assumption that in 1342–43 Petrarch underwent a religious crisis marked principally by the composition of the *Secretum* and the *Psalmi Penitentiales*. Originally a purely classical and secular humanist — so it was thought — Petrarch now felt the need of a religious conversion and a change in his work to a Christian humanism. That there occurred a crucial reversal of this sort in his life seemed indicated by the fact that his next major publications were the *De Vita Solitaria* (of 1346) and the *De Otio Religioso* (of 1347), both basically religious books. This was the picture of Petrarch's development outlined in Carlo Calcaterra's *Nella selva del Petrarca* of 1942.[10]

The discovery not only that the *Psalmi* were composed as late as about 1348 but that the *Secretum*, too, belongs to this later period, has cut the ground from under the conversion theory, not only in a chronological sense but by raising doubt whether there was any religious crisis in Petrarch's life at all. By the spring of 1347, both the *De Vita Solitaria* and the *De Otio Religioso* had been written, and hence the *Secretum* followed rather than influenced them. No sudden break can have occurred at that time in Petrarch's spiritual development. A highly persuasive illustration of this is the markedly gradual growth of Petrarch's biblical interests, especially in the Psalter, during those

[8] Ernest H. Wilkins, "On Petrarch's *Accidia* and His Adamantine Chains," *Speculum* XXXVII (1962), esp. p. 590.

[9] Informative is the careful essay by Siegfried Wenzel, "Petrarch's *Accidia*," *Studies in the Renaissance* VIII (1961), pp. 36–48.

[10] This is basically the same scheme I followed in *From Petrarch to Leonardo Bruni* in 1968.

very years. The *De Vita Solitaria,* in which many biblical examples appear, already concludes with the admission that "it was dear to me to give frequent place in my humble little book to the holy and glorious name of Christ, in contrast to the practice of the ancients, whom I am accustomed to follow in so many respects."

An exhaustive documentation of Petrarch's development is found in the *De Otio Religioso* — written, we know, shortly before the first draft of the *Secretum.*[11] Reviewing the history of his devotion to the Bible, Petrarch there relates that until rather recently he would not have admonished even monastic readers of the *De Otio* to study the Scriptures as constantly and avidly as he now advised them to do. Like others, he says, he had forgone the wholesome nourishment of the Bible, repelled by the "simplicity" and "insignificance" of its outward appearance. Because he had been educated by teachers "who derided David's Psalter . . . and the entire text of the Divine Scriptures as fables for old women,"[12] he did not begin to see the truth until recently. The decisive help came from Augustine's *Confessions,* and Petrarch puts emphasis on the slow progress he made in trying to emulate the church father in his own studies, initially with relapses, "revocantibus me studiis meis antiquis," but gradually sensing himself advancing more rapidly until the task "successit, agente Deo, felicius quam sperabam." Reading the works of other church fathers also helped. "Thus in the joyful company of the Holy Scriptures, I now move with awe in an area which I used to despise, and I find that everything is different from what I had presumed." In a later insertion in the *De Otio* of about (or not long after) 1350, he added the interesting idea that the "opportune necessity" regularly to participate in divine services had eventually taught him this — undoubtedly a reference to his obligations as a canon in Parma and Padua between 1348 and 1351.[13]

Just as gradually, so he maintained elsewhere, he became more reserved in his attachment to the classical poets and spent less time reading them. In his first *Ecloga,* written between 1346 and 1348 and

[11] I am in part using here what I first described in *From Petrarch to Leonardo Bruni,* pp. 41–44.

[12] ". . . qui psalterium daviticum . . . et omnem divine textum pagine non aliter quam aniles fabulas irriderent" (*De Otio Religioso,* ed. Giuseppe Rotondi, Studi e Testi 195 [Vatican City, 1958], p. 103).

[13] Ibid., pp. 103–105.

sent to his brother, Gherardo, in first draft in 1348 or 1349, he compares the poetry of Virgil and Homer with that of David. Here we
already find Petrarch full of praise for David's songs but still inclined
to seek his own place among the classical poets.[14] In 1353, in his *Invective Contra Medicum,* he finally "swore sincerely" that he had not
read the ancient poets for as long as seven years. Many of their
verses, he said, were of course indelibly fixed in his memory. But he
no longer read them; rather, he was trying to improve his mind
morally by writing useful things for posterity, "et in sacris literis de-
lector."[15] He made the same claim in his letter *Posteritati,* either at
that time or in a later addition. Originally he had shown talent — so
he describes his development — for both moral philosophy and poetry, but he had come to depreciate the latter in the course of his life,
"delighting in the *sacrae literae,* in which I now sense a hidden sweetness, while reserving the *poeticae literae* for adornment."[16]

These facts in Petrarch's autobiographical writings, together with
the redating of the *Secretum* from 1342–43 to 1347, clearly must affect
Carlo Calcaterra's theory of the nature of Petrarch's "crisis." As far
as his general program was concerned — to include the world of the
Bible and some patristic works in his humanism — much of it was
realized during the late 1340s in the course of an organic development. If there was also an element of suddenness — as is suggested
by some impassioned pages in the *Secretum* and *Psalmi Penitentiales* —
this involved only his performance, not changes in his religious
values. His "crisis" was a questioning of his own abilities, a profound
doubt whether he was, or ever would be, able to combine his kind of
studies — which demanded all his strength — with his religious strivings. But before we try to redefine the meaning of the *Secretum* crisis
in this light, we must take cognizance of still another recent, and
rather different, attempt at reinterpretation.

III

This approach is based on a theory that has served Rico as a guide:
that Stoicism, or more specifically stoic morality and rationalism —

---

[14] See Guido Martellotti's comment in Francesco Petrarca, *Rime, trionfi e poesie
latine,* ed. Ferdinando Neri et al. (Milan, 1951), pp. XV, 808.

[15] *Prose,* pp. 678–680.

[16] "... sacris literis delectatus, in quibus sensi dulcedinem abditam, quam ali-
quando contempseram, poeticis literis non nisi ad ornatum reservatis" (ibid., p. 6).

not really important for Petrarch before the middle of the 1340s — was the outlook that he was striving to adopt between 1347 and 1353 and that he employed in the construction of the *Secretum* dialogue. As Rico has it, "everywhere in the *Secretum* we find a struggle against peripatetic ideas"; the entire work shows "the taking of an intellectual position opposed to ancient and modern Aristotelianism and in favor of Stoicism allied with good rhetoric and . . . a current of medieval spirituality."[17]

The awareness that the stoic component of Petrarch's mind was an increasingly important force during those six years is a step forward in recent studies, and it is apparent how helpful it would be if more details of the debate in the third book of the *Secretum* could be traced to the advancing rigor of Petrarch's stoic attitude. Rico sees the debate as evidence that "Petrarch perhaps never overcame the conflict between stoic reason and peripatetic [recognition of] feeling. . . . When he wrote the *Secretum,* he embodied the truths of the *ratio* in Augustine and the impressions of the *sensus* in Franciscus."[18] He sees the two disputants as representatives of two successive phases in Petrarch's development, for "one must understand the dialogue between the stoic Augustine and the peripatetic Franciscus as a dialogue between the Petrarch of about 1350 (give or take three years) and the Petrarch of 1342 (in part real, in part drawn from the new perspective [of about 1350])."[19] Or as they are contrasted on the last page of Rico's book and in the summary of his conclusions later published in the *Giornale Storico della Letteratura Italiana:* "Augustine appears as the desired future . . . , Franciscus as the outmoded past"; "in Augustine is revealed the Petrarch of about 1350, whereas Franciscus is presented as [the illustration of] a phase already left behind in the intellectual evolution of Petrarch the writer."[20]

These differentiations have their attractions. Nevertheless, they conflict with the *Secretum*'s information about both disputants. If

---

[17] Rico, *Lectura,* pp. 532–533.

[18] Ibid., pp. 55–56.

[19] Ibid., pp. 51–52.

[20] ". . . Agustín aparece como el porvenir querido . . . Francesco es el pretérito superado" (Rico, *Lectura,* p. 534); "in Agostino ci si rivela il Petrarca del 1350 circa, mentre Francesco si presenta nel dialogo, drammaticamente, come una fase superata nell'evoluzione intellettuale dello scrittore" (Francisco Rico, "Precisazioni di cronologia petrarchesca: Le 'Familiares' VIII 2–5, e i rifacimenti del 'Secretum,'" *Giornale Storico della Letteratura Italiana* CLV [1978], p. 525).

Franciscus was intended to represent the Petrarch of 1342 and a past phase in his life, how does it happen that when Petrarch drafted the *Secretum* in 1347 he used the word *nuper* to introduce Augustine's presumed visit in 1342–43? As Petrarch uses the term, it may, of course, mean four or five years ago; but in a psychological sense it must be understood as "recently," or "not too long ago." Indeed, no one would use *nuper* to say that so much time had passed that the writer's values and outlook on life had changed. If the proem was intended to introduce a debate between a Franciscus representing Petrarch's "pretérito superado" on the one hand and his later beliefs on the other, it would not begin with *nuper* but with some such statement as: at a time when I was a different person, Veritas and Augustine appeared to me. Thus the interpretation of Franciscus as a representative of the "pretérito superado" cannot be correct.[21]

The theory that the Augustine of the *Secretum* must be understood as Petrarch's model for his own future — as the ideal he hopes to live up to in coming years — is also inherently improbable. If Augustine really represented the hoped-for Petrarch of tomorrow, how could Book III end with an acknowledgment of Augustine's inefficacy in the debate and the acceptance of Franciscus' plan to postpone his new life and continue working on the *Africa* and *De Viris* for the foreseeable future? Indeed, if Franciscus represented the "pretérito superado," and Augustine Petrarch's hopes for his future, the *Secretum* discussion would end with the victory of the vanquished past over the ideal embodied by Augustine — an ending which would not only be strange but incredible. The obvious alternative is that Franciscus and Augustine personify two conflicting strains of thought in Petrarch's mind (the conflict to which the title "De secreto conflictu curarum mearum" refers), Franciscus representing Petrarch in general (not a character from the past) and Augustine, the voice of Petrarch's conscience, a teacher who uncovers the secret thoughts which Petrarch tries to hide from himself, and at the same time a paternal friend who is prepared to let Petrarch's nature have the last word in his inner struggles. This may appear to be an old-fashioned view of the *Secretum;* still, it retains its validity if we follow the *Secretum* conversations as they unfold.

[21]"At a time when I was a different person" is the way in which Petrarch would, indeed, have expressed himself, for at the beginning of his *Canzoniere*, no. 1, verse 4, he talks of himself in the past, "quand'era in parte altr'uom da quel ch'i' sono."

But in order to judge these conversations realistically, we must first of all bear in mind the changing surroundings in which Petrarch conceived and afterwards revised and enlarged his work between 1347 and 1353.

(2) The *Secretum* and Petrarch's Changing Milieu

I

In the course of this discussion, it has often been observed that when Petrarch settled permanently in Italy in mid-1353, the atmosphere of the north Italian cities was bound to change his values to some extent, and that the change would affect the final outlook of the *Secretum*. This result, as we have found, especially affects two sections of Book II, which deal with the opposition between solitude and an urban milieu on the one hand and economic "mediocritas" and affluence on the other. But why did the impact of the Italian environment not already assert itself several years before, during Petrarch's previous long sojourn south of the Alps? It is a question which in turn suggests another: why are we sure that the initial irritation of city life reflected in the *Secretum* of 1353 must not be traced to Petrarch's urban experiences in the late 1340s?

By the latter part of 1349, Petrarch had been living in Parma for about two years, and we may well ask whether what we read in the *Secretum* about his imprisonment "in urbibus" as a result of his secret "avaritia" does not in part reflect his reactions at that time. Fortunately, we are given an answer by the priceless original (May 1349) draft of *Fam.* VIII 2–5, the letter in which Petrarch tried to persuade three of his closest friends to share a household with him in imitation of Augustine, who lived with coreligionists in a home at Cassiciacum. Now, the intimate expression of Petrarch's state of mind in this letter is the very opposite of the hatred for city life that characterizes the changes made in the *Secretum* in 1353. It shows him consciously turning to the attractions of the north Italian cities at the expense of his love for rural solitude. If we should decide to settle together in the Vaucluse, he tells his friends, we would find an abundance of streams and of flowery places in which to rest; but more is demanded of men than the enjoyment of these delights. "As Aristotle says, 'nature is alone insufficient for philosophizing; in addition, the body must be healthy and food and . . . servants must be available.'"[22] The Vaucluse, he goes on, might serve as a refuge at times, when life among urban pleasures becomes a bore, especially in summer; but "in the long run it would hold out no promise for what is needed, nor be superior." This is not meant to deprecate the Vaucluse, Petrarch apologizes; the Vaucluse has proved to be the most inspiring place for many of his works. "But a man has to make other provisions than a boy, and, young as I was, I had not yet seen anything else except in transit, and even if I had, blind love [for the Vaucluse] would have interfered with my objective judgment." Now, however, he sees things differently: "the veil which covered my eyes has been taken away, so that I can see what a difference there is between a secluded vale and Italy's open valleys and beautiful hills and pleasant, flourishing cities."[23] Thus Petrarch offered to his friends as common dwelling places the town houses he owned — or was entitled to occupy — in Parma and Padua, depicting in his letter how they would visit together some of the most attractive cities of northern Italy, such as Bologna, Venice, Treviso, Milan, and Genoa, and adding that he hoped his friends would accept this bewitching dream, although he would be content to use his little house in the Vaucluse if this was the only place where they could all be induced to gather together under one roof.[24] In 1349, then, Petrarch saw no problem in living "in urbibus" in northern Italy and felt anything but imprisoned by the thought of spending the remainder of his years in cities. He could not have been further from what he felt in the last months of 1353, when life "in urbibus" appeared to him to be an abandonment of his former solitude and a punishment for secretly having sought urban affluence.

Would the second part of Petrarch's diagnosis of his state of mind in 1353 — that *avaritia* had driven him to the city — have been any more probable in 1349? The 1349 version of *Fam.* VIII 2–5 answers this question as well. When he made his proposal to share a household with his three friends, Petrarch tried to allay any fears they might have that they would need to be rich in order to realize such a

---

[22] "'Non *est* per se sufficiens,' ut ait Aristotiles, 'natura ad speculari; sed oportet et corpus sanum esse, et cibum et reliquum famulatum existere'" (*Fam.* VIII 2–5, original γ version of 1349, Rossi's ed., vol. II, p. 197).

[23] ". . . apertas Italie valles collesque pulcerrimos et urbes amenissimas ac florentissimas . . ." (ibid., p. 199).

[24] Ibid., pp. 197–199, 202.

plan. There is no problem unless we are avaricious, his comment runs. "We have as much as suffices; whatever else we ask for springs . . . not from natural desire but from cupidity, which has no limit and no end. . . . For this is characteristic of *avaritia* and is its worst trait: it torments us with endless cares and inflames rather than satisfies the spirit." He knows well that his friends are free of avarice, and as for himself, "I have set a limit to my greed, in the true spirit of the Horatian verse 'semper avarus eget: certum voto pete finem.'"[25] "I have striven for this goal, I own, and have attained it with God's help." "And I shall not be afraid that my heir will reproach me for having been indolent. . . . For, why should I work so much? Fortuna has offered me more than necessity requires, and I fear that I am busier than I ought to be."[26] These are certainly not the words of one who feels he has been misled by *avaritia,* but rather of someone who is convinced that he is free of this sin, as well as endowed with a decent share of earthly possessions. If we look beyond Augustine's accusations against Petrarch's alleged avarice in the *accidia* and *avaritia* sections of the *Secretum,* we find in Book I a categorical assertion that he, Petrarch, has never been in danger constitutionally of succumbing to the temptation of wealth. In fact, he ventures to maintain that "I cannot recall ever having burned with desire for wealth and power, over which I see so many of my coevals, even mature men advanced in years, become passionate."[27]

However, to understand fully what Petrarch, during the period of the *Secretum's* growth, experienced and wrote regarding economic greed and satisfaction, we must again look outside the *Secretum.* In addition to *Fam.* VIII 2–5, we have the interesting *Epistola Metrica* II 18, which is now recognized as a product of the years when the *Secretum* was being written (1348–49).[28] There Petrarch tells us that he is engaged in building a house in Parma but is otherwise living in his usual simple manner, "even though a more benign Fortuna is hold-

---

[25] Horace, *Epist.* I II 56.

[26] *Fam.* VIII 2–5, Rossi's ed., vol. II, p. 200.

[27] ". . . quod opum magneque potentie desiderio, quo multos non modo coetaneos meos sed longevos homines et comunem vivendi modum supergressos exestuare videmus, nunquam arsisse me recolo" (Carrara, p. 62).

[28] Date established by Omero Masnovo, "La data di due epistole metriche di Fr. Petrarca," *Archivio Storico per le Provincie Parmensi,* ser. 3, I (1936), pp. 55–80.

ing out her hands and baring her bosom to me."[29] And a few weeks before he left Provence in 1353, he wrote cheerfully in another letter: "I have enough to live on, as people are accustomed to say . . . , [even] enough for some opulence. What, then, do you want me to wish or hope further? . . . I have what I need for short and long sojourns, enough to eat and drink, for clothes and shoes, for all the servants I require. . . . My possessions include books of all sorts, not the least of my riches. I have my talents, whatever these may be, my love of the *literae,* which bring such wonderful pleasures to my mind and of which I never tire. And to all this add yourselves, my friends, whom I count among my foremost goods."[30]

This was written during the difficult period when Petrarch was waiting in vain for invitations from Italy. Evidently, in those years his feeling that he was economically secure and free from insatiable avarice was independent of his worries about *solitudo* and city life, and we know very well what conditions were responsible for this attitude. The clerical prebends on which he depended before 1348 and which afforded him a relatively meagre living were supplemented at that time by two well-paid positions highly acceptable to him: the archdeaconate of the Cathedral of Parma on August 23, 1348, and a canonry in Padua in March 1349. These offices, used by him merely as benefices during his long absences, henceforth served as his major sources of income, allowing him a rather affluent life.[31]

This is the background against which we must view the ascent of *avaritia* to a dominant place in Augustine's accusations in Book II. When the *avaritia* and *accidia* sections were being enlarged, the years during which Petrarch had avidly sought to acquire more ecclesiastical benefices had passed and, consequently, also the time when he

---

[29]"Licet indulgentior ambas / det fortuna manus, gremioque invitet aperto" (*Metr.* II 18, lines 11–12, in D. de' Rosetti, *Poesie minori del Petrarca* [Milan, 1829–34], vol. II, p. 184).

[30]"Habeo unde vivam, quod vulgariter dici solet . . . habeo unde lasciviam. Quid me optare iubetis amplius, quid sperare? . . . habeo ubi breve tempus, ubi longum habitem, quid edam, quid bibam, quid calciem, quid vestiam, qui michi serviat . . . accedunt omnis generis libelli, divitiarum mearum portio non ultima; accedit hoc quantulumcunque est ingenium, hic amor literarum mira cum voluptate animum pascens et sine fastidio exercens; acceditis vos, amici, quos inter prima mea bona connumero . . ." (*Fam.* XVI 3 [5–6], March 28, 1353).

[31]See Ernest H. Wilkins, "Petrarch's Ecclesiastical Career," *Speculum* XXVIII (1953), esp. pp. 766, 767, 774.

ought to have appeared avaricious in his own eyes; but now a completely new source of bitter disappointment entered his life. Toward the end of 1353, Archbishop Giovanni Visconti wished to send Petrarch back to Avignon as his ambassador to the pope, and Petrarch, feeling more dismayed than he had at any time before, began to probe his past for the sin that might have been responsible for the mockery his life threatened to become. Because Giovanni Visconti soon gave up his plan, Petrarch's fear that he would be punished for secret "avaritia" — this being the sin that must have lured him from solitude into the world of cities — vanished as quickly as it had appeared. Nevertheless, its significance cannot be overlooked: in those few disruptive months, the ending of Book II assumed its strange and, without this explanation, unintelligible form. There is yet another observation worth making: although to us the idea that Petrarch had left his solitude for the urban world because of latent avarice seems absurd, it reveals the extent to which he remained bound by the fears of a period still dominated by the ideal of Franciscan poverty. There is, indeed, no other evidence from which we learn as much about the intimate contact of Petrarch's sensibility with the Franciscan world of values as this late addition to the *Secretum* text.[32]

II

There are other aspects of Petrarch's final work on the *Secretum* that cannot be understood without a close look at his contemporaneous life.

The first concerns the history of Petrarch's very gradual accommodation to city life after he settled in Milan in June 1353. His initial impression at that time was that city and country interacted there with unusual intimacy. "I am in touch with the tranquil country in the midst of the city, while the city is like a part of the countryside," he wrote shortly after his arrival.[33] In a description of this perfect combination made in August,[34] his emphasis is clearly on the cheer-

---

[32] For the relationship of Petrarch, his associates, and his acquaintances to Franciscan values (but without reference to the *Secretum*), see the sketch in Paul Piur, *Petrarcas 'Buch ohne Namen' und die päpstliche Kurie* (Halle a.d. Saale, 1925), pp. 68–77.

[33] "Rus michi tranquillum media contingit in urbe, rure vel urbs medio" (*Metr.* III 18).

[34] *Fam.* XVI 11, to Nelli in Florence.

ing fact that Archbishop Giovanni Visconti — "maximus iste Italus" — has granted him, as he promised on the first day, "in maxima frequentissimaque urbe solitudinem . . . et otium." As Petrarch describes his new life, it is the ease with which he can escape from the city and devote his full time to his work that makes him happy. Only now does he really understand the wisdom of the saying: "lost money returns, time once elapsed never returns."

In fixing his terms with the archbishop, Petrarch had made certain that his style of living would remain unchanged: his house alone would be altered, but not to an extent that would interfere with his freedom and *otium*.[35] He admitted that he did not know how long this agreement would last; knowing the archbishop and himself, he thought it would be brief. But meanwhile he had a house at the city wall, with a view to the snowcapped Alps and the Basilica of S. Ambrogio as his immediate neighbor. Indeed, these views from his windows were not all he had of rural solitude. As he told Guido Sette in October,[36] he had discovered not too far away, in the heart of Lombardy, the hill of S. Colombano with its ancient Castrum Sancti Columbani and a unique vista of the plain and all the old cities of Lombardy, itself a place of "dulce silentium." When he was writing his works in praise of "otium ac solitudo" in the Vaucluse (the *De Vita Solitaria* and *De Otio Religioso*), he told Sette in the letter of October, he was not composing them so much for others as for himself, because he feared that later fresh impressions might diminish his "otii ac solitudinis appetitus." The *De Vita* and *De Otio* had thus been written to help keep his old emotions alive.[37] The apprehension had totally disappeared by now, however, because his esteem for *otium* and *solitudo* had become ever warmer over the years and had eventually become a habit. Moreover, he still believed that the Vaucluse was the very breeding place of solitude ("solitudinis officina").[38]

We may say, then, that — in contrast to his easy accommodation to city life between late 1347 and mid-1351 — during the third quarter of 1353 Petrarch did everything possible to insulate the style of life

---

[35] "Cessi igitur hac lege ut de vita nichil, de habitaculo aliquid immutatum sit idque non amplius quam quantum fieri potest illesa libertate salvo otio" (ibid., [10]).
[36] *Fam.* XVII 5.
[37] See above, p. 196.
[38] *Fam.* XVII 5 (2-3).

acquired in the Vaucluse from the impact of urban Italy. It is not hard to find the reason for this different reaction. In the late 1340s, Petrarch's library and his emotional home were still in the Vaucluse, and he considered his sojourn in Italy (mainly in Parma and Padua) merely experimental. At no point did he have to choose between a future in urban surroundings and a permanent life of solitude. In the second half of 1353, the intended finality of his move to Italy and the fact that he had taken his library with him created a new situation. If any vestige of his experience in the Vaucluse was to remain — and we have just seen how deeply he longed for this — he had to act defensively, by not opening his heart and mind too fully to city life and by creating for himself, instead, a kind of Cisalpine Vaucluse; hence the conditions for freedom and a semi-rural life elicited from Giovanni Visconti, and the letters telling his friends that he had never been so eager for solitude and country life as now.

In the reality of Italian life, however, this castle in the air vanished after only a few months, when Giovanni Visconti broke his promise by making plans to send Petrarch to the pope as ambassador. We have seen the absolute despair which overcame Petrarch at the grotesque thought that, after struggling so hard to escape Avignon and Provence, he should be forced to return, of all places, precisely there; and how he speculated in the final version of the *Secretum* that secret avarice had driven him from his happy solitude in the Vaucluse and that he was now suffering the deserved consequences of his sin. "Since my youth," he wrote on New Year's day, 1354, as we know, "I have been such a great lover of solitude and woods, and now that I am older I must labor in the city among the crowd, and I feel ill at ease."[39] What should be added here is that this was not a rare outcry directed to some selected friends; rather, for several months, and perhaps longer, he considered his well-laid plans for a life in Italy to have failed. A letter written in late 1353 to a high official in Visconti service,[40] which touches upon the plans for Petrarch's embassy, is naturally more restrained than those to his confidants cited in our sixth chapter, but it nonetheless speaks of the shambles made of his dream of a Milanese Vaucluse by the archbishop's plan. We also have an *epistola metrica* (III 19) — definitively dated by Foresti and

[39] See above, p. 178.
[40] *Fam.* XVII 6, to Bernardo Anguissola.

Wilkins to those critical months[41] — which expresses better than any prose his sense of homelessness and uncertainty about the future so shortly after his return to Italy: "no country have I, no air is left for me, unsettled as I am, a stranger everywhere."[42]

We have no evidence that this discouragement poisoned Petrarch's life in Milan for any length of time, and of course the plan for his embassy to the pope was abandoned early in 1354. Nevertheless, as late as October 1355 he inquired through a member of his household sent to Naples, whether the grand seneschal of that kingdom, Niccolò Acciaiuoli, might not be willing to provide him with a dwelling place in the vicinity of Naples, where he could live the life of solitude so dear to him.[43] Although we have no further details of this strange inquiry, it tells us that even then he was not yet reconciled to a life in the cities of northern Italy and was still trying to discover an Italian Vaucluse.

Two years later, we find the first traces in Petrarch's correspondence of a fuller reconciliation with Milan and city life. Any student who tries to understand the *Secretum* as the expression of a definable period in Petrarch's middle years must consider the role of this new feeling.

III

We have repeatedly been induced to acknowledge the years around 1358 as the time when, at last feeling more at home in his new Milanese environment, Petrarch began to look back upon the *Secretum* with a sense of distance. In this connection I have quoted his statement in *Epistolae Variae* 52 — written about five years after the addition to the *Secretum* which deplored his imprisonment "in cities"[44] — that he had "learned to achieve solitude and leisure in the midst of

---

[41] Arnaldo Foresti, *Aneddoti della vita di Francesco Petrarca* (Brescia, 1928), pp. 304–308, early 1354; Ernest H. Wilkins, *Studies in the Life and Works of Petrarch* (Cambridge, Mass., 1955), pp. 236–240, late 1353–early 1354.

[42] "Nulla ... iam tellus, nullus michi permanet aer, incola ceu nusquam, sic sum peregrinus ubique."

[43] Ernest H. Wilkins, *Petrarch's Eight Years in Milan* (Cambridge, Mass., 1958), p. 107.

[44] Wilkins dates *Var.* 52 to 1357–59, or possibly 1354–55 (ibid., pp. 241–242). However, since all related letters (discussed in the paragraphs that follow) belong to the years 1357–60, and since Petrarch's correspondence of 1354–55 shows very different attitudes, we can assume that the date of *Var.* 52 is 1357–59.

city life."[45] Was this more than an isolated moment of rejoicing?

If one reads the relevant paragraph of *Var.* 52 as a whole, one sees that this comment was intended to indicate a design for Petrarch's future. He and the recipient of the letter, both lovers of the "vita solitaria et tranquilla," have lamented over Petrarch's urban existence, but Petrarch has at last found a solution to his problem. For you should be told, he informs his correspondent, that "as far as I am concerned, with God's help and an artful device not everyone can easily employ, when I am not able to do anything else I now know how to procure *solitudo* and *otium* for myself in the midst of city life: I shut my ears and eyes and finally my mind against a disgust for things and people. This is what I now value most. Otherwise I should clearly be lost and destroyed."[46] We find a second example in a *familiaris* of January 1358 (*Fam.* XX 10) which looks like a companion to *Var.* 52. This, too, is a note to a friend, briefly depicting Petrarch's mood and state of mind. He is again settled in an environment which is noisy and perilous for an old lover of tranquility, but he is convinced that he has the stamina to withstand a more complex style of living. "You should be told that in the midst of danger I stand secure," he writes, "that I keep myself so rested and tranquil among the waves that I forget I am surrounded by them."[47]

---

[45] "... in mediis urbibus ipse mihi solitudinem atque otium conflare didicerim." See above, p. 74f.

[46] "... quamvis, quod ad me attinet, et Dei munere et studio atque arte quadam non omnibus facili, quando aliud non possum, in mediis urbibus ipse mihi solitudinem atque otium conflare didicerim; contraque rerum atque hominum fastidia aures atque oculos et proinde animum obstruere. Quod nunc maxime facio: alioquin plane perditus et consumptus essem" (*Var.* 52, in *Francisci Petrarcae epistolae de rebus familiaribus et variae,* ed. Giuseppe Fracassetti [Florence, 1859–63], vol. III, p. 443).

[47] In dating Petrarch's achievement of solitude in the city to about 1358, I have neglected a retrospective statement of his that at first glance appears to point to an earlier time. In the *De Vita Solitaria* he tells us that "siqua me necessitas in urbem cogat," he had learned to control his senses within a crowd: "solitudinem in populo atque in medio tempestatis portum michi conflare ..., artificio non omnibus noto sensibus imperitandi ut quod sentiunt non sentiant." This is followed by a chronological clue: long after the fruits of his experience had grown to be a habit, he says, he found the same device described by Quintilian, whose long description he adds because it is not well known (*De Vita Solitaria,* in *Prose,* p. 336). Now, we know that Petrarch did not come into possession of Quintilian's *Institutio Oratoria* until 1350. Consequently, the entire passage is an interpolation in the *De Vita Solitaria* made during the 1350s or even later, and Petrarch may easily have learned to shut out the

The same cheerfulness, and even a satisfaction in being tested by a less than tranquil life, is found in the most complete portrait we have of Petrarch's urban existence, *Fam.* XIX 16, which was sent to Guido Sette, now archbishop of Genoa, during the summer of 1357. As Petrarch told this old friend of his youth, he was working ever harder, day and night, on old and new writings, "and to tell the truth, the very magnitude of the things I have undertaken in the short course of a lifetime is what frightens me." But he is confident that when God sees the utility of his plans for his soul he will come to his aid, so he strains every nerve, gaining strength from the very difficulty of his tasks. According to this letter, his equanimity is constantly increasing. If his fame does not reach posterity or even many of his contemporaries, "it will suffice for me to have been known to a few people or to myself alone." As for his financial circumstances, he is equally far from want and riches, but near to "safe, sweet, and carefree *mediocritas.*" He surpasses *mediocritas* only in having won greater fame than he would have liked.[48]

A special revelation of the letter is that it is his social standing in Visconti Milan that has created this balanced state in Petrarch's feelings and external life. As he says: "It is not only this archbishop [Giovanni Visconti] — to me the greatest of the Italians — along with his court, who loves and honors me more than I deserve, but the entire Milanese populace. For a full four years, as you can see, I have lived in the city of Milan, and I am now at the beginning of the fifth." "In this city, then . . . I have enjoyed all these years the benevolence not only of the leading men but of the people, and I think I will cling to it permanently, not only thanks to its excellent citizens but because of its land and air and, as it were, its walls and stones. Thus everything favorable embraces me here; I have the feeling that I am seen by many eyes and celebrated by many voices; and here . . . I know that I am welcome to the public."[49]

---

noise of the city during the very period, around 1358, when his letters repeatedly talk about his progress in this art.

[48]"Unum est in quo mediocritas me ista non sequitur, idque si invidiosum forte me fecerit, non mirer: honoratior sum . . . quam vel unquam optaverim vel semper optate sit expediens quieti" (*Fam.* XIX 16 [12–13; see also 5–6, 8]).

[49]"In hac urbe . . . non presidentium modo, de quibus nuntiatum tibi certus sum, sed totius etiam . . . populi benivolentia fui hactenus, ut non tantum civibus optimis, sed terre atque aeri ipsisque quodammodo parietibus urbis ac menibus in perpe-

This change in Petrarch's condition has come about without any damage to the substance of his former life: older experiences are continuing beside the new. Since his home is at the outermost edge of the city, he tells us, few visitors intrude there. His table remains frugal; he is still the lover of solitude and silence. A few miles outside the city walls he has found his new Italian Vaucluse, the village of Garegnano, to enjoy during the summer heat (although it is a weak parallel to the Vaucluse, he says). Most interesting to us, perhaps, is how Petrarch intends to reconcile the old with the new. Originally he had planned to live in the Certosa near Garegnano in summertime, together with its Carthusian inhabitants. "But I cannot exist without horses and servants, given my life as it is now, and I feared that the impertinence and noise of servants would be irreconcilable with religious silence."[50] So he has leased a house for himself and his household, knowing that the nearby Certosa will always be open to him for participation in religious services.[51] Similarly, in the city he has managed to solve the problem of being on social terms with people and yet preserving something of his inner solitude. "When occasionally I have to go out [into the street], either because I want to walk or because I have to visit my lord, I turn my eyes to right and left, salute from a distance by bowing my head without moving my lips, am saluted back in the same manner, and pass by, never allowing anything to delay me on my way."[52]

Whoever compares this self-portrait of 1357 with the sketch drawn by Petrarch on his last arrival in the Vaucluse in 1351 — when he envisaged completing his major works within the next two years and then beginning a more religious life — will recognize two crucially different phases in his development, or at least in his image of himself. In stark contrast to the earlier distinction made between a present dedicated to secular desires and obligations and a planned future of greater spirituality, the self-portrait of 1357 shows an acceptance

---

tuum me teneri arbitrer; is me omnium favor amplectitur; his me oculis videri, his vocibus concelebrari sentio; sic — ut amicitias singulares sileam, de quibus agere longum est — me vulgo etiam carum scio" (ibid. [15; see also 13–14]).

[50]". . . sed reputans me sine equis ac famulis — ut adhuc est vite modus — esse non posse, timui ne servilis temulentia ac strepitus religioso silentio obstarent" (ibid. [25]).

[51] Ibid. (26).

[52]". . . tum dextra levaque flexis oculis et labellis clausis nutu frontis eminus salutans salutatusque pretereo, nil in transitu patiens quo fatiger" (ibid. [18]).

of many things and of many intellectual pursuits at the same time.

The confrontation between present and future has also disappeared with respect to the relationship of classical studies and the *sacrae litterae*. Petrarch now feels that he can accommodate the latter in his life, and that he has less need to dream of a more spiritual future. In September 1360 he wrote to Nelli (in *Fam.* XXII 10) that he had achieved a balance in his studies for the first time. He had definitely found a place for the *sacrae litterae,* he said, and would not put them aside again until his last day, "si ex alto dabitur." He had not forgotten his old love for Virgil and Cicero, Plato and Homer; "but now something greater is at stake, and the salvation of my soul is a higher concern than eloquence. I used to read whatever pleased me, now I read what is profitable. This is what I have a mind for at present. . . . Before long my orators will be Ambrosius, Augustine, Jerome, and Gregory; my philosopher, Paul; my poet, David, whom, as you know, I compared with Homer and Virgil many years ago in the first eclogue of my *Bucolicum Carmen,* in such a manner that the result seemed uncertain. . . . Not . . . that I [now] prefer the one group and attach little value to the other, as Jerome wrote that he did, even though he did not act upon his words in his later work, so far as I can judge. I, it appears, can love both sides at the same time, even though I know very well whom to prefer when it is a question of expression and whom when it is a question of substance."[53]

It is not easy to evaluate this letter. The identification of the classical heritage with mere eloquence along with a belief that the church fathers are the true orators, that Paul is the philosopher, and David the poet is perhaps the purest expression of the spirit of medieval humanism that we find in Petrarch's writings. But in place of the image of two ladder rungs which must be climbed successively (the concluding idea in the *Secretum*), he now increasingly envisions

---

[53] "Sed iam michi maius agitur negotium, maiorque salutis quam eloquentie cura est; legi que delectabant, lego que prosint; is michi nunc animus est. . . . Iamque oratores mei fuerint Ambrosius Augustinus Ieronimus Gregorius, philosophus meus Paulus, meus poeta David, quem ut nosti multos ante annos prima egloga *Bucolici carminis* ita cum Homero Virgilioque composui, ut ibi quidem victoria anceps sit. . . . Neque ideo tamen quia hos pretulerim, illos abicio, quod se fecisse Ieronimus scribere potiusquam sequenti stilo approbare visus est michi; ego utrosque simul amare posse videor, modo quos in verborum, quos in rerum consilio preferam non ignorem" (*Fam.* XXII 10 [6–8]).

the coexistence of the *sacrae litterae* with Virgil, Cicero, Plato, and Homer — in his own words, "ego utrosque simul amare posse videor."

What kind of balance was to emerge from this coexistence can, of course, be learned only from Petrarch's actual literary activity, not from a single letter to a monastic friend like Nelli. In the *De Viris*, to give one example, the double thrust of the plan to include all ages and add a group of biblical *vitae* destroyed the Romulus–Titus version of Petrarch's youth, but nevertheless the new design did not prevent the finest fruits of Petrarch's Roman interests from ripening: the great biographies of Scipio and Caesar, both creations of the 1350s and 1360s.

This may be taken as typical of the kind of equilibrium that was to prevail in the period following the *Secretum*. From that time on, Petrarch managed to place both his classical humanism and the *sacrae litterae* on what was meant to be an equal level. As Martellotti puts it, one has to acknowledge that "in Milan ... and later in Venice, Pavia, and Padua a certain uncompromising moral extremism is mitigated, and Petrarch appears to have returned to his chosen studies with a tranquil mind."[54]

When such an equilibrium began to prevail — and we have seen that this occurred first in Milan around 1358 — the agitated period of the *Secretum* had come to an end.

[54]"... a Milano ... e poi a Venezia, Pavia, Padua, certe intransigenze morali si siano attutite e il Petrarca sia ritornato con animo tranquillo ai suoi studi preferiti" (Guido Martellotti, in *Annali della Scuola Normale Superiore di Pisa*, Classe di Lettere, ser. 3, VI [1976], p. 1399). See also Ettore Paratore's recent similar judgment that toward the last years of Petrarch's life "era avvenuta anzi finalmente l'equilibrata concilazione fra la componente religiosa e il desiderio della gloria poetica, il culto delle lettere" ("L'elaborazione padovana dell'*Africa*," in *Petrarca, Venezia e il Veneto,* "Civiltà Veneziana," saggi 21 [Florence, 1976], pp. 65–66). Finally, as Giles Constable has shown in "Petrarch and Monasticism" (in *Francesco Petrarca: Citizen of the World,* ed. Aldo S. Bernardo, Proceedings of the World Petrarch Congress, Washington, D.C., 1974 [Padua and Albany, N.Y., 1980], pp. 94, 59, 70, 78), it was Petrarch's relationship to monasticism that was primarily responsible for the difference in the two phases. As Constable puts it, all Petrarch's thought of entering a monastery "ended with his return to Italy in 1353, after which he seems to have found a new equilibrium less directly involved, though still not unconcerned with, monastic life and ideals.... These last twenty years marked in many ways a new stage in Petrarch's life, and there are fewer references to monasticism in his writings than during the decade from 1343 to 1353.... After his return to Italy in 1353 he seems to have accepted his fate as a prisoner and to have given up any thoughts of becoming a monk." Today, of course, we have to redefine the chronological boundaries some-

(3) On the Meaning of the *Secretum*

I

Against this sketch of Petrarch's changing attitudes and milieu, the
major results of our analysis of the *Secretum* debates fall into place.
Let us first examine more carefully the function performed by Augustine in these debates.

We will begin at the point in the first book where Franciscus confesses to Augustine that at night he has often tried to put himself into
the posture and state of mind of a dying person, hoping to free his
spirit from this world, but always finding the endeavor futile. As
Franciscus asks despairingly, "What hidden obstacle has thus far
caused all these meditations to bring me nothing but annoyance and
terror; I continue to be the same person I have always been . . . ?"[55]
From here on, Franciscus insists again and again that this is the
main question he wants Augustine to answer; indeed, he tries to
draw Augustine back to it whenever he digresses. On the next page,
he demands his answer: of course, he says, he will take Augustine's
various counsels to heart; "in the meantime, however, have you not
forgotten my first question?" Aug.: "Which question?" Fr.: "The
question of what is holding me back. I asked you why I am the only
one to whom intensive thought of death, which you said is so beneficial, brings no good whatever."[56] One page later, though Petrarch
has learned to relate everything in life to death, "the question still remains unanswered: 'quid ergo me retinet?'" When Augustine insists,
again a page later, that the will must be so strong "that it would
rather deserve to be called desire," and asks him if he knows "what
stands in the way of your meditation," he is urged on by Franciscus

---

what: the period in which Petrarch was toying with the idea of eventually becoming
a monk, or at least leading a semi-monastic life, began not in 1342–43 but in 1347
and was essentially over by 1352; but this does not affect Constable's interpretation
— that there was a brief central period in Petrarch's life, the period of the *Secretum,*
when his humanism and his desire for a monastic life threatened to diverge, followed
by the greater "equilibrium" which characterized the last two decades of his mature
humanism.

[55]"Que cum ita sint, quid ergo me retinet? quid latentis obstaculi est ut nunc
usque nil ista michi cogitatio preter molestias terroresque pepererit, ego autem idem
sim adhuc qui fueram prius . . . ?" (Carrara, p. 58).

[56]Ibid., p. 60.

once more: "This is what I ask you to tell me, this is what I so much desire to know."[57] And when the conversation threatens to bog down in joint admiration of the *Tusculans,* the dissatisfaction and sense of urgency of the disciple returns one final time: "But do, please . . . return now to our subject." Augustine, that is, should get back to the question, which he finally agrees to answer: "Your spirit suffers that same evil which befalls those who sow too many seeds on a small patch of land: namely, that the crops hinder one another by pressing each upon the rest." "And then the work that promised so well flags from too much vacillation, and there arises that inner discord about which we have said so much."[58]

As these quotations indicate, Augustine, at least in parts of the dialogue, serves Petrarch in a kind of socratic investigation of himself. This function can best be observed in the second book, where Franciscus is questioned by Augustine on his conduct in matters of political and social ambition. Boasting of having all his life shown his freedom from this sinful passion by fleeing public office as well as city life, Franciscus finally has to accept Augustine's conclusion: even this flight has been but another path for ambition. "Seeing clearly that you could not overcome nature, you turned your steps elsewhere" than to the competition for high social position. "For you assert your indifference not so much to honors as to the vexation of pursuing them, like the man who pretended not to want to see Rome because he could not endure the trouble of the journey. . . . But leave off trying to hide behind your finger, as the saying goes; everything you are thinking . . . is plainly before my eyes. You boast of having fled from cities and of being enamoured of woods; . . . there are many ways to reach an end, and believe me, though you have left the road trodden by the crowd, you are nevertheless hastening along a side path toward the same ambition which you say you have scorned. . . . The end and object is glory." And Franciscus has to admit that "you are driving me into a corner."[59]

How should we judge these illustrations of Augustine's function in

[57] Ibid., pp. 62–64.

[58] "Quod igitur evenire solet in angusto multa serentibus, ut impediant se sata concursu, idem tibi contingit. . . . Ex quo fit ut tam salutare propositum nimia mobilitate fatiscat, oriturque illa intestina discordia de qua multa iam diximus, illaque anime sibi irascentis anxietas . . ." (ibid., p. 68).

[59] Ibid., pp. 94–96.

the *Secretum*? Some of Petrarch's deeply ingrained persuasions — and doubts — are attributed to him there. He is the venerable critic of some of Petrarch's most personal traits. In other words, as I suggested earlier, in many places in the text he represents Petrarch's conscience. There is thus little substance to the theory that Franciscus symbolizes Petrarch's past and Augustine his future.[60]

Other parts of the *Secretum* dialogue consistently support this interpretation. The importance of the concluding scene — Franciscus' rejection of Augustine's advice to abandon the *Africa* and *De Viris* — can be understood only if we remember the preparations made throughout the work for Franciscus' challenge. In the third book it is the very contrast between spiritual concentration on the one hand and the pursuit of secular writing on the other which engenders the idea of two consecutive phases in Franciscus' life, and it is the same contrast which had already been adumbrated in the concluding pages of the first book. There, a metaphysical and cosmological framework is hammered out for the dualism that appears later in the discussion of the third book. Relying principally on Augustine's *De Vera Religione* — perhaps the most dualistic and pessimistic vision of the human psyche and man's earthly habitat ever set forth by the church father — the Augustine of the *Secretum* describes the misery of the human soul in this world: "Overwhelmed by phantasmata and forever struggling with its own cares, the weak [human] spirit is crushed, so that it has no strength to judge what it should ... cherish, what destroy, what repel."[61]

From this metaphysical explanation of why human beings find themselves confused and torn by endless cares and unable to rise up from them to the divine, the last page of Book I turns to a psychological diagnosis of the same situation: "energy and time" never suffice in this human world, least of all in Petrarch's life. As the seeds spring up, they choke each other; I have already cited this metaphor.[62] In the same way, Augustine charges Franciscus, "what is sown in your overcrowded mind can take no root and bear no fruit. With no considered plan, you are tossed now here now there in bewildering fluc-

[60] See p. 222, above.

[61] "Siquidem fantasmatibus suis obrutus, multisque et variis ac secum sine pace pugnantibus curis animus fragilis oppressus, cui primum occurrat, quam nutriat, quam perimat, quam repellat, examinare non potest ..." (Carrara, p. 66).

[62] See p. 237 and n.58, above.

tuation and can never put your full strength to anything."[63] This is the reason why his "meditatio mortis" has not helped him, "and there arises that inner discord. . . ." Fr.: "Woe is me! Now you have thrust your hand deep into my wound." Aug.: "It is well! The numbness has ceased."[64]

From the end of Book I, a bridge stretches to Book III, spanning the second book with its test of Franciscus' involvement with the Seven Deadly Sins. When we have crossed the bridge, we encounter passages in which "amor et gloria" are described by Augustine as the "remaining adamantine chains [adhuc adamantinis cathenis] . . . that prevent you from meditating on either death or life." Fr.: "You call these chains? And you would break them if I let you?" "Yes, I mean to try," Augustine replies, "but I am uncertain whether I shall succeed. The other things that held you back were less strong and also less pleasant to you, and so you helped me to break them. These, on the contrary, are pleasant though they injure, and they deceive you by a false show of beauty; they will demand greater effort, for you will offer resistance as though I wished to rob you of some great good. Nevertheless I mean to try."[65]

Despite the uncertainty of the outcome inherent in these introductory words, Augustine finds Franciscus ready to lay down his arms with respect to *amor* — although a reader who recalls that parts of the *amor* section stem from 1349, when Laura was no longer alive,[66] may wonder whether Franciscus had surrendered so meekly in the draft of 1347. From the very opening of the *gloria* section, however, Franciscus is just as doubtful about the result as Augustine: "Though I have not been completely freed from my other evils," he tells Augustine, "I do feel blessedly released from a great part of them, but I am

---

[63]". . . vigorque . . . omnis ac tempus, parca quod tribuit manus, ad tam multa non sufficit. Quod igitur evenire solet in angusto multa serentibus, ut impediant se sata concursu, idem tibi contingit, ut in animo nimis occupato nil utile radices agat, nichilque fructiferum coalescat; tuque inops consilii modo huc modo illuc mira fluctuatione volvaris, nusquam integer, nusquam totus" (Carrara, pp. 66, 68).

[64]"Nunc profunde manum in vulnus adegisti" (ibid., p. 68).

[65]Fr.: "Has ne tu cathenas vocas, hasque, si patiar, excuties?" Aug.: "Hoc molior, sed incertus de eventu; relique enim omnes, quibus tenebaris, et fragiliores erant et inameniores; ideoque dum confringerem favisti; he autem nocendo placent ac fallunt specie quadam decoris, ideoque plus negotii subest; reluctaberis enim, ceu de summis bonis spoliare velim. Aggrediar tamen" (ibid., p. 132).

[66]See Chap. 4, passim, esp. pp. 95-97.

unable to find any remedy whatsoever for my desire [for glory among men and the immortality of my name]."[67] And, indeed, at the end of the *Secretum* Augustine's advice is shown to be ineffectual. No adequate meaning can be found for the *Secretum* without giving this climax of the work its due weight. The heart of the discussion is not the establishment of Augustine as Petrarch's model or ideal but the attempt to set a limit to the church father's powerful impact. Since Augustine has proven that man's dissipation in this world is not compatible with a vigorous religious life, the only solution for Franciscus is first to complete the work which has been the core of his existence and only afterward to find religious quietude for his soul.

This was anything but an easy solution for Petrarch, because we know from his *Epistola Metrica* I 14, "Ad se ipsum," that the sudden death of so many of his friends during the plague of 1348 made him long to change at once and not delay the start of a new life.[68] We should also recall that when, in the early 1350s, he revised for the book form of the *Familiares* his letter of 1349 inviting three friends to settle down with him in a semi-monastic life, he chose as one of the letter titles a warning not to delay the new start ("non differenda consilia melioris vite").[69] It is thus obvious how deeply the concluding problem of the *Secretum* — the decision to postpone a stricter religious life until after the completion of the *Africa* and *De Viris* — was rooted in his "conflictus curarum," and how profoundly the entire architecture of the *Secretum* dialogue is in the service of its crowning scene.

Now, it has sometimes been asked why, after all, Franciscus insists so obstinately on continuing his work on the *Africa* and *De Viris* against Augustine's advice. If the most recent "psychological" theory is repudiated[70] — namely, that Augustine is made to ask Franciscus to abandon those two works because Petrarch has failed to complete them to his satisfaction — should we assume that Petrarch's desire to

---

[67] Fr.: "Age, pater mitissime, nam reliquis etsi nondum plene liberatum, magna tamen ex parte me levatum sentio." Aug.: "Gloriam hominum et immortalitatem nominis plus debito cupis." Fr.: "Fateor plane, neque hunc appetitum ullis remediis frenare queo" (Carrara, p. 188).

[68] The dating of this *metrica* to 1348, the time of the plague, rather than to 1340, was suggested by Wilkins in 1957 and confirmed by Giovanni Ponte (1349, if not the last months of 1348) in "Datazione e significato dell'epistola *Ad se ipsum*," *La Rassegna della Letteratura Italiana* LXV (1961), pp. 453–463.

[69] In *Fam.* VIII 4 of the revised version.

[70] In particular, Fenzi's and Rico's; see above, pp. 125–128.

win glory with them is the only explanation for Franciscus' resistance to Augustine at the end of the *Secretum*? If we accept this explanation, the conclusion of the third book becomes a paradox. For
Franciscus' insistence on continuing with his two *magna opera* is then
tantamount to the final triumph of his impassioned desires — his
cupiditas gloriae — over Augustine's superior wisdom. Consideration
of all the elements involved shows that the situation is more complex
and is open to a different interpretation.

To begin with, the text of the *Secretum* suggests that Franciscus'
passionate longing itself serves to some degree as an excuse: "I am
well aware that . . . it would be much safer for me to . . . relinquish
the bypaths altogether and follow the straight path to salvation. Sed
desiderium frenare non valeo."[71] Furthermore, this admission is surrounded by highly positive expressions of Franciscus' belief in the
intrinsic value of his humanistic epic: "For I could hardly bear the
thought of leaving such an important and exacting work half completed," Franciscus says in its defense;[72] and elsewhere even Augustine is made to agree that the *Africa*, would be a "preclarum nempe
rarumque opus et egregium," if only it could be completed.[73] Moreover, after Franciscus has vowed that once his writings have been
finished he will most seriously concern himself with his soul, he does
not refrain from adding: "But even while we converse, a host of important affairs, though only of this world, is awaiting my attention."[74]
Finally, if the reader of the *Secretum* wishes to explore the extent to
which Petrarch had already articulated the thought that the life he
was leading was justified by the inherent worth of his secular *labores*
and *negotia,* he should consult the letters to Gherardo, in which Petrarch tried — during the very years of the genesis of the *Secretum* — to
explain what it was that differentiated him, the scholar and writer,
from the Carthusian monk. He formulated his explanation most
clearly in *Fam.* X 3 of 1348: whereas Gherardo had found his way out
of the dark suddenly, with God's help, "I am one who ascends step by
step and with much labor" (*ego sensim multisque laboribus assurgo*).

[71] Carrara, p. 214.
[72] "Tantum enim ac tam sumptuosum opus vix possum equanimiter medio calle deserere" (ibid., p. 206).
[73] Ibid., p. 194.
[74] "Sane nunc, dum loquimur, multa me magnaque, quamvis adhuc mortalia, negotia expectant" (ibid., p. 214).

Although in Petrarch's eyes this was not a rival means of achieving what Gherardo had achieved — perhaps God wanted to show him that a "repentina mutatio," like that of Gherardo, does not come about with the "help of studies or as an offspring of natural gifts, but is entirely an act of God" — at this point in his life at least, the ascent through difficult secular labor was his personal way.[75]

If the last pages of the *Secretum* are read, as I have tried to do, with its final climax considered as the logical outcome of the three dialogues, the interpretation of its meaning given here will be seen to have at least as much validity as any of those suggested in earlier approaches to Petrarch's work.[76]

II

It has been intimated in the course of this study that the late 1340s were too late a period in Petrarch's life for the kind of "conversion" crisis that students after Carlo Calcaterra thought had occurred in 1342–43 — the start of a greater religious earnestness, that is, which deeply influenced Petrarch's views of the relationship between the classical world and the Christian heritage. By 1347, so many of Petrarch's basic ideas about the role of Christianity had already found expression in his writings that whatever crisis he may have undergone at that time would have taken a very different form from the sudden turn to spirituality envisioned for 1342–43 by Calcaterra and his school. Let us clarify Petrarch's spiritual situation about 1347 by unraveling some of its major strands.

Shifting our attention from the *Secretum* of 1347 to the *De Vita So-*

---

[75] The whole passage in *Fam.* X 3 (17) runs: "... te de tantis errorum tenebris eduxit repentina mutatio dextere Excelsi; ego sensim multisque laboribus assurgo, credo ut intelligi detur nullum his adminiculum literarum, nullum opus ingenii, sed totum Dei munus esse, qui forte et michi manum porriget imbecillitatem meam ingenue confitenti."

[76] An interpretation basically not unlike the one given in the present study is intimated in Francesco Bruni's review of Rico's work in *Medioevo Romanzo* III (1976 [1]), pp. 146–152. Two of its major conclusions are as follows: (1) It is incorrect to say that the *Secretum* points to an impending "conversion" of Petrarch's. Whereas this term applies to the lives of Augustine and Gherardo, Petrarch's life was one of labor and secular pursuits. (2) One should pay attention to "non solo la norma indicata da S. Agostino, ma anche il parziale rifiuto di P. di seguirla ..." (p. 148). Augustine is not the only "victor" in the debate; while Petrarch accepts Augustine's doctrine as correct, he does not sacrifice his own way of life: there is evolution instead of conversion in Petrarch's life.

litaria of 1346, we find a striking variation in Petrarch's thinking.
According to the *Secretum* of 1347, there can be no real peace between
Petrarch's literary goals and his "desiderium Dei"; the whole *Secretum*
dialogue and Petrarch's two-stage design for his future years derive
from his belief in this disharmony. In the *De Vita Solitaria,* on the
other hand, everything had been based upon the idea that solitude is
the breeding place equally of secular studies and religious meditation.
The *De Vita* begins and ends with this very thought. The first chapter
starts with the creed "I believe that a noble spirit will never find re-
pose save in God, in whom is our end, *or* [my emphasis] in himself
and his private thoughts, *or* in some other spirit united by close sympathy with his own. . . . But whether we are intent upon God, or
upon ourselves and our *honesta studia,* or whether we are seeking for a
mind in harmony with our own, it behooves us to withdraw as far as
may be from the haunts of men and crowded cities." In one of the last
chapters of the concluding second book of the *De Vita,* we read again
in retrospect: "Whether our desire is to serve God, which is the only
freedom and the only felicity, or by virtuous practices to develop our
mind, which is the next best application of our labor, or through reflection and writing to leave our remembrance to posterity and so
arrest the flight of days and extend the all too brief duration of our
life, or whether it is our aim to achieve all these things together, let
us, I pray you, make our escape at length and spend in solitude what
little time remains."[77]

There is, no doubt, some difference between the third items in
these two summaries — the search for intimate contact with minds
other than our own. In the introductory statement, Petrarch is speaking about intellectual contact with friends, whereas in the passage
near the end of the work he is thinking of posthumous contact with
future generations through surviving works. But both formulations
are pervaded by the same spirit of reconciliation, inasmuch as solitude is seen to be equally fruitful for the spiritual life, for personal
introspection, and for *honesta studia* of every sort. This deliberate rap-
prochement of divergent elements is also evident throughout the
second book of the *De Vita,* especially in the balanced selection of
Christian examples of the love of solitude to accompany the classical
models.

[77] The *Life of Solitude,* trans. Jacob Zeitlin (Urbana, Ill., 1924), pp. 105, 301.

Much of this seems to anticipate the attitude of those later Renaissance humanists who are known to have been adherents of a religious universalism, although in the case of the *De Vita* it should rather be termed a "solitudinarian universalism" (a universalism of solitudinarian values, to be precise), which goes beyond the limits of Roman and Greek classicism to bring together the representatives of many ages. Thus it would be a serious misunderstanding of what really took place in the years 1346–47 to believe that Petrarch was then a secular-minded classicist who underwent a religious conversion a year after he wrote the *De Vita*.

There is one possible obstacle to viewing the Petrarch of the *Secretum* period from the perspective emphasized here: it is the sudden transformation of the *De Viris* from a book based on classical authors to one based largely on the Old Testament. Does not this abrupt change in the structure and content of what was originally an almost strictly Roman *De Viris* suggest, after all, that Petrarch's attitude toward classical antiquity and the Judeo-Christian tradition changed substantially during the years when he was composing the *Secretum*?[78] One vital observation ought to prevent us from making this mistake. During the time when he was restructuring the *De Viris,* Petrarch seems never to have given a religious motivation for his addition of biblical *vitae;* rather, he put all the stress on the necessity of including "all ages and peoples" in the study of history. He does this in Book II of the *Invective Contra Medicum,* where the great figures of the *De Viris* are defined as "ex omnibus seculis illustres."[79] He does the same in his letters during the early 1350s. In *Fam.* VIII 3 (between mid-1353 and mid-1356) he emphasizes his universal historical interest: "ex omnibus terris ac seculis illustres viros in unum contrahendi."[80] In *Fam.* XV 3, of February 1353, in which he writes to Zanobi da Strada from the Vaucluse about the ties binding him to the great men of the past, he says: "I often gather them, from every land and every age, here in this little valley."[81] The humanistic roots and general appeal for Petrarch of the idea of all ages and all lands are perhaps most

---

[78] A theory to which I still adhered in *From Petrarch to Leonardo Bruni,* p. 25.

[79] Ibid., p. 26.

[80] For the date, see ibid. and the clarification above in the Appendix to Chap. 4, pp. 115–116.

[81] I am using Wilkins' translation in *Petrarch at Vaucluse: Letters in Verse and Prose,* ed. and trans. Ernest H. Wilkins (Chicago, 1958), p. 178.

convincingly attested by its appearance long before its consequences destroyed the Roman version of the *De Viris*. For in one of the early *metricae*, of 1338 or 1339,[82] we already read the following characterization of his books, which he calls his friends: "They come to me from every century / and every land . . . , / bringing to my mind / ages long past." And in the *Secretum*, in a passage at the beginning of Book II to which Rico first drew attention, Augustine is made to castigate Franciscus' idle curiosity with the words "cum omnis evi clarorum hominum gesta memineritis."[83]

There is no doubt that the new 1351–53 preface to the *De Viris*, on Adam and the creation of the world, is weighted toward the religious and biblical side. But the consistency of Petrarch's interest in the historical amplification of the *De Viris* spanning "all ages" must serve as the decisive basis for determining why the plan was changed. This inevitable conclusion undermines the belief that the vicissitudes of the *De Viris* in 1351–52 had much to do with the religious "conflictus curarum mearum" analyzed in the *Secretum*. Rather, Petrarch came to the conclusion, as a historian and biographer, that a book about "illustrious men" would be too narrow if it did not include more of mankind than Romans from Romulus to Titus and a few of their antagonists. That Petrarch longed to broaden his scope beyond Roman classicism during his last stay in the Vaucluse we know, too, from the development of the *triumphus Fame*, in which the original restriction to Romans came to an end at the very same time.[84]

A similar expansion of Petrarch's interests and tastes occurred in his response to the Scriptures during the 1340s, and especially to the poetry of the Psalter, as we have seen from his report in the *De Otio Religioso*.[85] In his youth, he tells us there, he used to deride David's Psalter; the only poetry he read and loved was that of the classical poets. But gradually he entered into "the joyful company of the Holy Scriptures," and "I now move with awe in an area which I used to despise." When we add this report in the *De Otio* on the growth of

[82] *Metr.* I 6. I am using Ernest H. Wilkins' translation in *Life of Petrarch* (Chicago, 1961), p. 20.

[83] Carrara, p. 72.

[84] This was discovered by Guido Martellotti, "Linee di sviluppo dell'umanesimo petrarchesco," *Studi Petrarcheschi* II (1949), pp. 51–80. See Baron, *From Petrarch to Leonardo Bruni*, pp. 27–29.

[85] See above, p. 219.

Petrarch's interest in the *sacrae litterae* to the impressive exposition of his solitudinarian universalism in the *De Vita,* we begin to understand his variegated intellectual world in the 1340s and early 1350s — the steady, gradual growth of his humanism, contemporaneous with, yet independent of, the identity crisis of that period to which he gave voice in the *Secretum.*

III

How, then, should we define the place of the *Secretum* in the sum total of Petrarchan humanism?

Two statements should be made at the outset. In the first place, since the *Secretum succeeded* the *De Vita* and the *De Otio,* it is not necessarily an expression of the same state of mind; quite apart from the fact that if the *Secretum* is no earlier than 1347 it came too late to mirror the religious conversion of a still secular-minded classicist. Secondly, if the *Secretum* followed the *De Vita Solitaria* by little more than a year, it has to be viewed against the persuasion of the *De Vita* that a true life of solitude must prove its fruitfulness in three ways: not only by encouraging introspection and affording a psychological proximity to friends and posterity but also by bringing us closer to God. The nagging problem that led to the conception of the *Secretum* was Petrarch's realization by 1347 that in solitude he was not able to experience God as fully as he was experiencing the two secular components of the solitudinarian life.

This does not mean that Petrarch became uncertain about the indivisibility of the program set forth in the *De Vita Solitaria;* we have observed that a combination, or rather juxtaposition, of classical letters and *sacrae litterae* was becoming more and more the hallmark of his humanism. But in the *Secretum* he asked himself whether he was personally fit to carry out what he had made his goal, and whether he would be capable in future life of conforming to the principles of medieval thought as personified by Augustine. If this is still to be called a "crisis" in his life, it should in any case not be confused with the kind of sudden conversion to religiousness long imagined to have occurred about 1342. What Petrarch experienced in 1347 was rather a doubt concerning his personal way of life: he wondered what kind of activity would allow someone with his humanistic values and

occupations who also longed for a profound experience of the divine
to live in both worlds. If we read the *Secretum* with this question in
mind, most of its puzzling aspects become intelligible: his dualistic
view of the world and life, his plan to begin a more or less monastic
existence after the completion of his humanistic work, and his idea of
a "secret" book that would not be part of his published work or serve
to enhance his name.

It is from the perspective of these considerations that one becomes
aware of the place of the *Secretum* in Petrarch's many-sided literary
endeavors. Whereas in the *De Viris Illustribus* and the *Africa* epic he
had begun his humanistic career as a pioneer philologist and historian, by the time of the *De Vita Solitaria* his humanism had grown to
be more than simply Roman and secular, and it developed organically in the direction of greater variety throughout the rest of his life.
After his acclimatization to Italian city life, about 1358, his interests
in secular history and moral philosophy on the one hand and the
sacrae litterae on the other were allowed to mature side by side. His
humanistic work could have evolved in this form even if the *De Otio
Religioso* and the *Secretum* had never been written. These two guides
for Gherardo and himself, when all is said and done, represent an
independent realm in his writing, as his Volgare poetry constitutes
another; like the latter, they represent a rival or companion sphere
rather than an inherent part of Petrarch's humanism. Unlike his vernacular poetry, however, the *De Otio* and *Secretum* show a singular
preoccupation with medieval values, which is characteristic mainly
of Petrarch's middle period between 1347 and 1353. This was a time of
transition, when his brief reunion with Gherardo in the Carthusian
monastery of Montrieux in early 1347 put him in a dilemma and induced him to marshal the remnants of his medieval heritage against
the classicism of the *Africa,* the *De Viris,* and some of his early letters.

We might well wonder what would have become of Petrarch's later
development as a humanist if during the six years from 1347 to 1353
he had somehow succeeded in completing the two major literary
projects of his youth: the *Africa* and the *De Viris.* It is conceivable that
he might eventually have followed Gherardo's example, at least to the
extent of settling down in the shadow of a Carthusian monastery,
dismissing his servants, and leading an existence antithetical to Italian city life. He might then have written the missing three books of

the *Secretum* concerning his inner peace, with the anticipation of finally achieving an Augustine-like conversion in old age.

The mere possibility of posing this as a serious question shows
that the *Secretum* is more fruitfully read not primarily as a piece of literary art but as a book of intimate confessions, in which humanism
not only fuses but eventually disaccords with Petrarch's medieval
legacy.

Index of Names /

Index of Works of Petrarch
(other than the *Secretum*)